JOANNE LIEBELER'S
do it herself

DISCARD

By JoAnne Liebeler

with Bridget Biscotti Bradley

Sunset Books, Menlo Park, CA

This book was produced for women, by women!

managing editor: Bridget Biscotti Bradley
art director: Amy Gonzalez
principal photographer: Michele Lee Willson
photo editor and stylist: Laura del Fava
technical illustrations: Melanie Powell,
  Studio in the Woods
comic art: Tracey Woods
copy editor: Vicky Congdon
proofreader: Sandra Beris
indexer: Nanette Cardon
production specialist: Linda M. Bouchard
prepress coordinator: Danielle Johnson

Sunset Books
vp, general manager: Richard A. Smeby
vp, editorial director: Bob Doyle
director of operations: Rosann Sutherland
marketing manager: Linda Barker
art director: Vasken Guiragossian
special sales: Brad Moses

10 9 8 7 6 5 4 3 2 1
First printing January 2007
Copyright © 2007, Sunset Publishing
Corporation, Menlo Park, CA 94025. First edition. All rights reserved, including the right of
reproduction in whole or in part in any form.

ISBN-13: 978-0-376-01808-3
ISBN-10: 0-376-01808-9
Library of Congress Control
Number: 2006934591
Printed in the United States of America.

For additional copies of *JoAnne Liebeler's Do It Herself* or any other Sunset book, visit us at www.sunsetbooks.com or call 1-800-526-5111.

Cover: Photography by Michele Lee Willson, styling by Laura del Fava, design by Vasken Guiragossian.

CONTENTS

My friend Michelle bought her first home a couple of years ago, and she promptly assumed the role of drill sergeant in maintaining it. When a mouse appears in her basement, she launches an all-out ground-force assault. Every nook, crevice, cranny, and opening is sealed and shut down. There's no clutter on her counters, the towels are fresh, the beds neatly made. She's proud of her home, and rightly so. It's lovely, warm, and inviting.

Michelle has millions of kindred spirits. Single females are the second-largest group of first-time home buyers, right after married couples. We've traded apron strings for purse strings, and we're opening those Coach bags to make a huge and smart investment—a home.

Owning a home is a big responsibility. And because most of us aren't lolling around on big piles of cash, we need to judiciously allocate our home maintenance dollars. That's where this book comes in. It's designed to guide you through the practical aspects of home ownership. You won't find instructions on how to sew café curtains or stencil pansies in your kitchen. This is in-the-trenches stuff. My goals for this book are to:

- Empower you with a general working knowledge of how your home functions.
- Show you simple, easy ways to keep your home and its inhabitants safe.
- Help you determine when you can fix something yourself, and when it's best to call a pro.
- Save you money with repairs and improvements you can do yourself.
- Make you laugh! Stuff goes wrong in our homes. It's not funny at the time, but afterwards it can make great comedy material.

Perhaps the most important thing I want to do is to convey information clearly. One thing that rankles me is when contractors blast you with their jargon-filled shoptalk. This book aims to cut through the gobbledy-gook and explain things clearly and simply. Understanding how house systems work gives you knowledge. Knowledge gives you power. Power enables you to do things on your own and save money.

I hope you enjoy the book and that you'll also pay a visit to my website, jojosdoitherself.com. You'll find more helpful hints as well as links to other useful websites. Stop on by, we're open anytime!

JoJo Fiedal

chapter 1

ANATOMY OF A HOUSE

....

TAKE A GOOD LOOK at your friends and family, and you'll see we come in all shapes and sizes. Yet, human anatomy bonds us all. We all have a heart (with the exception of certain jerky ex-boyfriends and -husbands). We all have bones, skin, a respiratory system, a nervous system…and a brain (with the exception of certain jerky ex-boyfriends and -husbands).

Well, a house is a lot like a human body. It combines a number of components and systems to make it a functioning entity. Even though it's more interesting to examine what's on your walls—like silk shantung wallpaper—it's a lot more important to know what's behind those walls. Just as in *Alice's Adventures in Wonderland*, there's an alternate reality thriving behind your walls, ceilings, and floors.

That alternate reality includes the buzz of electricity, the gurgle of plumbing pipes, and the deep breathing of your heating and cooling systems. Metaphorically speaking, your house is alive. So let's milk this anatomical analogy for all it's worth and pay a house call to the home to dissect its systems.

chapter contents

HOME OWN(HER)SHIP 101

Back when I was in junior high school, we girls had to take a class called Home Economics. Home Ec taught us how to sew and cook. I'm glad I learned how to stitch on the bias and double-sift flour, but as a single female homeowner, I need a more comprehensive body of home knowledge. I need to know why the faucet leaks, why the door won't latch, and why the window keeps jamming. I need a class on Home Ownership—a how-to on how to own her own ship.

Like any class, Home Own(her)ship starts with the basics. You can't bake a cake without the right ingredients. By the same token, good home maintenance means understanding the recipe behind your home's construction.

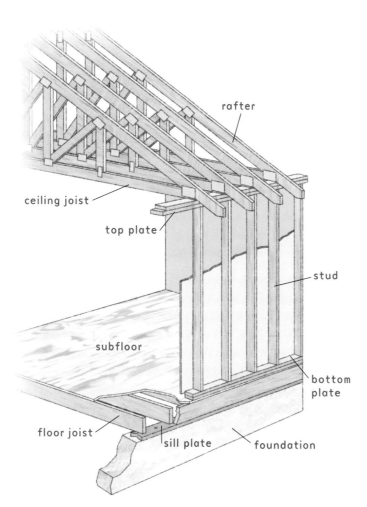

rafter

ceiling joist

top plate

stud

subfloor

bottom plate

floor joist

sill plate   foundation

framing: the bones of a house

Just as bones form the framework for our bodies, lumber forms the framework of a house. Many of us have seen homes in midconstruction. That orderly layout of lumber creates the home's walls, floors, ceilings, and roof. This lumber skeleton is called the house's *framing*.

If you've ever played with Legos or built structures using a deck of cards, you have a crude idea of what framing is all about. Vertical and horizontal pieces are needed to construct the whole of the structure. If you're going to build two or more stories, the only way to do it is to top off the first level (to create more structural integrity) and build up from there.

Framing is an art that's based in both architecture and construction. A good architect knows exactly what limits of weight a wall can bear. A good framer will give form to those specifications on site. Houses with imaginative angles or curves have a lot of framing artistry behind those walls. When you comprehend the amount of logic, skill, and brute strength it takes to frame a house, you appreciate the folks who do it for a living.

In this book, you are not going to learn how to frame up your own house. But a crash course in framing jargon might be helpful, so here goes.

STUDS Studs are the handsome hunks who frame a house—usually shirtless, with pearly beads of sweat gleaming on their ripped abs…Oh. That's right. This isn't a Jackie Collins book. In framing, *studs* refer to the vertical pieces of lumber that form the house walls. Lined up like lumber soldiers during the framing process, the studs are placed so that the center of each one is 16 inches (or 24 inches) away from the center of the neighboring stud. This standard of framing is called "16 inches on center" or "24 inches on center." (Framing 16 inches on center is the norm, but as a material- and cost-saving measure, 24 inches is acceptable in certain applications.) So why do you care? Well, in a lot of home repair work, you have to locate the studs hiding behind walls. If you find one, you can simply measure over 16 or 24 inches in either direction and find its neighbor.

JOISTS The horizontal equivalents of studs; *joists* are what hold and support floors and ceilings. They're almost never made of 2 by 4s. Joists require beefier cuts of lumber—like 2 by 6s, 2 by 8s, or larger. Just think of how heavy one 12-inch ceramic tile can be. Then imagine a whole floor of that tile. Wimpy framing can't support that kind of weight.

You can see what a joist is by looking underneath a deck. The long framing members that run perpendicularly from the house wall are the joists. Many times these deck joists rest in metal pockets called joist hangers. The deck boards are then nailed to the joists.

RAFTERS AND TRUSSES The roof of a house has its own glossary of terms. In the old days, the pitch—or slope—of a roof was hand-framed with *rafters*. The top ends were cut on an angle, which created the roof's slope. A sloped roof is desirable because it helps water run off the surface instead of pooling and sitting stagnant.

These days, roof framing is more commonly done with *trusses*, which are pitched roof configurations constructed off-site and delivered to the job. When a framing crew is ready to frame the roof, the trusses are hoisted up by a crane. The framers, balanced precariously on top of the stud walls, then steer them to their proper locations and secure them. Yikes! "Flying in the trusses" is a *Fear Factor* challenge, if you ask me.

2-BY-4 TRIVIA

A 2 by 4 (often seen as 2 × 4) is a piece of lumber commonly used for studs. These lumber dimensions—2 by 4, 2 by 6, 2 by 8, and so on—refer to the measured depth and width of the lumber. If you measured a stud, you'd expect it to be 2 inches thick and 4 inches wide, but it won't be. It'll be more like 1½ inches by 3½ inches. That's because when lumber is first milled, its true size is as advertised. But after it's planed and dries out, it naturally shrinks to a smaller size. I guess they didn't change the name because there's not as much ring to "I got hit over the head with a 1-and-one-half by 3-and-one-half!"

siding and roofing: the skin of a house

Skin covers the bones of our body. Over the bones—or framing—of a house, you'll find the *siding* and *roofing*. Both come in a variety of materials and need to be extremely weather resistant. They're like a suit of armor your home wears to protect itself from rain, sleet, snow, wind, and withering heat. Now mind you, the siding and roof shingles are the outer gear. There are all kinds of inside layers designed to keep a house warm (or cool) and zipped up tight.

• *Insulation* is kind of like a down comforter for your home's walls and roof. There are several different types of insulation, with blown-in cellulose and fiberglass being pretty common. Fiberglass insulation, which looks like cotton candy, helps sweeten your energy costs. It comes in rolls or in precut "batts" that nestle in between each stud cavity. Insulation is rated by something called *R-value.* The "R" stands for resistance to heat flow. The higher the R-value, the more resistance the insulation has against heat loss. Insulation doesn't stop the heated or cooled air from escaping from your home, but it sure slows it down.

• *Sheathing* is the first covering of boards, plywood, particleboard, or similar material that goes over the house framing. New generations of house sheathing are being introduced that give the material more strength, and, in some cases, include pesticides to deter termites and wood-boring insects.

• *House wrap* is a paper-thin additional layer of protection that helps keep Mother Nature from intruding into your home. If it's properly installed, with all the seams taped and airtight, it can significantly reduce outdoor air infiltration. On roofs, you will find tar paper or a rubber membrane designed to provide insurance against moisture infiltration.

All these preparatory layers are the undergarments for what people see from the street—your roofing and siding. Know how your home is cloaked in case you need to make repairs.

TYPES OF SIDING Brick and stone siding will never go out of style. If you examine the brickwork on older homes, many times you'll find the mason created patterns like herringbone or semicircles. Brick and stone are expensive siding materials, but they're also fireproof, durable, and solid.

Like brick and stone, stucco siding requires an artisan to apply it. One advantage to stucco is that it's seamless, which gives the house one more defense against Mother Nature's worst moods.

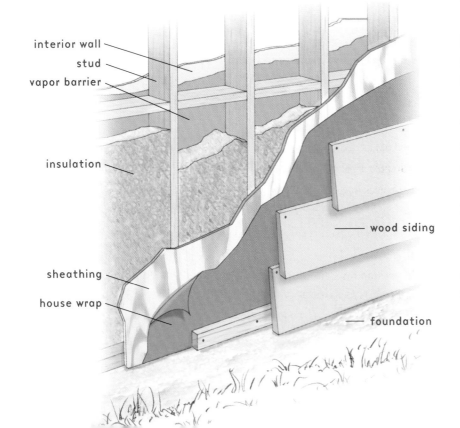

interior wall
stud
vapor barrier
insulation
sheathing
house wrap
wood siding
foundation

Vinyl siding can look just like wood but is much easier to maintain. Asphalt roof shingles work with almost every architectural style.

Whether it's applied to the house as boards, shakes, or shingles, wood siding imparts a look of quality. But it's not exactly low maintenance. The paint on wood needs to be maintained. If the wood stays in its natural state, you need to keep up with staining and sealing. If you don't mind upkeep and are willing to pamper your siding material, wood is a great-looking, architecturally diverse product.

Unlike wood siding, vinyl is basically maintenance free. Vinyl can look like classic wooden clapboard from afar, so you might not know it's vinyl until you actually touch it. It's a form of plastic, so it's resistant to rot, rust, and blistering. The color is applied at the factory, so you never have to paint vinyl.

Like vinyl, aluminum and steel siding have coloration that's factory applied. Insects and pests aren't into metal, so these materials won't rot. Aluminum is softer than steel, so if you live in an area that gets a lot of hail, better think twice about aluminum. It can dent.

There are also a lot of different composites available for siding. Composite means that the product is a blend of different materials. For instance, fiber-cement siding (popularized as a brand by James Hardie) has cement, cellulose fibers, and resins in it. Fiberboard has wood fibers and synthetic resins. Composite materials can be made to look like wood or even stucco. Many wood composites cost less than the real thing.

TYPES OF ROOFING Asphalt shingles are the most commonly installed roofing material in the United States because they are affordable, versatile, and durable, lasting 20 years or longer. The color and style choices have come a long way in terms of enhancing the design and character of a home. From a distance, some asphalt shingles can even look like wood shakes or slate.

As you can imagine, a roof with slate, fiber-cement, or clay tiles needs some Schwarzenegger-strong framing support. If you're considering one of these materials for your new roof, do your home-work. Residential homes might not have the structural strength to withstand all that weight on top. But there's no doubt these are durable, attractive, fire-resistant options.

Other roofing materials include metal and wood. Metal roofing can range from a corrugated "tin shack" kind of look to a sleek and seemingly seamless style. Wood roofing—usually sold as shakes or shingles—can impart a distinctive design to a house. The wood shingles and shakes manufactured these days are treated to ensure that they are fire retardant and moisture resistant.

plumbing: the circulatory system

If you remember high school physiology class, you know that arteries carry fresh, oxygenated blood away from the heart and distribute it throughout the body. The veins then carry "used" blood back to the heart, where it can be pumped up with oxygen and then pumped back out again.

Your house plumbing system works in a similar way. Just as with your circulatory system, you can't see the inner workings. But *supply* pipes are busily carrying fresh, clean water to sinks, toilets, the washing machine, showers, and tubs. Meanwhile, another system of pipes carries away the waste-water. This system of water supply lines and *drain/waste/vent* (or DWV for short) pipes travels up, down, and around behind your walls and ceilings, and under your floors.

You'll see the supply lines are marked in the illustration to the right in red (they're the arteries, after all!) while the drain/waste/vent lines are in blue. Water comes into your home via a main supply line—often called the *main*. Go to your crawl space or basement and find this main supply (sometimes the water main is located outside the house next to the foundation). This is your fountainhead—the headquarters for your water supply. If this thing ain't working, there's no hot soak in the tub tonight! You should be familiar with this source and mark it with a big red sign saying "Main" if it isn't marked already. If there's some sort of crisis, like the washing machine hose blows and sprays water everywhere, this valve is where you'll turn off the water supply to the house. There should be other shutoff valves sprinkled throughout the house underneath sinks and behind appliances, but familiarizing yourself with the main is key.

The main shutoff valve is usually a flat type of lever (see photo on next page). You don't want to wear it out, for Pete's sake, but turn it off and on at least once so you're familiar with how it operates. It's important that everyone in your household learns about this valve. You never know when you're going to need the knowledge!

HOW TO SHUT OFF WATER AND GAS

Water and gas supply lines have similar shutoff valves. There's usually a lever that's capable of making quarter turns only. If the lever is running in a direction parallel to the main supply line, that means the water or gas is flowing. Turning it perpendicular to the line shuts off the flow.

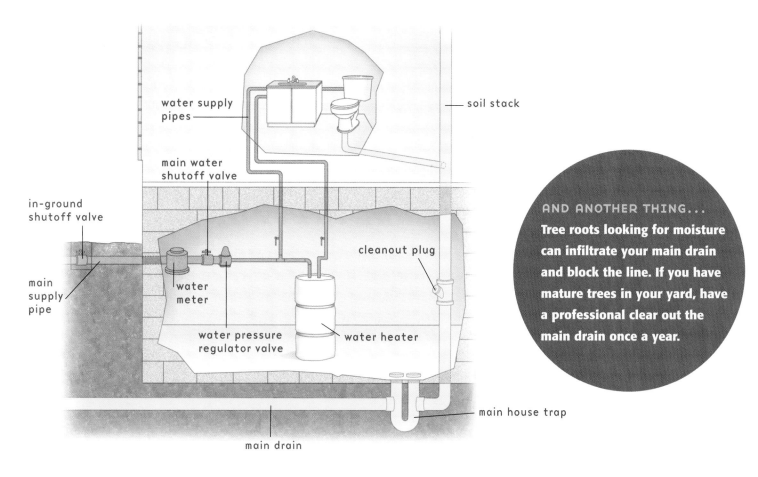

water supply pipes

soil stack

main water shutoff valve

in-ground shutoff valve

main supply pipe

water meter

water pressure regulator valve

cleanout plug

water heater

main house trap

main drain

AND ANOTHER THING...
Tree roots looking for moisture can infiltrate your main drain and block the line. If you have mature trees in your yard, have a professional clear out the main drain once a year.

WHERE THE WATER GOES: DWV LINES All the used water in your house travels through a network of small drains to a larger main drain in your home. Just as you have a main water supply, your *soil stack* is headquarters for the waste. Typically there will be a cleanout plug or drain in the lowest point of your house. (It's low because drains depend on gravity to help move waste from your house.) If there's a severe backup in your house, this is where your friendly "rooter" professional will come and root out your problem. And yes, it's gross.

For city slickers, the waste in your soil stack ends up in a municipal sewer system where it's likely cleaned, treated, and redistributed. If you have a well, the waste likely goes to a *drain field* and *septic tank*. The drain field (also called a leach

MAIN WATER SHUTOFF VALVE

field) is a well-filtered area in your yard that absorbs the liquid waste. The septic tank is designed to handle the solids. Septic tanks need to be pumped out or cleaned periodically. That's also a job for a professional. And yes, it's gross.

WATER-SUPPLY SOURCES For those who live in an urban or suburban area, the water that feeds your house probably comes from your city or town. Your municipality invested in a vast network of underground lines that carry water from its source all the way to your hacienda. The city's source might be a body of water like a river, or a large municipal well or reservoir that pulls water from an aquifer.

If you're a rural homeowner, you most likely have your very own well buried right in your yard. A pump draws the groundwater out of the well and delivers it to your home's main supply line. Poor you if you're a homeowner living in a rural area that's quickly turning into a municipality! The city will eventually build water supply and sewer lines and want you to be connected to them. Can you say "assessment?"

WATER-TREATMENT OPTIONS If you've already gotten familiar and cozy with your main water supply, you might have noticed the line hooks up to various contraptions before it branches off to the water heater and other locales. These devices might be whole-house water filters, water softeners, or iron filters. Their jobs are to "treat" your water so it's more potable and usable. After all, undesirable elements can hitchhike into your water supply—things like iron, arsenic, lead, cadmium, and chromium. (Remember the chromium in *Erin Brockovich*? Yikes!) Municipalities test their water frequently to ensure these amounts are within the EPA's mandates (see www.epa.gov for more info). But if you're a water snob and demand the best, or if you have well water and you're curious about what might be in it, go on the Internet and get a kit to test your drinking water. Or have a water-treatment professional do it for you. These companies often give free consultations where you can ask lots of questions.

"Hard" water means there is a significant concentration of minerals in the water. It isn't

WATER WOES FOR WESTERNERS

I live in a state that brags it's "the land of 10,000 lakes." The supply of fresh water isn't a problem here. That's not the case in some of the more arid western states. Elaborate water-import systems run hundreds of miles from mountains and rivers to slake the thirst of cities like Las Vegas, Los Angeles, and Phoenix. The demand for fresh water keeps growing as more and more people move in. If you live in one of these areas, it behooves you to do all you can to conserve water in your home, including using water-saving appliances and fixtures. In some municipalities out West, homeowners have to abide by water "budgets." When they exceed their designated household amount, the surcharge can be hefty. So…hey, maybe living in a state with 6 months of winter—and lots of fresh water—isn't so bad after all.

necessarily bad for you, but it can be tough on fixtures, pipes, skin, hair, and even your laundry. For one thing, the minerals (typically calcium and manganese) can slowly accumulate inside your water lines and compromise water flow. Hard water doesn't do much to stretch your soap-products dollar either; it takes more detergent to wash your dishes, clothes, etc. If you notice that you have rust stains or corroded surfaces on your fixtures, a metallic taste to your water, and laundry that looks dull, while your hair never seems to feel squeaky-silky clean, you might need to condition your water.

Water conditioning is like dialysis for your water; it's cleaned and treated before it's distributed to your fixtures and sinks. Here are some of the things a water-treatment professional can do for you:

WATER SOFTENERS It seems like a weird term—"softening" water. But considering how harsh hard water is on fixtures, appliances, plumbing lines, etc., it makes sense. A water softener uses technology called *ionic transfer* to supplant the mineral ions with sodium ions. That's why softeners need to be regularly supplemented with clean salt pellets. If you have a conditioner, lift the top off the salt drum to see if there's enough salt. If there's at least a foot of it covering the bottom, you're OK.

A water softener is equipped with a timer and clock that will tell the system when to condition the water—usually in the wee hours of the morning. If your power should go out for any reason, the clock will need to be reset or the system might

Adding a water filter means you will have fresh, clean water to drink and wash fruits and veggies with.

recharge your water at an inopportune time. Unless your softening system has twin resin tanks, your sweet, velvety-soft water won't be available to you while the system is conditioning the water. You'll just have the hard stuff to contend with.

WATER FILTERS AND PURIFIERS The simplest water filters screw onto your tap in a matter of minutes and cost about $30. There are also countertop water filters that work the same way, last longer, and don't require specialized tools to install. Or there are reverse osmosis—simply called R.O.—systems that are installed underneath sinks. An R.O. system uses a semipermeable membrane to purify water and requires that you periodically replace the filter/membrane. Whole-house water filters are for those who want the Tiffany's of water quality. These can remove sediments, and even bacteria and germs. Complete systems are a big investment, but they're of particular benefit if you have a private well because you never quite know what might be leaching into your groundwater.

electricity: your home's nervous system

Turn on a light and chances are you're not thinking of the hydroelectric, nuclear, or coal-fired generating plant that has helped produce your instant illumination. "This chandelier was brought to you by...Ohm to Home Power! We're here to brighten YOUR day!" It's good to know how your utility generates its power, but what should concern you most is where power enters your home. The utility's transmission lines snake their way into the brains of your electrical system: the *service panel* (where there are switches called *breakers*) or the *fuse box* (where you'll find old-style fuses).

SERVICE PANEL

FUSE BOX

Fuse boxes and service panels are not to be trifled with. Just as with your water supply, there is a main switch that will shut down power to the entire house. Learn where it is and how to turn it off. Whenever you do any electrical work, shut down the circuit to that area (see page 175). When in doubt, shut down all the power. Tough toenails if you have to reset your digital clocks afterward.

The electrical system can be likened to the body's nervous system. If you flip a switch, an impulse of power instantly flows to the fixture and you have illumination. Just like synapses firing in your body, it's pretty instantaneous. It's not as if the power goes away when the light's off. It's always there, you just haven't told the "brain" to release it.

The electricity of your home is mapped out into mini "neighborhoods," called *circuits*. Some circuits demand—and get—more power than others. For example, a washer and dryer will gobble up more amps of power than the little powder room down the hall. The washer and dryer probably each have their own circuit (a "dedicated" circuit). Meanwhile, the powder room probably shares its power with the hallway and maybe a couple of bedrooms. The key is, there's only so much load that a single circuit can handle. Too much power on one circuit and ZAP! The breaker *trips* or the fuse *blows* (both built-in safety measures), and you lose power to that part of the house. It's the electrical equivalent of stubbing your toe—the synapses fire and the brain immediately responds with a pain-riddled "Ouch!"

Like the plumbing lines, the wires that carry power to all your lights and appliances are hidden behind the walls. So if you get a wild hankering to bust through a wall someday, hold up there, pardner. There's power in them thar walls! Any demolition work needs to take several factors into consideration; electrical power is just one of them.

While you may not need to fully understand the inner workings of your home's electrical system, you do need to know how to reset a flipped circuit breaker, or replace a fuse. When a breaker trips, it flips itself to the "off" position, shutting off the flow of electricity to that circuit. To reset it, switch it back to the "on" position. If the same breaker keeps tripping repeatedly, and you feel you're not overloading the circuit, have an electrician look at it. It might be symptomatic of a bigger problem.

When a fuse blows, its face is no longer clear. Carefully unscrew the fuse and replace it with the exact same amperage. (The numbers "15" or "20" will be marked on the fuse.) When you buy replacements, get a couple of spares so you won't be left in the dark. And keep your fingers far and away from the fuse socket, or your nervous system will be in for a shock! See Chapter 7 for more information on working with your home's electrical system.

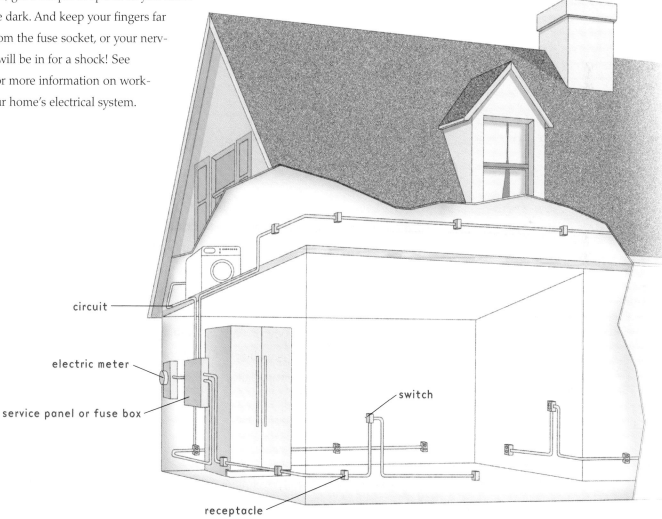

circuit

electric meter

service panel or fuse box

switch

receptacle

heating, ventilation, and air-conditioning: the respiratory system

It's not as if your house actually huffs, puffs, and gasps for air. But figuratively, your house does breathe. Outdoor air infiltrates your home, and the indoor air slowly vents outdoors. More important, during winter and summer, the air in your home is probably conditioned—meaning there's equipment that heats or cools it.

The heating, ventilation, and air-conditioning in a home are called the *HVAC system*. In newer construction, a lot of the HVAC ductwork is tucked unobtrusively behind walls, floors, and ceilings. But in older homes, the components might be obvious—like a radiator or window air conditioner.

In general, there are three energy sources that fuel heating and cooling systems:

• *Natural* or *propane gas* is carried via underground lines into your home and into your gas-fueled appliances like the furnace. Propane doesn't come directly from a utility company; a storage tank for it is located on your property and an underground line carries it into the house.

• *Fuel oil* is used to heat air, steam, or water to provide heat in the house. Gas and oil fumes can be noxious, so good ventilation is essential with these types of heating systems.

• *Electric furnaces* and *heat pumps* are more commonly found in temperate climates. An electric furnace heats a house almost as if it were a giant toaster. A heat pump (see page 20) functions like an air conditioner in reverse. Electricity is used to power all refrigerated air-conditioning systems.

These systems need to be treated with respect. If your furnace goes on the fritz, do not poke and play around, trying to figure it out on your own. This equipment is best left to the professionals. Do, however, learn how to shut down the system if you have to. Gas furnaces usually have a shutoff valve right in the gas line leading to the furnace, plus a main shutoff valve at the meter. Electric systems should have a switch. There will also be a dedicated, or single, breaker or fuse for that appliance in your electrical system. There is usually a shutoff valve located near the bottom of a fuel-oil tank.

Heating and cooling equipment is rated based on its efficiency. For furnaces, the acronym *AFUE* (annual fuel utilization efficiency) rates how efficiently the unit delivers warmed air into the house. If your furnace has an AFUE of 78 percent,

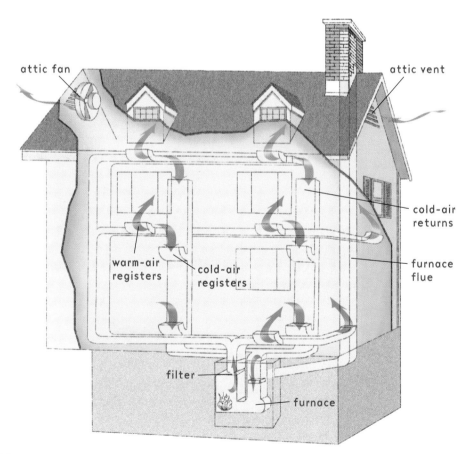

attic fan

attic vent

cold-air returns

furnace flue

warm-air registers

cold-air registers

filter

furnace

which is the minimum by federal standards, it means that 78 percent of the heat the furnace produces actually gets into your house, and the other 22 percent goes up the flue. High-efficiency furnaces can deliver as much as 96 percent.

For cooling units, the acronym is *SEER*. The seasonal energy efficiency ratio follows the same idea: a higher number equates to better cooling efficiency. Recent federal law dictates that new central air-conditioning systems should have a SEER of at least 13. So if you need to buy new HVAC equipment, don't gamble with the inefficient stuff. Instead say, "I'll see yer SEER and raise you to a 96 AFUE."

HOT-WATER AND STEAM HEAT The operating principle behind hot-water and steam heat systems is similar. A boiler heats water, which is then fed through pipes—as either steam or hot water—to radiators (or convectors) throughout the home. These systems can be durable! Boilers that are 80 years old or older are still chugging away, heating homes. An advantage to this type of heat is that the moisture content feels good to our bodies—especially when humidity levels can zap to zilch during cold snaps.

GRAVITY FURNACES Warm air rises and cold air falls, and that's the principle behind how a gravity furnace works. You'll find them in homes built during the '30s and '40s and they're easy to identify—the furnace looks like a giant octopus. Tentacles extend every which way from a big, chunky, imposing belly, which is the heat exchanger. These furnaces aren't manufactured anymore because they're not very efficient.

FORCED AIR These common systems are affordable and flexible. As with most heating systems, the process begins with your thermostat. You set it to a desired temperature and the thermostat then calls down to the basement, "Yoo-hoo! Mr. Furnace! The mistress of the house has called for 72 degrees. Better get busy!" The furnace heats air in a chamber, which is then blown, or forced, into rooms through ductwork and registers.

ALTERNATIVE ENERGY SOURCES

An uncertain supply of oil and unstable prices have reinvigorated the alternative energy market. Sun Belt states have the option of solar power. Parts of California and some of the Plains states can take advantage of wind power, and earth-sheltered homes are an old concept getting contemporary designs. Efforts to harness these "free" resources are still in their swaddling clothes, but are worth exploring and supporting. After all, the oil market promises to be more wildly unpredictable than your appetite during a PMS attack.

Ductwork throughout the house has some advantages, especially if you want to add central air-conditioning. As a rule, you can use the existing ducts and registers from your heating system to deliver air-conditioning. If you own an older home without the ductwork of a forced-air system, it's a hefty price tag to retrofit for central air.

RADIANT HEAT You'll have no need for slippers with radiant heat. In *hydronic radiant* systems, plastic tubing called PEX is installed on top of the subfloor. Hot water is pumped through the tubes, which heats your floor. The heat then rises to warm up the air in the room. Hydronic radiant heat is best installed when the house is being built. You can retrofit a house by running the tubes underneath the subfloor in a crawl space or basement, but this type of installation can be very expensive. Make sure you hire someone with a lot of experience installing this type of system.

There's also *electric radiant* heat, which works in a similar way to hydronic systems, except the heat source laid on the subfloor is a pad or other flat material and it is powered by electricity. For a whole house, this kind of system would be expensive because electricity costs more than gas. But if you're adding a room to your house, it would probably be less expensive to use radiant heat than to extend the existing ductwork. People most often use electric radiant heat in bathrooms because the rooms are small, the system works particularly well under ceramic tile floors, and the bathroom is a nice place to have warm feet.

HEAT PUMPS The name is almost a misnomer because a heat pump is really an air conditioner. But it can work in reverse and deliver heat, too. There's a valve that enables it to switch from the air-conditioning mode over to heat. Heat pumps are extremely efficient in climates where the temperature rarely goes below freezing. As the temperature falls, the heat pump's efficiency falls with it. Shoot, a heat pump would probably blow its coils and walk away in disgust if it had to heat a typical Minnesota home in January. But this could be changing. The technology is available to make heat pumps efficient in cold-weather climates. The key lies in a backup, or "booster," compressor, which kicks in as temperatures go down.

EVAPORATIVE (OR SWAMP) COOLERS
In arid climates, adding water to air can be an efficient way to cool a home. Hence, the evaporative cooler is a hot (or should I say a cool?) HVAC ticket. A swamp cooler works by drawing in hot outdoor air and distributing it over special pads soaked with water. As the water evaporates, the hot air is cooled down. The cool air is then delivered

ULTRAVIOLET LIGHT PUTS THE HEAT ON MOLD

In the last decade or so, ultraviolet lights have been used in forced-air systems to combat mold. Mold spores won't live if they come in contact with ultraviolet light. This technology is of particular value for hot, humid areas where the air-conditioning runs for weeks, sometimes months, at a stretch. They can be retrofitted into ductwork and above the air-conditioning coil for about $200 to $300.

into the home. Swamp coolers can be cheaper to operate than comparable air conditioners that use refrigerants to cool, so they're a good option in the Southwest.

indoor comfort systems

New homes are built to be more weathertight than ever. The good news? You can save on utility bills. The bad news? Newer homes can be so air-tight, indoor pollutants can get trapped indoors. I'm talking pollutants like pet dander, smoke, mold, and pollen. Not exactly sweet-sniffin' stuff. As a result, there's a whole array of "comfort equipment" designed to custom-condition the air you breathe. Most of them need ductwork as a delivery system.

HUMIDIFIERS Think of what 80 degrees feels like in Arizona compared with how it feels in Florida. Florida feels warmer. That's why some forced-air systems are equipped with humidifiers. Adding humidity to your wintertime air has other benefits, too—it can prevent wood from becoming overly dry and splitting, and it cuts down on elec-trostatic shocks. There are evaporative pads in the humidifier that should be checked at the begin-ning of each heating season. If they are not changed on a regular basis, they'll look like some-thing straight out of *Creature from the Black Lagoon* as they fill with mold and mildew.

AIR-TO-AIR EXCHANGERS (HEAT-RECOVERY VENTILATORS/ENERGY-RECOVERY VENTI-LATORS) Having this equipment is like having an electronic traffic cop to bring fresh air into your home, while making sure that the stale stuff going out doesn't take the heat with it. Some homes are built so weathertight, the easy-breezy exchange of indoor and outdoor air is lost. These units will handle that job. You can accomplish the same thing by opening windows, but that's not the best approach when it's 8 degrees below zero outside.

WHOLE-HOUSE ELECTRONIC AIR CLEANERS Back in the old days when people used to smoke in bars, you'd occasionally hear the zap, crackle, pop of the smoke-eating equipment. A similar (but quiet) apparatus can be installed on your HVAC system. A good electronic air cleaner will remove pet dander, mold spores, dust, smoke, and pollen so all those nasty things aren't distrib-uted through your ductwork.

A whole-house electronic air cleaner attaches to your furnace and provides fresh, clean air for the entire house. Be sure to change or clean the filter regularly (check the manual).

chapter 2

HOME SAFETY

. . . .

I WAS TRYING TO IMPRESS a guy during the holidays once and figured the best way to do it was to have him eat my sister's home cooking on Christmas. The backdrop was perfect. Her holiday decor was so all-American, Norman Rockwell could've cribbed notes from it. Outside, animatronic deer dipped their antlers in the snow, and white mini-lights framed the colonial-style home. Inside, the aromas of pine boughs, roast beef, and...was that smoke? Yep. Partway through the evening, a hazy film of blue-gray smoke filled the first floor. Within minutes, we were shooing smoke out the front door and windows.

It turns out something was clogging the chimney—and it wasn't Santa. The damper was open, but a critter had wedged itself in the flue. My sister doused the logs with a fire extinguisher and the minor home emergency was over. Dinner went on as planned, and my date was impressed because now he had a good story to tell.

We all like happy endings, so why not do everything you can to ensure your feathered nest is safe? Home safety encompasses everything from security to smoke detectors. So here's to keeping the home fires burning...safely!

SAFETY FIRST (AND SECOND)

I don't like to perpetuate paranoia. Fretting and freaking out over "what might happen" isn't my idea of a ticket on life's joyride. There's nothing wrong, however, with practicing preventive maintenance and making your home as safe as possible. That's just good horse sense.

Later chapters will focus on maintenance for specific areas of the house, but there are some general things you can do to keep your home safe. These aren't labor intensive or difficult. They're simple, smart measures that are for your ultimate protection. Whether it's making sure the smoke alarms work, or keeping lights on automatic timers while you're out of town, these strategies will keep your house humming happily.

detectors, sensors, alarms, oh my!

The technology around home safety alarms, detectors, and sensors has come a long way. Home smoke detectors used to be rare—as well as a bit of a luxury at about $125 a pop. But technological advances have brought the prices down, and smoke detectors are now the norm in most American homes.

Home security systems have become more sophisticated. Some systems interface with your home lighting and heating, and can be controlled or changed via your phone. Advancing just as rapidly are the detectors and alarms that can sniff out leaks, smoke, or noxious gas. Consider these safety tools as the watchdogs of the twenty-first century. They're ready to bark, lest you get bitten.

SMOKE DETECTORS We've all been annoyed by the hypersensitive smoke detector that freaks and shrieks when we overbroil a burger. But the fact is, smoke detectors save lives. In most new construction, smoke detectors are hardwired into the electrical system. If your detector dangles from wires when you unscrew it, you've got a hardwired detector. Other detectors are stand-alone devices that need to have their batteries replaced. They will usually chirp at you when the battery's weak, but that's not always the case, so it's a good idea to test the alarms monthly to make sure they're working. Fire-safety professionals recommend that the batteries be replaced every 6 months.

CARBON MONOXIDE DETECTORS Carbon monoxide (CO) is an odorless, colorless gas that can be deadly. When an unsafe quantity accumulates in a home, it can produce flulike symptoms in the inhabitants. If you have any fuel-burning appliances—a stove, oven, furnace, water heater, fireplace, dryer, space heater—there's a possibility CO gas could accumulate in your home.

In 2001, the Consumer Product Safety Commission recommended that every home have a CO detector. Some experts recommend that you have a CO detector on each floor of the house, and in every bedroom. Like smoke detectors, CO

SMOKE DETECTOR

detectors can be hardwired or wireless. Some models plug into a standard receptacle and have a battery backup. Place CO detectors at least 5 feet away from a fuel-burning appliance, or you might get false alarms.

Of course, regular professional tune-ups and checkups for all your fuel-burning appliances is something every homeowner should do. Have the professional pay special attention to the venting for these appliances to be sure it is safe.

RADON DETECTORS Radon is a naturally occurring radioactive gas that is found in soil, rocks, and water throughout the U.S. It has no color or odor and is a "heavy" gas—meaning if it's going to collect in a home, it's going to hang around in the lower levels. Like a sulky teenager holed up downstairs, radon is up to no good. Long-term exposure can lead to lung cancer, so it's a good idea to test for it.

Radon test kits are available on the Internet, or at hardware stores and even some health food stores. Remedying high levels of radon might not be as easy as testing for it. It involves sealing up cracks and gaps along the foundation, and under

concrete slabs, floors, and walls. Getting access to those areas is a hassle and potentially expensive.

WATER-LEAK DETECTORS With an extensive network of water supply and drain lines throughout your home, a leak can happen in almost any area. Luckily, there are a number of detectors you can buy that will alert you to a leak.

The least expensive water-leak detectors are battery-operated, stand-alone units that are placed in high water use areas (near a toilet, under a sink, in the laundry room, or near the water heater). An alarm will sound if the unit detects a water leak. (Of course, you need to be home to hear the alarm. Otherwise, all it will do is freak out the dog.) More expensive and sophisticated systems are categorized as "active" leak detectors. These shut down the flow of water automatically as soon as they detect a leak.

DEALING WITH ASBESTOS This mineral fiber was commonly used in insulation materials and building products prior to the 1970s. If you have a newer home, you've likely dodged this construction bullet. Long-term exposure to the small fibers in asbestos—which can be released as the material deteriorates, or when it is damaged or disturbed—can lead to lung cancer. The EPA recommends that unless asbestos is severely damaged, leave it alone. If you're planning a major remodel that could disturb it, have an asbestos-abatement professional recommend the best course of treatment.

WATER-LEAK DETECTOR

There is asbestos in the material wrapped around this old pipe. But as long as you don't disturb it, it shouldn't disturb you.

keeping intruders out

If you were a burglar, what would you look for in a target home? Probably one without exterior lights, one well hidden from the street and neighbors' homes, and one with no obvious security devices such as an alarm system, dead bolts, and window locks. Of course, you can't help the location of your house. If you're living out in the middle of nowhere, all you can do is get a security system that contacts an outside service, and equip the doors and windows as best you can. But if you do live in a neighborhood where other houses are nearby, you may want to sacrifice some privacy for security. How? Here are some tips:

- Thin out foliage between your house and the neighbors, so they can see if something fishy is going on.

- High fences and tall plants provide a privacy screen from the street, but they also block the view of passersby, who could spot an intruder.

- Install motion-sensor lights next to all doors and windows that intruders could easily reach. If burglars are suddenly bathed in light, they'll probably lose their nerve.

- Get an alarm system that you can hear from outside the house. For added expense but more security, invest in a system that calls an outside service when the alarm is activated. And make sure you put the alarm placard in your front yard—that alone might scare a burglar away.

EXTERIOR DOORS Exterior doors should be made of solid hardwood or metal—these are the hardest to kick in. Make sure the door fits in its frame correctly, and that the dead bolt is installed with screws that are at least 3 inches long. (See page 210 for more information on what to look for in a dead bolt.)

If your front door has a small amount of glass in it, you can cover the glass with polycarbonate panels so it can't be shattered to gain access.

You should be able to see who is knocking on your door without having to open it, and, ideally, without that person being able to see you. Peepholes can be installed in existing doors, so have one put in unless you can see visitors knocking from a nearby window. I know it can feel as if you're being rude, but you should never open the door when you don't know who it is and/or weren't expecting someone. Employees from a utility company or a repair service that you are expecting should have a visible name tag or be wearing the correct company name on their shirt. Call the police immediately if someone you don't know starts walking around the side of your house when you don't answer the door.

SLIDING GLASS DOORS Look for special security locks made for sliding glass doors at your local home center. There are a variety of metal stops that you can install on the bottom track that will keep the door from opening wide enough to allow access. There are also bars that slip into the bottom track, or are installed in the middle of the glass door. Dead bolts specifically designed for glass doors and sliding-door pins make it so the burglar can't lift the door from its track.

Consider replacing the glass with laminated glass, which is very hard to break. Laminated glass is not the same as tempered glass. Tempered glass is designed for safety—when it breaks, it won't shatter into little shards, while laminated glass is designed for security.

Don't have an alarm system? If you're worried about your sliding glass door in particular, there are products that you can install on the glass that will sound an alarm if the door is opened.

WINDOWS Keyed and nonkeyed locks are available for all types of windows. There are hundreds of options in a wide range of styles and finishes, so if your windows don't currently have locks, you will be able to easily find something that works for your needs.

You might also be interested in window alarms, which go off when they detect the window glass is being broken. A high-decibel sound will alert you to the problem so you can run the other way! If you're getting new windows, buy ones with laminated glass.

KEYED SASH LOCK

SLIDING WINDOW LATCH

SLIDING-DOOR PIN

BEING SMART

*B*eyond securing your home as best you can, you can be smart about keeping your home from becoming a target. Remember that locks don't work if they aren't being used! Make it part of your daily routine to lock doors and windows before you leave the house, and at night. Don't leave house keys in your car, or "hidden" outside of your house. Burglars know to look under pots, over door trim—all the usual places.

If you go out of town, ask someone to pick up your mail and newspaper, or have these services put on temporary hold. Consider putting a few lights on timers so it looks as if someone is home at night. You might even put the radio or TV on a timer. Also turn down the volume on your phone so that someone standing outside can't hear that the ringing is going unanswered.

FIRE HAZARDS AND PREVENTION

Unless it's the spark of new romance or a spicy-hot Thai meal, none of us really want to invite fire into our lives. A fire can devastate your home and wrench your emotions. It's no wonder most of us got to know "Sparky the Fire Dog" and received fire-prevention training as kids. Thanks to that, most of us know the basics of fire prevention. But talking to a firefighter about fire safety in the home is an eye-opening experience that made me realize the very simple things we can do to prevent fires.

fireplace maintenance

Let's admit it. The thought of cozying up with a sweetie in front a wood-burning fireplace on a cold night is—in the words of Paris Hilton—"hot." The smoky smell of wood…the dancing flame …the bearskin rug…candles. *Screech!* Hold up there, Casanova. There are potential fire hazards all over this romantic scene.

Ditch the politically correct faux bearskin rug; it's a combustible. Any combustibles need to be well away from a wood-burning fire. As for the candles? We all love how the soft flicker of candles creates a mood. But according to Minnetonka Fire Chief Joseph Wallin (and this is his professional side, not his romantic side, talking), "We firefighters hate candles. If you want to set the mood, put on some Barry White." He noted that unattended candles are frequent culprits of house fires—perhaps even more so if you're a cat owner. Cats are more likely

Keeping the area around the fireplace clear of combustibles—and keeping those screens or glass doors closed—is the best way to enjoy a cozy fire.

JUST SO YOU KNOW …
Some utilities offer financial incentives (sometimes up to $500!) to homeowners who convert their wood-burning fireplaces to gas.

to leap onto surfaces and investigate things they shouldn't—like burning candles. Those candles can be accidentally knocked over, whereupon the guilty cat will immediately flee the scene, hide, and then blame the dog when interrogated later on.

Of course, the biggest fire hazard in our romantic scenario is the fireplace. If you live in a home with a wood-burning fireplace, use it frequently, and can't remember when the chimney was last cleaned, make the appointment NOW! The average wood-burning fireplace can handle about 60 fires before the chimney should be swept and cleaned. The reason for the scrub down is because creosote builds up inside the chimney and too much of it can ignite a fire. Plus, a good professional chimney sweep will get on the roof to inspect the exterior and interior condition of your chimney for safety, as well as to make sure critters can't crawl in.

Another cause of chimney fires is when the chimney is poorly constructed. Although there's no obvious outward sign of improper construction, some fireboxes and chimneys have been built with inadequate clearance. The creosote builds up more quickly than normal, and the temperature needed to ignite a chimney fire drops down significantly. That's more evidence for the need to keep your chimney swept and clean.

Before building a fire, make sure the damper operates and the flue is open. A way to see if the flue is open and drafting is to light a match and blow it out while holding it in the fireplace—the smoke should easily vent up the chimney. Finally, use the screens and doors when burning a fire.

As logs burn down, they shift and could potentially roll out, ruining your floor. Now that you've gotten your lecture, spin a cut of "Can't Get Enough of Your Love, Babe," snuggle with your sweetie, and enjoy the fire safely.

appliances and fire safety

Appliances can malfunction. Appliance users malfunction, too. You probably don't give a second thought to using the toaster and coffeemaker each morning while blow-drying your hair, but these seemingly benign little appliances can cause big problems if a cord is damaged or frayed. Keep an alert eye on all your electrical cords; faulty ones should be replaced. And not tomorrow—today.

You also need to be mindful about not overloading circuits (see pages 174–175). Firefighters

REMEMBER THE EMBERS

It's common sense to keep combustibles away from the fireplace opening. What you may not know is that fire embers can quietly smolder for a couple of weeks. Yep, weeks! So, when cleaning out the firebox, place ashes in a noncombustible container—like a coffee can or metal pail. Let the ashes cool outside for 2 weeks before throwing them in the garbage. Believe it or not, plastic garbage cans have caught fire from smoldering embers (and here you thought those garbage cans were self-immolating).

Keep the area around your water heater clear of any combustible material. It should also be elevated off the floor, and if you have doors around it, they should be louvered.

say that an overloaded circuit is a common cause of electrical fires. They don't recommend loading up power strips and using multiple receptacles on your average household circuit. Share the electrical load; don't put all the stress on one circuit.

The biggest energy-guzzlers in your home are the furnace, air conditioner, and water heater. Typically, electric models will have their very own circuit (a "dedicated" circuit) so they don't stress the electrical load in your home. Gas appliances need to be inspected annually (yes, I know you've heard that before). But just as important is to keep combustibles out of the area—especially oil-based paints, solvents, and household chemicals.

Most house fires start in the kitchen. This statement may conjure up visions of an overcooked turkey charred down to its bones and filling the kitchen with fowl (heh-heh!) smoke. The oven,

WHAT TO DO IF YOU SMELL GAS

Natural gas is colorless and odorless. The sulfuric "rotten egg" smell is actually an additive called mercaptan. So, if you walk through your door and smell gas, turn around and walk out. Call the fire department using your cell phone or a neighbor's phone. The slight charge caused by turning on a light or using the phone can be enough to spark a gas leak into an explosion. Now you spunkier types may think you can nip the problem in the bud by shutting down the flow of gas at the main. But don't. If you're smelling gas, let your utility or fire department handle it.

however, is a bit player in the kitchen fire-hazard drama. If smoke is coming out of your oven, turn it off and keep the door closed. Oxygen fuels fire. If the oven door, with its airtight seal, remains closed, the fire will go out.

The more common kitchen fire culprit is the cooktop. Or at least the cook. Overheated grease and combustible materials that are too close to the cooktop are to blame for many house fires. Don't keep pot holders or paper towels next to that pan of sizzling bacon. Don't reach over the cooktop if you're wearing loose-fitting clothing. Most important, if you're cooking, don't space out and walk away. (I recently did that with some pine nuts I was toasting. I got distracted and came back to a smoldering, smoking, ruined Calphalon pan.) The best tool you can keep handy whenever you cook is a lid that will completely cover the pan you're using. It's the same logic as the oven; if there's fire, smother it by depriving it of its oxygen.

DRYER VENTS A special "potential fire hazard honorable mention" goes to the dryer vent, normally an unobtrusive piece of equipment.

All dryers produce warm air that must be exhausted outside. An aluminum, steel, or plastic duct carries the air from the vent in the back of the dryer to the outdoors. Lint accumulates in the ductwork and if too much builds up, it can ignite a fire. Fortunately, it's a fire that can be prevented.

Common sense—and your dryer's instructions— tell you to clean the lint screen every time you use the dryer. Every time—no exceptions. Then, every 6 months give a thorough "dusting" to the ventilation system. Start with the outside exhaust area.

Use a long-handled brush to reach inside the duct and pull out as much lint as you can. Make sure the vent hood is lint free. Then head inside to finish the job. Remove the lint screen and use the brush or the crevice tool on a shop vacuum to remove the lint. Shine a flashlight down in the area to make sure it's clean. Finally, you'll need to unplug the dryer and pull it away from the wall to access the ductwork. Disconnect the ducting from the dryer and exhaust area. It might be screwed in, taped, clipped, or secured with metal collars. If the duct is rigid metal, take it outside and clean it there. If it's the flexible variety, you're probably better off spending the $10 or so to replace it. This is especially true if you've been using an old-style plastic duct (they're usually white). Take the old one with you so you get the right diameter.

FIRE EXTINGUISHERS A fire extinguisher will not be your knight in shining armor that rescues your home from a Big, Bad Fire. Even if you have a weensy little fire, you should exit your home and call the fire department. Firefighters aren't real keen on homeowners trying to take matters into their own hands. Frankly, we just don't have the training to do it safely.

Nevertheless, an occasion might arise where you could use an extinguisher. So make sure you have one and keep it close to an exit. If you have an attached garage, the entry door there is best because the extinguisher can cover fires inside and out.

Fire extinguishers are rated for the types of fires they can put out and the area they can cover. The letters A, B, C, and K represent the common residential fire types.

A is for "ash," meaning a fire caused by combustible materials like paper or cloth that will leave an ash residue.

B is for "boil," meaning any kind of liquid fire, such as from grease or gasoline.

C is for "current," meaning an electrical fire.

K is for "kitchen," meaning a fire specifically related to cooking.

The numbers give an approximation of how many square feet the extinguisher can handle. The average homeowner needs a 2-A:10-BC fire extinguisher, which means one that covers a 2-foot area for an ash fire and 10 square feet for liquid or electrical fires. If you have to use one, here's a clever acronym to remember how to operate it properly—PASS.

P—Pull the pin.

A—Aim at the base of the fire. That's the heart and heat of it.

S—Squeeze the handle. You might need a little hand strength for this.

S—Sweep the area in a back-and-forth motion and empty the entire contents of the canister.

Fire extinguishers should be placed in easily accessible areas. In a garage, consider mounting one near the entry door.

EMERGENCY PREPAREDNESS

As I said earlier, I don't want to perpetuate paranoia. We've got the nightly news for that! But it can seem as if we live in an age of disasters, with the media constantly warning us to be prepared for the "big one." Depending on where you live, the "big one" might be a hurricane, tornado, earthquake, wildfire, or flood. Heck, let's throw in locusts and hail made of fire just for good measure.

We may get warnings of natural disasters, but are we really prepared? Probably not. So set aside an afternoon to assemble everything you'd need for an emergency kit.

The first thing to do is buy a storage container for all your gear. Some experts recommend keeping everything in a locked, waterproof container outside—the logic being that if your garage collapses, you can still get at your emergency kit. But depending on where you live, there might not be a safe outdoor place to put it, or extreme weather may make keeping it dry a challenge. So you'll have to determine for yourself where you want to keep this stuff. But do think about accessibility. For example, if you're putting it in the garage, place it close to the door.

Once you have your container, be it metal, rubber, or plastic, you can load it up with goodies. The following list should cover you in any major disaster where water and power have been shut off, and should keep you up and running for a while. Yeah, it's an extensive list and if you got everything, it'd take

two storage containers. But if the worst should happen, you'll sure be glad you have these supplies.

- Portable radio
- Flashlight
- Candles and strike-anywhere matches
- Batteries
- Bottled water (at least 4 gallons per person)
- Ready-to-eat food, including high-calorie snacks, to feed you and your family for one week
- Manual can opener, if needed for the food
- First-aid kit and handbook
- Prescription medications
- Pain medication
- Emergency cash
- Car keys
- Important phone numbers
- Copies of personal identification
- Wood or charcoal for a fire
- Hot plate with full propane tank
- Portable heating device that runs on batteries or propane
- Portable toilet or 5-gallon container with tight-fitting lid
- Toilet paper
- Personal necessities (diapers, hearing aids, spare glasses, toothbrush)

- Sleeping bags and blankets
- Warm clothes
- Tarp
- Heavy-duty plastic garbage bags
- Basic nonelectric tools: hammer, saw, pry bar, wrench, pliers
  - Several pairs of work gloves
  - Pet food and leashes
  - Comfort items (crayons, paper, teddy bear)

PREPARING YOUR HOME FOR AN EARTHQUAKE Not all of us live in an area where huge underground plates get themselves in a mood to shift and shimmy around. Maybe they got tired of holding one position—kind of like voguing—and it was time to move. Anyway, if you've ever been in an earthquake, you'll never forget it. During a big earthquake in Los Angeles, a friend of mine ran past her desk hutch filled with books and a radio, smartly heading for the safety of the doorway. As the temblor trembled, the hutch toppled over, barely missing her. When the movement stopped, the first thing she heard was Debbie Gibson singing from the radio under the rubble. If that hutch had been bolted to the wall, it never would have fallen.

All bookcases, entertainment centers, and armoires should be securely fastened to studs in the wall using metal L-brackets and long screws. You should be able to install these on the top or sides where they won't be noticeable. And don't screw through a flimsy, glued-on back panel—it will most likely just detach from the rest of the unit during a strong quake.

Look around your house and locate any items that you'd like to prevent from being thrown across the room. There are various products on the market such as straps and latches that will hold down computer equipment and keep cabinets shut. Delicate collectibles can be "glued" in place with removable putty made for this purpose.

AND ANOTHER THING ...
Buy a radio and a flashlight with winding mechanisms that generate electricity so you don't have to stock batteries or worry about running them down.

WHEN THE LIGHTS GO OUT

No matter where you live, there's probably at least one time during the year that the power goes out. Maybe a car hit a power pole. Or maybe a nearby line got hit by lightning. The blackout could last 5 minutes, or 10 hours. Be prepared by having candles and matches (or a fueled lighter), and even a battery-powered lantern in a spot in the house that's easy to find in the dark. There should be enough candles to illuminate the necessary rooms, unless you want to carry the candles around like Ebenezer Scrooge. You may want to keep an old-fashioned hardwired phone around too, because cordless phones stop working when the power goes out. And you homeowners with private wells should keep some bottled water on hand; your pump runs on, you guessed it, electricity.

chapter 3

FINDING HELP AND PICKING TOOLS

AW, FORGET THE VICTORIA'S SECRET DAINTIES, diamond necklaces, and Godiva chocolates. The wish list for the "can-do"-it-herself homeowner includes tools and a BlackBerry full of reliable, honest contractors.

Finding a quality contractor is like striking oil. There are plenty of them out there, but also intangibles to consider, like personality and the ability to see your "vision." Just as important is determining when—or if—you've got the chops to make a repair yourself. Are you willing to take the time? Do you have the strength? The determination? There are dozens of tasks you can handle; this book is chock-full of them. But there are other times when the best tool is the pen that signs a check for a pro.

In this chapter, we'll help you decide when to attack a project with guts and gusto, and when it might be better to retreat like a yelping puppy. Plus you'll learn what tools you absolutely must have to manage your household. So if you never thought you'd be asking for a "variable-speed 14-volt cordless drill with keyless chuck and gel grip," think again.

DOING IT YOURSELF

When people learn what I do for a living, they figure I grew up with a hammer instead of a pacifier in my hand. Or that my dad was an avid do-it-yourselfer and I tagged along, absorbing every nuance of home improvement. Uh…far from it. About the only exposure to building I had was to erect elaborate Barbie dream houses. I'd use books for walls and adorn the rooms with miniature furniture and fabric scraps. I really hit the jackpot when a neighbor threw out some linoleum floor samples. Now Barbie had flooring! If only Ken had enjoyed the decorating as much as she did.

The fact is, I learned everything I know by working on television home improvement shows. Skilled craftspeople taught me how to use hand and power tools. Asking the proverbial "dumb questions" about what terms meant helped me understand what I was doing. And finally, by researching, writing, and producing television episodes, I completed my education in Tool School.

There are tasks that still stump and stupefy me. Ask me to lay out drain, waste, and vent lines for new plumbing and I'll stare back with that deer-in-the-headlights look. But ask me to add some R-value to the garage walls and I'll know exactly what to do.

stuff you can tackle

So if you too are willing to go to Tool School, welcome to your freshman year. The projects in this book are designed for beginners. But if you've never completed a home improvement project, never held a drill, or never painted a wall, then even the simple projects may be a challenge. If you're comfortable with tools and have successfully tackled small projects in the past, then you may feel ready to fix that leaky faucet or install a ceiling fan.

With repairs, remember that there's almost always a way out. Say your sink is clogged, but you're not totally comfortable with fixing it. You can always give it the old college try, and if you don't succeed, a plumber can bail you out. There's a big difference between repairs that need to be done for practical reasons, and improvements that beautify your house. Most repairs don't need to be gorgeous, just efficient. Patching a hole in the closet wall is one thing, but patching a hole in the middle of the living room is another. You'll never get good at patching the hole in the living room if you don't practice on other holes. So if you're a true beginner, and you have a hole to patch in your closet, go for it! You'll get the experience and confidence you need to try again in a more conspicuous place.

So the big essay question is, how do you decide whether you should tackle a particular project in this book? First, read through the instructions from start to finish. Read 'em two or three times if you have to. Visualize your own project while you read, and see if a lightbulb goes on over your head. Look at the tools list. Do you feel comfortable using what's on there? If you can mentally see your way from the start of the project to the end, then you should go for it.

SPECIALTY TOOLS Doing a job well often requires using the right tools. If you don't own a tool you need for a specific project, look in the phone book for a tool rental center near you. Before rushing over to pick up a floor sander, however, consider the cost of the tool rental (including renting a truck to get it to and from the job site, if applicable) and your comfort and skill level in using the tool. It's possible that it would cost the same amount or less, and it'd get done faster, if you hired out the job.

DO YOU HAVE THE TIME? Throughout the book, you'll find boxes called "Time & Talent." These include approximations of the amount of time that each project will take. But of course, there are always complications. You could tackle something easy like cleaning out gutters, and then run into rotting woodwork on the eaves, or a hole in your roof. Simple projects sometimes have a way of becoming more involved.

Ask yourself whether what you're about to do really needs to be finished by the end of the day.

Say you're fixing a leaky bathtub faucet. If your tub doesn't have a shutoff valve, then you'll have to turn off the water to the entire house to do the repair. Therefore, if you start this project in the late afternoon, run into some trouble, and aren't finished by the end of the day, you won't be able to turn the water back on that evening. That means you can't do the dishes, flush the toilet, or brush your teeth until you finish the project, which may take the majority of the next morning. So consider the possible ramifications of not finishing, and take them into account when deciding how long to give yourself.

Besides the time, think how you'll feel about living with the chaos and mess for weeks on end. If you're painting a spare bedroom, you could feasibly work at a snail's pace and it wouldn't interfere with your daily life. But let's say you want to retexture the walls in your living room and you can only tackle the project on Saturdays. In that case, you might be living with moved furniture and dust for weeks, whereas if you hired a professional, the project could be completed in a few days.

Of course, the biggest reason for doing it yourself is to save some serious ka-ching. So consider tackling smaller projects (especially if you're honing brand-new home improvement skills) and leave the bigger projects that disrupt your home for weeks to a professional. Remember that you don't have to do it all yourself. If you're remodeling a bathroom, you could hire out the major plumbing and electrical work, then tile your own floor and paint your own walls. It doesn't have to be all or nothing.

what are you comfortable with?

Many homeowners, especially female homeowners, have never tried their hand at electrical or plumbing

work. We all know that electrical work is dangerous, and plumbing work is gross. So why bother? Even if you can afford to call a professional every time the faucet drips or you want a new wall sconce installed, it's good to know how to handle the basics yourself. Who knows? You may be able to fix the problem in 15 minutes and save yourself a $200 repair bill.

The electrical and plumbing chapters in this book cover basic projects that most homeowners will at some point need or want to do. These projects are all safe for you to try, provided that you follow the safety instructions. Electrical work is dangerous only if you don't turn off the power first!

Beyond wires and clogs, novice do-it-yourselfers are often nervous about certain power tools. While they can take some getting used to, power tools are your friends. They make life easier. But using them is an acquired skill. When you're doing a project that requires a tool you've never used, practice on some scrap material before using the tool for real. Also read the instruction manual, or have someone experienced in using that tool give you a demo. Most of the tools used in this book are explained on pages 42–55. Check out that section for basic instructions and buying advice before you start tearing into a project.

prioritizing projects

So you've been dying to paint your kitchen and wallpaper the den. But there's a cracked tile on your bathroom floor and you're pretty sure the gutters haven't been cleaned out in years. All homeowners go through this push and pull. You want to do the fun stuff, but repairs and maintenance keep rearing their nagging heads.

One thing to remember is that most repair and maintenance projects take less time than improvement projects. You could have that cracked tile fixed in an hour, whereas it might take two weekends to paint the kitchen.

Determine whether the repairs are doing any harm while waiting to get a little attention from you. A slowly leaking faucet might not be impacting your life, but that little drip is wasting tons of water. Also consider if the fix affects your safety. If the receptacle you plug your hair dryer into blows a fuse once a month, that's unsafe. You shouldn't delay that type of repair.

There are also things we all know we should do, but rarely get around to. For example, the best way to keep bugs and critters out of your house is to make sure every point of entry outside the house is sealed. Of course it's a good idea to take care of that. It's a great idea, in fact! But until you actually have a mouse in your house, or start seeing spiders every day, you just might keep letting that particular chore slip to the bottom of the list.

Sometimes it helps to promise yourself an "improvement" reward for every "repair" you tackle. Get some of the mundane stuff out of the way, and then paint your kitchen. If you need motivation for that, move all those painting supplies into the kitchen. Climbing over paint cans to make your toast every morning will inspire you to get the job done!

working alone

You can do most of the projects in this book by yourself. When an extra pair of hands is needed, it's mentioned in the "Time & Talent" box. Depending on the project, working alone can be enjoyable and even relaxing. But sometimes it's best if someone else is around in case of an emergency. Keep the following tips in mind before embarking on a project on your own.

- If you're going out to the garage to use a power tool, bring a phone with you. That way you can call for help if you injure yourself.
- Don't attempt to lift more than is comfortable. Get a helper for that part of the job, rather than throw your back out. And lift with your legs!
- Get a dolly to transport heavy items. Or do what my friend Suzu does: she totes materials in her daughter's wagon.
- Make sure there's plenty of ventilation when working with strong fumes. If you start to get dizzy, leave the area immediately.
- Wear the recommended safety gear for each task. You won't look like Heidi Klum, but you'll be protected.

THE DIRTY BUSINESS OF TRASH

Those who are new to do-it-yourself projects often don't consider the hassle of getting rid of whatever they're ripping out, or even of extra supplies they don't use. Drywall, containers of joint compound, cement, scrap wood, and other leftover materials can't be thrown into the regular garbage. Call your local waste-management service to find out what can and can't be thrown away. Some areas offer special pickups for scrap like your old baseboards and window trim, as long as they're cut into short lengths and bundled together. Hazardous materials must be disposed of responsibly. If you have leftover oil-based paints, solvents, or cleaners that contain toxins, ask around to see if any of your friends or neighbors can use the rest. Schools will sometimes take leftover paint and lumber to use in their theatrical productions. If you can't give away building supplies or old fixtures, try leaving them outside your house for a day or two with a "free" sign on them. There are also used building-material supply stores across the country that will accept usable materials in exchange for a tax deduction. Think creatively about how you can get rid of what you don't want. When all else fails, you'll need to take toxic materials to a hazardous-waste disposal facility.

HIRING A CONTRACTOR

There are some things you just can't or don't have time to do yourself. That's when you need to find an independent contractor. Wouldn't it be great if a stud finder worked for this? You could just place the tool on the project and a hunky, talented contractor would magically appear!

Finding a reputable, reliable contractor can be hard. Some don't like to bother with small jobs that will only take a day or two; it might not be worth their while. Most of them are juggling several jobs at once—including recurring gigs with builders or architects—and might not make your job a priority. And some live up to their "independent" contractor moniker. They show up when they want.

First, ask your friends for recommendations. Then when you make the calls, tell the contractors who recommended them. It may inspire the contractors to call you back, but this technique doesn't always work. The best-case scenario is to know at least one contractor who will refer you to someone else. Dropping another professional's name will often guarantee a call back, and could possibly get you speedy and attentive service. After all, most contractors want to keep getting referrals from their colleagues. What can I say? It's all about who you know. If all else fails, you can start calling people in the phone book.

what type of company should I call?

When your toilet, sink, or tub is backing up and you need it fixed NOW, call a 24-hour emergency plumbing service. For most other jobs, you'll have a choice between calling a company with a business name, or one listed under an individual's name. Try to find someone who has an assistant to answer phone calls, which can be invaluable when you're trying to get work scheduled.

Ask if the contractor is licensed, bonded, and insured. That sounds like "blah, blah, and blah," but here's what it means. The *license* means the contractor has registered the business with the state, so he or she likely knows and subscribes to building codes and regulations. If there's shoddy workmanship or a dispute over the contract, and the whole mess goes to arbitration, it's the contractor's *bond* that would pay out. If there's damage to your home, or an injury due to the contractor's negligence, his or her *insurance* will cover it.

what should I say?

Once you get a live person on the phone, tell them what needs to be done and by what date. Ask if the crew will be on the job every day until it's finished. If the company is juggling multiple jobs at once, you might end up with someone who shows up a day at a time here and there.

If the person sounds agreeable and is willing to work on your schedule, ask him or her to come out and bid on your project. Don't choose a contractor based purely on money. The person who offers services for the least amount of money might be new and inexperienced, or might rope you in with a good deal and then tell you the job took longer or required more materials, so he or she has to raise the price.

Ask your top two choices for a list of references of past clients. Call those references and ask if they were happy with the work; if the crew showed up on the days scheduled; if the crew finished by the agreed-upon date; if they cleaned up at the end of each day; if the contractor was good about calling back; if the crew was respectful of your house; if the price was fair; and if the crew was easy to communicate with.

Just so you know, the contractor you hire may send less experienced employees to do the job for them. Be sure to ask if this will be the case.

finalizing the deal

Now that you've interviewed the candidates and picked your favorite, give that contractor the gig! For small jobs that will only take a few days or less, the contractor might not give you a contract. If this person has come highly recommended, then that's probably OK. But if you feel at all uncomfortable, ask for a contract that lists the specifics of your arrangement. (Large jobs like kitchen remodels or room additions require detailed legal documents, which is not what I'm talking about here.)

You should know whether the contractor is doing the job for a fixed price, or for time and materials. "Time and materials" means that the contractor is charging you an hourly rate for the actual work, and will include additional amounts for materials. A fixed price might cover labor only and you provide the materials, or it might include everything.

The down payment that secures a spot for you on the company's work schedule generally shouldn't be more than 20 percent of the total job. An exception is when you're paying the contractor to buy expensive materials (like a new window), in which case they may need more money up front. Ask to see the receipts if you think the amount sounds inflated. The remaining payments should be tied to defined milestones of the project. For short projects, the balance is due when the job is done.

Be sure to ask whose responsibility it is to remove any debris from the job site. If you want the contractor to take it, make sure that's understood and don't make the final payment until it has all been removed.

building codes and permits

Some projects—like a room addition—require a building permit. The fee is typically a small percentage of the project's overall value. Don't skip this step to save a few bucks! Building permits and inspections ensure the work is up to code. You'll know the work has been carried out safely, and it also puts the improvement "on the record" should you decide to sell your home later on.

JUST SO YOU KNOW ... Visit the Better Business Bureau at www.bbb.org and type in your contractor's company name to see if there has been a history of complaints or legal actions taken against it.

THE ESSENTIAL HOUSEHOLD TOOL KIT

This will sound dorky, but I believe that acquiring an essential tool kit for your home is a *fun* shopping expedition. In this section I'm going to tell you what hand and power tools should be in your tool box, what to look for when shopping, and how these tools work. You'll also find lists of tools you may need for certain types of projects, such as tiling, plumbing, and electrical.

the five essential hand tools

People assume I have a museum-quality collection of tools. They imagine I lead tours of a sparkling workshop, pointing out the highlights like a curator: "This is a plunge-cut router circa 2000 with a collection of quarter-inch shank bits…" But my tool kit is pretty average looking. I still use my ratty-looking wood-handle hammer that I've owned for 17 years. My power drill is 12 years old. The print on my tape measure is worn and my power handsaw is battered. But these are tools I use over and over and over and over again. They're reliable, and more important, versatile.

As you tackle projects in this book, you'll see there are specialized, one-trick-pony kinds of tools and then there are really versatile, all-purpose tools. Your essential tool kit should combine both hand and power tools that are versatile—they can do many jobs equally well.

HAMMER There are more varieties of hammers than you think—there are framing hammers,

HAMMER

sledgehammers, roofing hatchets, drywall hammers, tack hammers, ball-peen hammers, Arm & Hammer, MC Hammer…you get the drift. All *you* need is a 16-ounce curved claw hammer. It's got enough weight to handle most nailing jobs, but it's not so heavy your arm will wear out after the ninth nail.

I learned how to hammer the hard way—by doing it wrong. I was so focused on hitting the nail square on the head (which is the goal) that I tap-tap-tappy-tapped in short strokes, using my wrist as the fulcrum for the swing. Wrong! Use your full forearm and the weight of the hammer to fuel that swing. You get much more momentum and force

The hammer's curved head can gouge materials. Place a wood scrap behind the head to protect surfaces when prying off trim or pulling nails.

SCREWDRIVER

by doing it that way. Practice hammering with this technique. You might miss the nail many times at first, but it won't take long before you perfect your aim and get good at it.

The hammer's claw is used for more than just pulling nails; it's a great demolition tool. The blades of the claw can bust through drywall pretty easily and give you a "starter hole" for tearing down the rest of the wall. Or the claw can function as a lever when you need to pry off wood trim or baseboard. I've even seen contractors use the claw to straighten out a crooked saw blade.

SCREWDRIVER There are so many battery-powered screwdrivers available, you'd think the manual screwdriver was as outdated as petticoats and corsets. But you still need one—because there will be a time when a big ol' power drill-driver is too big for the space you're working in. Plus, the screwdriver can perform many roles in home repair dramas. It can pry off lids, pry behind wood baseboard or trim, or poke stiff, unruly wires back into an electrical junction box (power off, of course!).

Go for a model that has interchangeable magnetic heads. That way you can easily switch from a Phillips head (looks like a +) to a standard or flat head (looks like a –).

UTILITY KNIFE Most of us are familiar with this handy little tool, and its cousin, the box cutter. The metal or plastic case houses a retractable cutting blade. A utility knife is used to cut materials like drywall, carpeting, tile backer board, screening, and wood shims. It can also be used to dig out and cut away old caulk or sealant.

You can buy a utility knife for two bucks or less. But it might pay to spend a little more on one with a nonslip grip and an easy blade-changing feature. To replace most blades, you have to disassemble the body of the knife with a manual screwdriver (See? Another use for that tool!) and set a new blade in place. Sometimes it takes a little fussing to ensure the blade is placed properly and on track. But you'll be surprised how often you'll use this tool, so consider springing for a good-quality one.

UTILITY KNIFE

SLIP-JOINT PLIERS

NEEDLE-NOSE PLIERS

TAPE MEASURE Even if you plan to contract out every little thing that goes wrong with your house, you're still going to need a tape measure. Subcontractors will want to know the size of your window, door, floor, wall, whatever. So, my friend, you'll have to measure it.

A 25-foot tape measure is a good basic model for your tool kit. When the blade is extended on a 25-footer, it'll stay stiff up to 6 feet. Why does that matter? Because when you're measuring up the side of something, like window casing, it's nice if the blade doesn't collapse down on you.

On most tape measures, an inch is divided into $\frac{1}{16}$-inch increments. All those little lines make for tricky reading at first. Just know that the longest line dividing each inch is the $\frac{1}{2}$-inch mark. The next longest lines are the $\frac{1}{4}$-inch marks, then the $\frac{1}{8}$-inch marks, then the wee, little, need-your-reading-glasses-to-see-them $\frac{1}{16}$-inch marks. There are even some tape measures that go way down to $\frac{1}{32}$-inch marks. Gimme a break! Anything that needs to be cut with that much precision can beat it.

There's an old carpenter's saying about measuring: measure twice, cut once. Take this to heart. If you've bought some fancy, expensive wood trim for a window or door, you don't want to waste a piece. Measure twice, cut once. And if, like me, you tend to forget measurements, write them down.

PLIERS Pliers are like extensions of your hands; they grip onto things good and tight, so you can use the grips as leverage to turn, pull, or crimp something. My favorite pliers are needle-nose pliers because the long, slender jaws work for lots of different things. I've used needle-nose pliers to repair jewelry, to reattach and secure the lift chain in my toilet tank, and to reach down the drain and fish out clumps of hair (hope you aren't eating lunch when you read this). Needle-nose pliers are also perfect for electrical work (see page 55).

Slip-joint pliers will put you in good stead if you're leaning toward plumbing repairs. The jaws adjust to varying widths to grab onto different-sized nuts and fittings.

essential power tools

Power tools can be scary for a first-time user. They're noisy, they vibrate, and they look as if they could hurt you. I'll admit some power tools are scary. (You won't catch me near a chain saw.) But once you've learned how to use a power tool safely, you'll never turn back. Using a handsaw to cut a 2 by 4 can take a minute; using the power version of the same tool will take seconds and give you a clean cut.

Now…a few words from Mama JoJo before you begin: use all tools mindfully. Using tools isn't like running the vacuum where you can space out while working. You need to focus on what you're doing and give it your full attention. Keep the following tips in mind:

• If you're using electric power tools, don't get tripped up by the cord.

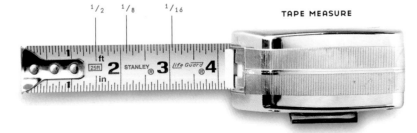

$\frac{1}{2}$ $\frac{1}{8}$ $\frac{1}{16}$ **TAPE MEASURE**

• If the cord is frayed or worn, don't use the tool.

• Don't use electric tools near water.

• Make sure your grip is steady and firm and that you're not over-reaching to perform a task.

• If you're cutting, be sure the wood is held firmly in place before you start.

It's overconfident, cocksure familiarity that will trip you up with power tools. The minute you don't pay attention to what you're doing is when accidents happen. I know a woodworker who's been using power tools for two decades. He spaced out while using the table saw—a tool he's used thousands of times—and sheared off part of his thumb. So, if you feel your mind wandering or you're getting tired, take a break. The project will wait for you.

POWER DRILL-DRIVER It's a drill! It's a screwdriver! It's both! Every power-tool manufacturer makes a combination "drill and screwdriver" that enables you to drill holes, and, with a simple change of the bit, drive screws.

An example of an application for this two-fer tool might be installing a drapery rod. You'd use one bit to predrill the holes for the screws. Then you'd use a screwdriver bit to secure the brackets. Same tool, two jobs.

Drill-drivers can be electric (corded) or battery operated (cordless). The advantage to electric power tools is that they don't need to be recharged. They keep going as long as there's juice. The batteries on cordless tools do need to be recharged, but you don't have a pesky cord getting in your way.

I could wax poetic about my 12-volt cordless drill-driver. It's not too heavy, so I can work overhead without muscle fatigue. It has enough power to handle all manner of jobs. It's variable speed, which means I can start driving a screw slo-o-o-o-wly to get it seated, and then zip!—drive the sucker home. And finally, it just feels good. The handle has gel padding so it cushions the grip.

When drilling, you want to approach the surface at a perfect 90-degree angle. This can take some practice. To help you, some drills come with level bubbles that indicate whether you're steering straight on or heading off course.

CORDLESS DRILL-DRIVER

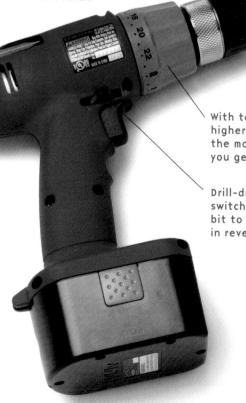

A keyless chuck allows you to change bits without using a special "key."

With torque control, the higher you turn this dial, the more turning power you get.

Drill-drivers have a switch that enables the bit to drive forward or in reverse.

POWER SANDER

DRILL BITS A discourse on drills isn't complete without a bit on bits. Bits are fitted into the drill's chuck (see photo on page 45). When you turn the chuck to the left, it opens the jaws to accept the bit. Turn it to the right to secure the bit.

Most drills will come with a bit for driving screws, but you'll have to invest in a couple more to complete your collection. If you're going to be drilling into wood, buy a "pilot point" drill bit set. These are the bits you'll use whenever you see instructions for "predrilling a hole." Use a size slightly smaller than the fastener when you're predrilling. A good quality set of bits will cost around $20 to $25 and will include a variety of sizes.

DRILL BITS

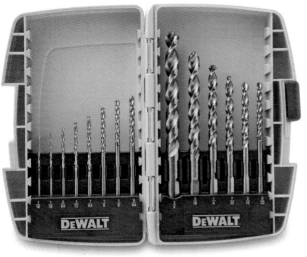

POWER SANDER If you never plan to paint wood or do so much as a lick of wood refinishing, skip this section. But if you would love to make your hollow-core doors with cheap stain look better, or get rid of the chipping paint on a nightstand, you want a power sander.

An electric palm sander is a good bet. It's a nifty square or round jobbie that allows you to clip on sandpaper of the desired grit and go to town. There are also sanders that use a hook-and-loop system (aka Velcro) to swap out the sanding pads.

TECHNIQUE
When using an extension cord with a power tool, tie both cords together with a loose knot where the plug meets the extension cord so they don't come apart.

With some of the old cordless models, the batteries would die after 30 minutes of constant use. But newer models have more long-lasting power. Power sanders also have creative designs. I have one shaped like an iron that works beautifully for getting into corners as well as for making wide passes.

When you use a power sander, the key is to apply even, light pressure and to go over the work with consistent strokes. Don't bear down on the sander with all your weight; let the tool do the work. You just need to keep it under control.

Oh, and it might be a Kindergarten Sanding Lesson to say this, but sand *with* the grain of the wood—not against it.

POWER SAWS OK, here comes Mama JoJo again with this public service announcement. Saws have blades; blades cut. Powered blades can be dangerous. Learn how to use a power saw responsibly and safely. Some of the rules include:

• Always wear safety glasses.
• Make sure your workpiece is stabilized and anchored before making your cut.
• Don't operate the saw with it directly in front of your body; keep it to either your left (for southpaws) or your right.
• Keep the cord out of the way.
• Keep the base plate firmly planted on the work surface.

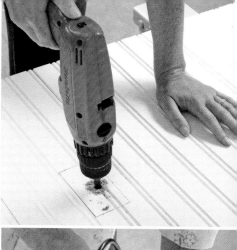

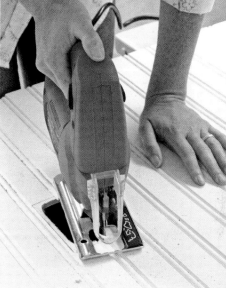

POWER HANDSAW

Don't wear jewelry or loose-fitting clothing that could get caught up in the tool, and if you have long hair, tie it back.

Now let's talk about which saw you want. There are two "starter" saws I like: the jigsaw and the power handsaw. They're kind of like Lady and the Tramp. Lady, the jigsaw, uses thin, delicate blades and makes a variety of cuts, including elegant scrolled cuts. Tramp looks like a stubby short hand-saw and is great for rough 'n' tumble work. Both are lightweight and easy to maneuver.

The jigsaw will be a snap to master if you've ever worked with a sewing machine because these tools have similar operating principles. When you sew fabric, the needle moves up and down and you move the material around as needed. With a jigsaw, the blade moves up and down and you move the tool around the material as needed.

The power handsaw I like is called the Navigator. It's such a staple in my household, I practically set a place for it at the dinner table. True to its name, the Navigator has sailed through tasks as varied as pruning tree branches and slicing into gutters. It won't give you an elegant, crisp cut such as you'd need for finish carpentry, but for general, all-purpose versatility, this saw rocks.

If you're using a jigsaw to cut out an opening in a piece of plywood or wainscot, you have to drill a pilot hole first (top photo). This allows the jigsaw blade to slip its slender self into position and make the cut (bottom photo).

PLEASE PASS THE PINK HAMMER

It seems more and more companies are coming out with tools marketed specifically to women. These tool lines typically feature lighter-weight drills and hammers, and ergonomic handles made for smaller hands. If you run across any of these tools while you're out shopping for your toolbox, pick them up and see what you think. Perhaps one of them will work better for you than a standard tool. Check out the resource guide on page 248 for some companies to look into.

JIGSAW

base plate

SAFETY GLASSES

WORK GLOVES

EARPLUGS

RESPIRATOR

DUST MASK

safety equipment

STAGE DIRECTIONS: [Read this in the effete tone of a fashion show commentator.]

"New this construction season! Accessories to safely complement your every home improvement task! Our first entry…oooh! I spy with my little eye…

Safety glasses! You'll be Geek Chic with these fabulous goggles that protect the fronts and sides of your eyes. Frames come in all colors, including black for a dramatic evening look!

Next? *Work gloves!* Vinyl textured grips are the rage this season and a value at only $5. Remember, ladies, those brown cotton jersey work gloves are so-o-o-o yesterday.

No home improvement maven who boogies in her off hours should be without *earplugs!* Available in electric blue, fuchsia, and parrot yellow, these cushiony foam pads will protect precious eardrums from nasty construction noise!

Finally, the *dust mask!* You will look like a surgeon…and darlings, you can consider yourself the Doctor of Home Repairs! Elastic bands tuck behind the ears for a snug fit. If you're working with noxious fumes or very fine dust particles, then upgrade to the popular *respirator!* Available now at your local home center or hardware store!"

But seriously, you need this stuff. You only need to be hit in the eye with a nail one time to realize that safety glasses aren't overkill. Lay in some fiberglass insula-tion without gloves and you'll itch like crazy. So spend $15 or so on these accessories. (The respira-tor is more expensive, so don't buy one unless your project demands it.)

other miscellaneous equipment

• Stepladder. For about $60, you can get a sturdy, reliable 6- or 8-foot stepladder that will reach most places you need to get. A stepladder is easier to work from than an extension ladder and it's not as scary. Always keep safety in mind. When using

STEPLADDER

ROLLER TRAY

DROP CLOTHS

MASKING TAPE

PAINT ROLLER

a ladder, make sure its legs are firmly and evenly planted. If you need to excavate a little dirt to get the ladder level, do it. A wobbly, tipsy ladder is a recipe for an accident.

• Drop cloth. Even minor home repairs can trash your floors with dust and debris. So it pays to have a good drop cloth or tarp to protect them. Plastic tarps and coverings are cheaper, but they are slippery. So spend the extra money for a good drop cloth with moisture-resistant backing. If you're in a pinch, use old sheets (but be aware that paint spills and drips will soak right through).

• Whisk broom. Whether it's removing leaves and debris from outdoor vents, knocking down spider webs, or simply getting better leverage for sweeping up construction debris, this little tool is another versatile must.

painting tools

You could spend a small fortune outfitting yourself with state-of-the-art painting tools. There are power sprayers that create a fine finish on cabinetry, or paint applicators that work like giant syringes by drawing from the can directly into the roller. If you plan to do a lot of painting, explore some of these tools. But for most tasks, the ones shown on this page ought to do the trick.

1¹⁄₂" ANGLED SASH BRUSH

2" TRIM BRUSH

4" PAINTBRUSH

PUTTY KNIFE

FOAM BRUSHES

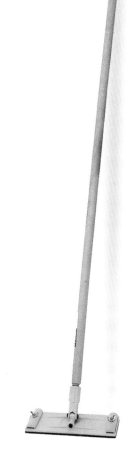

tools for walls and ceilings

This looks like a lot of tools, but consider that some are for minor patches and repairs, while others are for beautifying and making improvements. Some of the tools on these pages are specifically for finish carpentry (a term that refers to putting up trim around windows, doors, ceilings, etc.). In finish carpentry work, you need a really good saw for making precise cuts where two pieces of wood are joined. You can use a jigsaw (see page 47), but the power miter saw (pictured at right) is best for this kind of work.

A GOOD TOOL COLLECTION INCLUDES

Assortment of taping knives, pole sander, mud pan, utility knife, can opener, hammer, tape measure, drill, stud finder, level, sandpaper or power sander, nail set, pry bar, chalk line, carpenter's pencil, caulk gun, combination square, bevel gauge, and power miter saw.

A power miter saw's blade is adjustable so it can make either straight cuts or angled ones, such as 45 degrees for corners. The broad base helps stabilize the wood and the blade is pulled down to make the cut. See pages 107–109 for more information.

POLE SANDER
Cuts down on shoulder and arm fatigue. The extra length gives more leverage, enabling broader passes over ceilings or walls.

COMBINATION SQUARE
Invest in this versatile tool if you plan to do a lot of woodworking. It's used for marking square and angled cuts.

STUD FINDER
This device locates framing members (studs and joists) behind walls and ceilings.

MUD PAN
The sharp edge can be used to wipe a taping knife clean.

CAULK GUN
Press the release trigger to stop the flow of caulk or you'll have a gooey mess on your hands. Wipe the tool clean after each use and it'll last for years.

TAPING KNIVES
The wider the blade on a taping knife, the smoother the finish you'll get. Most often used to apply joint compound, but also handy for wood putty and anything else that needs to be smeared on.

PRY BAR
A versatile demolition tool worth owning, this is used to pry away materials.

The teardrop-shaped opening is for pulling nails.

NAIL SET
Helps you drive nail heads below the surface (a technique called countersinking). Use the nail set at a 90-degree angle to the surface.

LEVEL

The end bubbles read whether a surface is sitting perfectly vertical, or "plumb."

The center bubble indicates when a surface is sitting perfectly horizontal, or "level."

STANLEY
FatMax

tiling tools

The tools for tilework are pretty specific. None of them will send you to the poorhouse, but a wet saw is something best rented unless you're doing a lot of tilework.

The wet saw (or tub saw) looks and sounds scarier than it is. The blade doesn't have serrated cutting teeth like the ones you see on most saws. Instead, the grinding wheel is designed to cut through stone or ceramic surfaces.

A GOOD TOOL COLLECTION INCLUDES

Power drill, mixing paddle, chalk line, tape measure, pencil or marker, utility knife, level, rubber mallet, notched trowels, margin trowel, rubber grout float, wet saw, snap cutter, and tile nippers.

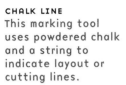

CHALK LINE
This marking tool uses powdered chalk and a string to indicate layout or cutting lines.

TILE NIPPERS
The sharp blades can make tiny nips in tile and are used for irregular cuts, such as curves around tub faucets.

RUBBER GROUT FLOAT
The padded face helps push grout into tile joints.

HOW TO USE A WET SAW Wear eye protection and earplugs when using a wet saw. Once you've marked where the tile should be cut, place the tile on the saw table. Without starting the saw, push the tile forward until it's up against the blade. You may have to adjust the tile to the right or left to get the blade directly on the cut mark.

Clamp down the guide so it's holding the tile in position. Pull the tile back, and start up the saw. Use your hands to hold the tile steady on its outside edges as you slowly move it forward under the grinding wheel (as shown above).

When it has cut all the way through, turn off the saw. The water cools down the heat caused by the friction, so make sure there's enough of it in the tray.

NOTCHED TROWELS

Small notches comb out mastic, which has a glue-like consistency.

Large notches are used for combing out mortar.

The flat side is used for spreading out mortar.

MARGIN TROWEL
Used to get mortar or mastic into tight spaces, and to back-butter tiles.

MIXING PADDLE
This drill attachment helps mix large quantities of mortar or grout.

SNAP CUTTER
A small circular blade scores the tile and the handle snaps down to make the cut.

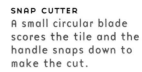

RUBBER MALLET
A rubber mallet can gently tap tiles level without marring the surfaces.

the essential household tool kit   53

plumbing tools

You can be a wench with a wrench if you do your own plumbing repairs. Whether you're disassembling a faucet handle to replace a worn O-ring or replacing a toilet handle, there's a lot of wrench work in plumbing. There are plenty more plumbing tools, but the repairs in this book are pretty basic. You probably won't be running out and buying a power snake any time soon.

A GOOD TOOL COLLECTION INCLUDES
Adjustable wrench, closet auger, drain-and-trap auger, crescent wrench, slip-joint pliers, needle-nose pliers, screwdrivers, sink plunger, socket wrench, tape measure, toilet plunger, caulk gun, and utility knife.

SINK PLUNGER
Designed specifically for sinks and drains.

TOILET PLUNGER
Designed specifically for the john.

SOCKET WRENCH
This is another way to loosen nuts. Interchangeable sockets come in many different sizes.

DRAIN-AND-TRAP AUGER
Works almost like a fishing line and reel—only you're fishing out clogs.

ADJUSTABLE WRENCH
The turning mechanism adjusts the jaws to custom-fit nuts.

54

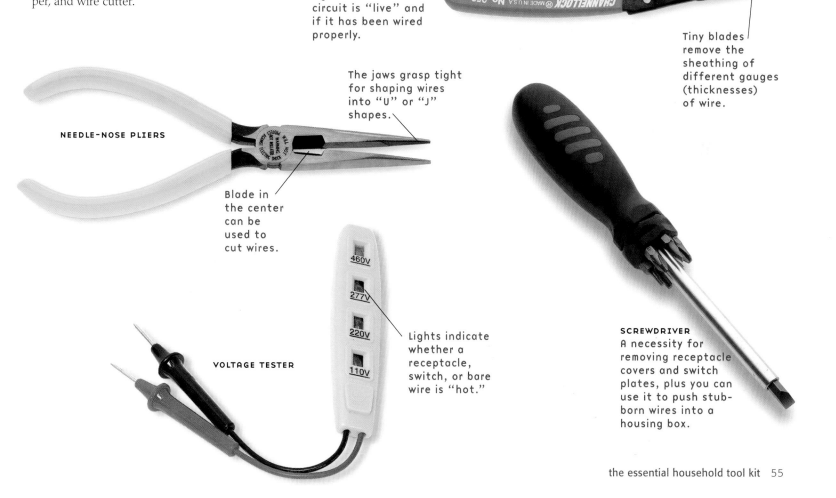

electrical tools

Electrical work doesn't require heavy lifting as a rule, but some of the wires you work with are stiff and unruly, so you want pliers that will grip tight. It's tempting, but it's not a good idea to try to bend wires with your fingers. I've tried and gotten poked. Ouch! Use needle-nose pliers instead.

A GOOD TOOL COLLECTION INCLUDES

Screwdrivers, needle-nose pliers, circuit tester, voltage tester, tape measure, ladder, torpedo level (see page 195, step 4), utility knife, drill, wire stripper, and wire cutter.

WIRE CUTTER

The sharp tips make clean cuts on wires.

CIRCUIT TESTER

Lights indicate if a circuit is "live" and if it has been wired properly.

WIRE STRIPPER

Tiny blades remove the sheathing of different gauges (thicknesses) of wire.

NEEDLE-NOSE PLIERS

The jaws grasp tight for shaping wires into "U" or "J" shapes.

Blade in the center can be used to cut wires.

VOLTAGE TESTER

460V
277V
220V
110V

Lights indicate whether a receptacle, switch, or bare wire is "hot."

SCREWDRIVER
A necessity for removing receptacle covers and switch plates, plus you can use it to push stubborn wires into a housing box.

CAUTION
WET
PAINT

Quality Paints

chapter 4

WALLS, CEILINGS, CABINETS, AND DOORS

HOME IMPROVEMENT PROJECTS can be a lot like your hair: you have good days and bad. I had a lousy home improvement day while installing a kitchen shelf.

I was predrilling holes through stubborn plaster walls when I smelled something burning. It wasn't toast; it was the drill bit smoldering from friction. The drill itself sounded as if it was about to explode from the effort.

So that's when I decided to compromise the project and use shorter screws. I knew it was wrong, but I wanted the job done before I was eligible for Social Security. I screwed in the brackets, popped on the shelf, and admired my work. It looked good—at least until a friend who'd had a little too much wine leaned on it. The whole thing crashed down, taking cookbooks, candles, and Chardonnay with it.

Of course, there's a moral to this story: don't let your tipsy friends lean on your cruddy home improvement projects.

In this chapter, you'll learn the right way to fasten shelves to a wall, as well as how to repair and spruce up walls, and how to complement your work by giving ceilings, trim, cabinets, and doors a face-lift.

chapter contents

REPAIRING WALLS AND CEILINGS

Unless you're a recovering claustrophobic, walls and ceilings create a sense of psychological security. We feel cocooned and nestled within these surfaces. But they take some nasty hits, bruises, and abuse. Think about the last time you moved furniture. *Boing!* So it's good to know how to heal the wounds and smooth over the scars.

Before you begin any work on the walls or ceiling, you need to determine what they're made of. If you live in a home constructed before 1940, chances are you have plaster walls. They sound solid when you knock on them. The surface can be swirled, stippled (speckled with small touches during application), or smooth.

Homes built since 1940 most likely have walls made of drywall. Knock on drywall and it'll sound hollow in places. The surface is almost always smooth, but might have a slightly textured layer of joint compound, or "mud," over it.

minor plaster repairs

If your plaster wall is Frankenstein-ugly with major jagged cracks and chunks missing, you probably can't patch the plaster yourself. That's because plaster is built up with three applications of a wet lime or gypsum mixture, and it requires artistry and skill to match it to the existing surface. But you can cut out a larger hole around the damaged area and fill it in with a piece of drywall. If you want to do this, follow the instructions for patching large holes in drywall on pages 62–63. To repair small holes and cracks in plaster walls, it's best to use joint compound rather than traditional plaster, because it's readily available and easy to work with.

It seems counterintuitive, but to get the best results, you might need to do a little more damage to plaster cracks and holes before filling them in. You also need to make sure the damaged area is completely free of any debris or dust particles, or the patching compound will plop out faster than Janet Jackson's you-know-what during the Super Bowl.

TIME & TALENT

It should only take about 15 minutes to patch; then you'll have to come back the next day to sand the area after it dries. Don't let the plaster scare you; this is a piece of cake.

STUFF YOU'LL NEED
- Drop cloth
- Can opener with a sharp, triangular point
- Small brush
- Spray bottle
- Taping knife
- Premixed joint compound
- 220-grit sandpaper or drywall sanding sponge and bucket of water
- Clean rag
- Paintbrush
- Primer
- Paint

HOW TO FIX PLASTER WALLS

1. Spread out the drop cloth to protect the floor. If you have a crack, use the sharp, triangular point of the can opener to gouge out a V-shaped channel in it. Thoroughly remove the loose material with the brush. If you have a hole, scrape the edges with the triangular point of the opener and then brush out the loose material.

2. Dampen the plaster around the damaged portion with the small spray bottle. This helps the patching material adhere.

3. Using the taping knife, fill the crack or small hole with joint compound. Spread it in an X pattern to make sure it fills the recessed area. Feather the edges as shown so the patch blends with the surrounding surface.

4. When the joint compound is dry, lightly sand the repaired area until the surface is flush with the rest of the wall. You can either use 220-grit sandpaper or a drywall sanding sponge (the latter will not kick up any dust). If you use the sponge, dip it in a bucket of water, squeeze out the excess, and rub the area until it's smooth.

5. Wipe off the dust with a clean rag (if you used sandpaper), or let the area dry (if you used the sponge). Prime and then paint the area.

59

minor drywall repairs

Drywall is made of gypsum sandwiched between two layers of paper. Gypsum isn't exactly diamond hard, so it's easy to dent or even gouge drywall.

If you have a small hole, make sure there's enough of an indentation to fill in. In some instances, you may actually need to use a hammer to pound the hole deeper. Just try to do it gently so you don't break through the drywall's paper shell.

If you have a crack, use the triangular point of a can opener to lightly etch out a V-shaped groove. Again, don't tear up the paper.

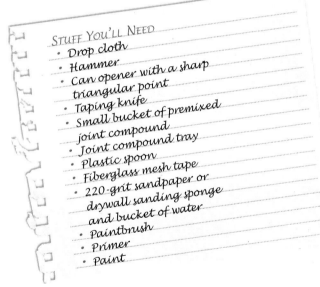

STUFF YOU'LL NEED
- Drop cloth
- Hammer
- Can opener with a sharp triangular point
- Taping knife
- Small bucket of premixed joint compound
- Joint compound tray
- Plastic spoon
- Fiberglass mesh tape
- 220-grit sandpaper or drywall sanding sponge and bucket of water
- Paintbrush
- Primer
- Paint

TIME & TALENT

Easy-schmeasy. Takes 5 minutes, unless you need to do multiple coats, in which case it will take a series of 5 minutes over a couple days to allow for drying time.

SHORTCUT

Very small holes (under ½ inch) can be filled with spackling compound (Spackle is a common brand) instead of joint compound.

HOW TO FIX MINOR DRYWALL DAMAGE

1. Spread the drop cloth. If necessary, use a hammer or can opener to prepare the hole or crack as described at left. Then scoop a small portion of joint compound into the tray, thin with a few drops of water, and mix to the consistency of frosting with a plastic spoon.

2. Use the taping knife to fill the crack or hole with joint compound. Hold the knife at a 45-degree angle and wipe off the excess material in an X pattern. Try to get it as smooth as possible to avoid excess sanding.

3. Let the area dry completely, then apply a second coat if needed.

4. Sand the area so it's flush with the surrounding wall; then prime and paint the area (see steps 4 and 5 on page 59).

USING MESH TAPE Drywall holes larger than 1 inch but smaller than 4 inches, and cracks longer than 1 inch, will need fiberglass mesh tape. This special tape is sold alongside joint compound and other drywall supplies. Tear off a piece big enough to cover the damage and press it to the wall. It will stay in place by itself—it's tape after all! Make sure it lays flat with no puckers or ridges. Then use a taping knife to apply three coats of joint compound over the mesh tape, letting each coat dry before applying the next. Be sure to feather out the edges so the patch blends with the existing wall surface.

Lightly sand the repaired area until the surface is flush with the rest of the wall. You can either use 220-grit sandpaper or a drywall sanding sponge (the latter will not kick up any dust). If you use the sponge, dip it in a bucket of water, squeeze out the excess, and rub the area until it's smooth.

Wipe off the dust with a clean rag (if you used sandpaper), or let the area dry (if you used the sponge). Prime and then paint the area.

WHAT'S "FLUSH"?

Flush isn't always associated with the toilet or hot flashes. In the realm of home improvement, it means to have a smooth, continuous plane or surface. Whenever I complete a repair, I run my fingers or hand over it to see if it's "flush." Check out some of the home-repair TV shows after the pros have joined two pieces of wood or patched a hole. They all stroke the repair to make sure it's flush.

patching large holes in drywall

Mesh tape won't be enough of a bandage if a large piece of drywall has been damaged. You'll need to cut out the area around the damage and replace it with a new piece of drywall (this technique is the same for walls and smooth ceilings). Make sure you get the right thickness. Drywall is typically ½ inch thick on walls and ⅝ inch thick on ceilings.

TIME & TALENT

It takes guts to cut a hole in your wall, even if it's already damaged. But once you get over that fear, the fix itself is relatively painless. You'll have a patched wall within an hour.

STUFF YOU'LL NEED

- Drop cloth
- Stud finder
- Pencil
- Tape measure
- Metal yardstick or other straightedge
- Utility knife with a fresh blade
- Scrap piece of drywall (usually ½" for walls, ⅝" for ceilings)
- Drywall saw
- Drill with screw bit attachment
- Drywall screws
- Handsaw or circular saw
- Scrap wood, either plywood strips or 1 x 2s
- Fiberglass mesh tape
- Taping knife
- Small bucket of premixed joint compound
- Joint compound tray
- Plastic spoon
- 220-grit sandpaper or drywall sanding sponge and bucket of water
- Paintbrush
- Primer
- Paint

HOW TO FIX MAJOR DRYWALL DAMAGE

1. Spread the drop cloth to protect the floor. Use the stud finder to locate studs on either side of the damaged area (see page 101 for instructions on using a stud finder). If the damage is directly over a stud, you can screw your new piece of drywall directly to it.

2. Sketch a square on the wall that extends slightly beyond the damaged area. If the damage is between two studs, mark the locations of the studs to the immediate left and right of the damage. You can either cut out a large section of wall that will span those studs (so you have something to screw the patch into), or cut out a smaller hole and construct a simple wooden brace to support the new piece of drywall (see steps 9 and 10). Mark your square on the wall accordingly.

3. Measure the height and width of your sketch and mark those dimensions on the new piece of drywall. This is going to be your patch.

4. With the straightedge as a cutting guide (a metal yardstick works well for this), use the utility knife to score the drywall along your pencil lines. *Score* means to cut it deeply, but not so deep you go through to the other side. Score each side of your patch.

5. Snap the drywall along the score lines. It should break easily. The paper backing on the other side will still be hanging on, so flip the piece over and cut along the seam with the utility knife to finish the job.

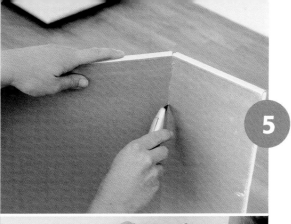

6. Hold the piece of drywall up to the damaged area and if your old sketch doesn't exactly match the patch, trace its contours onto the wall. Set down the patch.

7. Score along the trace lines with the utility knife, then use the drywall saw to cut out the damaged area. If you're cutting over a stud, you may run into some old nails or screws that held the drywall on, and you'll have to remove those as well.

8. If there's a stud (or studs) visible in the wall opening, all you need to do is fit the patch into place and secure it to the stud(s) with countersunk drywall screws ("countersink" means driving the screw until it's slightly below the surface). Use 1 screw every 8 inches.

9. If your damage isn't located between studs, you'll need to create a support brace. Measure the dimensions of your hole. With a hand saw or circular saw, cut two pieces of plywood or 1-by-2 wood so that they will extend horizontally a few inches beyond the opening on both sides.

10. Hold one of the wood pieces inside the hole toward the top, pull it tight against the back of the drywall, and secure it with one drywall screw on either side. Countersink the screws. Then do the same with the second piece of wood toward the bottom of the hole.

11. Screw the drywall patch to the wood backing, countersinking the screws. Then tape the seams and apply layers of joint compound with a taping knife as described on page 61. Once the final layer of joint compound is smooth and dry, prime and then paint the area.

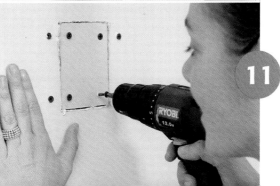

textured wall repairs

As a kid, my childhood bedroom had textured walls that fascinated me. The walls' pattern swirled, whirled, crested, and crashed like waves on an ocean. The texture not only helped the walls be more durable, it was a nice design upgrade as well.

Once you fix the damage on your textured walls using the techniques described on pages 58–63, you'll have to match the surrounding texture, which can take artistry and practice.

Give yourself some time to practice on a scrap piece of drywall first. Use a drywall knife, a damp sponge, a whisk broom, or even a finely notched trowel to play with finishing techniques. Personally, I think this is fun. You may get in touch with your inner artist—the Mud Diva!

COOL PRODUCT TO TEXTURE WALLS Some walls are such a mess, there's no choice but to give them a full makeover. You could tear down the wall and start over, retexture the wall (see pages 70–73) and then paint, or cover up the mess with a product called Manda Mudd, which gives your walls texture and color. Start the process by paint-ing your walls a solid color. The second coat, in a coordinating color, has a mudlike texture and is randomly applied with a trowel over the paint. The third coat of "mud" has a slightly different color than the paint and the second coat. The end result is an open-plaster look that disguises flawed walls and creates an Old World European feel. See all the color choices at www.mandamudd.com.

Patching a distinct wall texture takes practice. To create craters like this, make quick passes with a dry-wall knife and don't go back to fill in areas that were missed.

Manda Mudd hides flaws, leaving you with color and texture that looks as if it cost a fortune. Kind of like a good makeup job.

textured ceiling repairs

Most often, ceiling damage is caused by water. It happened to me once. My guest bedroom ceiling looked like a wet diaper when the shower above it leaked. Obviously, plumbing problems need to be fixed before you repair the ceiling.

TEXTURED CEILINGS If your ceiling has a smooth finish, you can use the same techniques outlined in the wall-repair section to make minor repairs and patches (see pages 58–63). A textured ceiling can either have a popcorn-like finish, or something called "knock down," which means the surface has some texture—almost like the craters of a moonscape—but not quite the nubby look of popcorn.

Fortunately, there are readymade products that make repairing textured ceilings a snap. Before you start, be sure to cover the floor and any furniture that can't be moved out of the way with drop cloths. Also, wear a respirator and goggles so you don't inhale any dust (especially if it might contain asbestos) or get a piece of "popcorn" in your eyes as you're looking up at the ceiling.

WATCH OUT!

If your home was built before 1980, the popcorn may contain asbestos. Send a sample to a lab for confirmation first, as breathing asbestos dust is hazardous to your health.

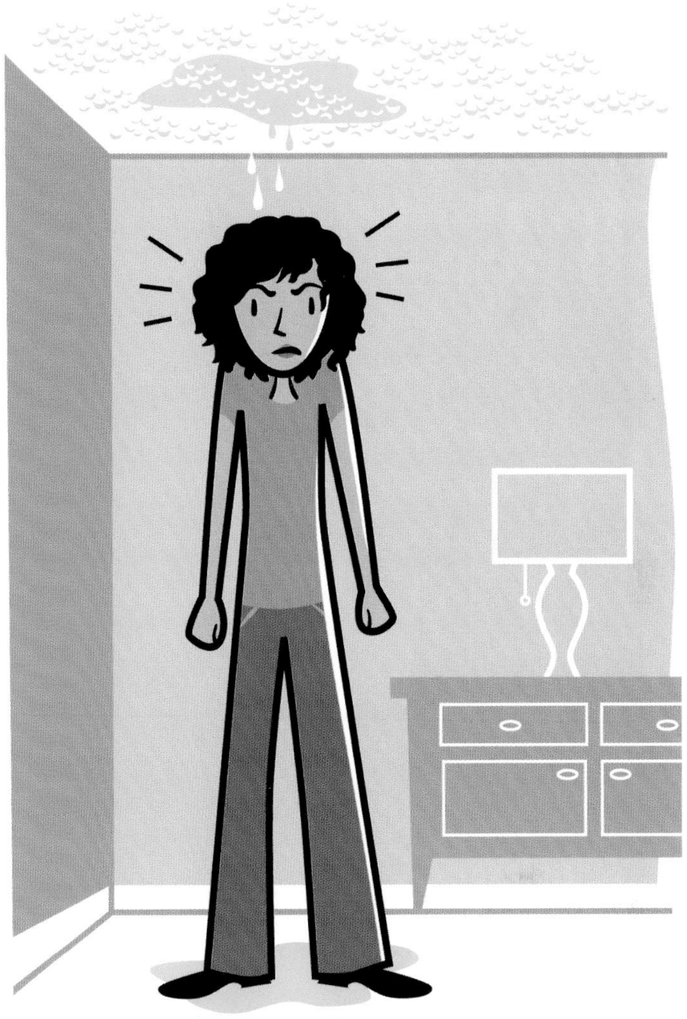

AN EDITORIAL MOMENT...

There are some ceilings that have a nubbled, sprayed-on texture—the so-called popcorn ceiling. Let me just say this about popcorn ceilings: they suck. They're ugly and cheapen the look of a room. Ceilings comprise one-sixth of a room's area. A room can go from "wow" to "whoa!" when a ceiling has a beautiful smooth finish, or has beams or painted scenes. So I say reserve popcorn for long winter nights watching *Seinfeld* reruns. Choose smooth ceilings wherever, whenever, however you can.

STUFF YOU'LL NEED

- Drop cloths
- Whisk broom
- Taping knife
- Safety glasses
- Respirator
- Spray-on ceiling texture
- Scrap piece of cardboard
- Stepladder
- Paintbrush
- Primer
- Paint

The biggest part of the job will be protecting everything in the room and cleaning up. The rest is just point and spray.

HOW TO PATCH A POPCORN CEILING

1. Spread the drop cloths. Use the whisk broom to clear away any loose particles in the damaged area. You may want to use the taping knife to scrape the area down a bit.

2. Wearing your stylish safety glasses and respirator, test out the spray pattern of the canned texture on the scrap of cardboard. That way you'll see how far away you should be and how much you should use to match the existing finish.

3. Spray the texture onto the ceiling with a back-and-forth motion. Use a light touch. It's always easier to add material than to scrape it off and start over. To match knock-down texture, take your taping knife and hold it almost flat against the ceiling surface after you've sprayed it. While the material is still wet, lightly draw your knife across the texture in a smooth movement. For popcorn texture, leave the material alone.

4. Let the texture dry completely before priming and painting. Popcorn likes to pop off the ceiling when it's wet. So it's best to dab on small quantities of primer and paint, and let each coat dry thoroughly before applying the next (all the while muttering "Popcorn sucks!" under your breath).

REPLACING CRACKED TILES

If you have tile in your bathroom or kitchen, you already know it's a durable material that looks good. But over time, tile can crack—usually because of structural stresses or water damage.

Repairing cracked tiles isn't a sweat-inducing, labor-intensive chore. But locating matching tile and grout might be. Ideally, previous homeowners have left behind spare tiles, so then your detective work is limited to matching the grout. If, however, you have to sleuth out matching tile, don your trench coat and best Humphrey Bogart accent and try these tips:

• Take a sample of your damaged tile to a tile showroom. If the pattern is still available, the tile can be ordered.

• Contact local salvage yards. Some of them harvest materials such as doorknobs, molding, and tile from old homes and buildings. They might have what you're looking for.

• Hire a tile artisan to custom-match your tile. There are many companies that specialize in restoration work and these experts can match just about anything.

• Buy coordinating tiles and create a new accent strip. You'll have to remove perfectly intact tiles to make the strip, but it's a great way to update your design. Make sure the new tiles are the same thickness as the existing tiles.

• For grout matches, visit a tile showroom and take a piece of your existing grout with you. Let someone at the store help you find a color that will blend with your existing grout.

As you remove damaged tiles, especially around showers and tubs, you might find water damage underneath them. The surface behind the tile may either feel damp or spongy to the touch, or might have evidence of mold or mildew (black spots). If you have water damage, it's a waste of time and effort to slap up some replacement tile and walk away. You need to do a bigger excavation to get to what's causing the damage so you can have the problem repaired. You might even have to replace portions of the surface underneath the tile. In that case, consider calling a tiling contractor. If there is no water damage, you can replace the damaged tile with no worries.

STUFF YOU'LL NEED
• Safety glasses
• Cold chisel
• Hammer
• Grout saw
• Margin trowel or putty knife
• Premixed mastic
• Paper towels
• Plastic tile spacers
• Painter's tape
• Grout
• Rubber grout float (optional)
• Sponge
• Clean cloth

TIME & TALENT

Finding replacement tiles can be as tough as finding the Holy Grail. Otherwise, this repair's a snap (unless there's water damage, which complicates things).

HOW TO REPLACE A CRACKED TILE

1. Put on the safety glasses so that flying shards of tile don't hit your eyes. Position the edge of the cold chisel in the grout line above the damaged tile, and hit the handle edge with the hammer. You may have to do this a few times on each side before the tile comes loose. Once the tile is out, remove any remaining grout with the grout saw.

2. Use the margin trowel or putty knife to scrape the surface clean of any residual mortar or mastic.

3. Back-butter the new tile (this means to spread the mastic directly onto the back of the tile) and press it into place. Wipe off any mastic that oozes out around the edges with a wet paper towel. Put plastic tile spacers or piece of cardboard underneath the new tile to keep it from sliding down.

4. Put two strips of painter's tape over the new tile to hold it in place while the mastic dries.

5. Once the mastic is dry (check the label on the can for dry times), mix a small amount of grout and press it into place with your fingers or the rubber grout float. Let it set for about 20 minutes, then come back and remove excess grout from the face of the tile with a damp sponge. Once the grout is completely dry, wipe away any remaining "grout haze" with the clean cloth.

REMOVING WALLPAPER

Many times, wallpaper is applied over old wallpaper, so stripping down to the bare wall takes patience. The key is in dissolving the glue with moisture. You can rent steamers for this. But I've found this technique works just as well.

STUFF YOU'LL NEED

- Drop cloth
- Serrated scoring tool, such as the Paper Tiger (made by Zinsser)
- Safety glasses
- Rubber gloves
- Wallpaper stripper (I like the gel type made by DIF)
- Plastic paint tray and foam paint roller
- 4" wallpaper scraper or drywall knife
- Garbage bags
- Large sponge
- Bucket of water

TIME & TALENT

For a small room, set aside a full day to complete the job. If the wallpaper comes off easily, you'll barely break a sweat. If not, you'll be cursing the previous homeowners by lunchtime.

HOW TO REMOVE WALLPAPER

1. Spread out the drop cloth to protect the floor. Run the scoring tool in a circular motion over the wall to create small holes in the wallpaper.

2. Put on your safety glasses and rubber gloves. Pour some of the stripper into the plastic paint tray and use the roller to "paint" the stripper onto the wall. Really saturate it. The stripper will seep through the holes and dissolve the glue. Leave it alone for the amount of time indicated on the stripper label.

3. Use the wallpaper scraper or drywall knife to peel away the paper and throw it away. Be careful not to damage the drywall as you scrape. If there's more than one layer of wallpaper, you might have to remove them one at a time.

4. Use a wet sponge to completely clean off any remaining glue.

RETEXTURING WALLS

If walls could talk, they might complain about the indignities they've suffered over the years. They may have cracks from uneven settling and foundation movement, or botched patching jobs. Whether you need smoother walls for a certain decorative paint technique, or you'd just like to cover up years of wear and tear, it's possible to get a clean slate by retexturing the walls with a thin layer, or "skim coat," of joint compound.

It takes lots of practice to get a thin layer of joint compound to be absolutely smooth. The key is to work in small sections and then fix the uneven spots by sanding when the surface is dry. But you don't want to rely completely on sanding to get a smooth surface. Sanding joint compound makes a huge mess. You'll be covered in white powder from head to toe. So will everything else in the room. While some sanding is inevitable (and there are ways to minimize the dust; see page 73), you want to keep it to a minimum by spreading the joint compound as smoothly as possible to begin with.

Maybe you don't want smooth. Maybe you want a light or heavy texture. Practice first! Experiment on scrap drywall with swirling motions, making short swipes with your taping knife, or by using a notched trowel to create grooves.

If your walls have any holes, dings, or cracks, you need to fix those before you retexture (see pages 58–63). Popped nails should be hammered in so the heads are slightly below the surface and then patched. Remove any receptacle and switch covers and store them in a ziplock plastic

STUFF YOU'LL NEED
- Hammer (if necessary)
- Screwdriver and ziplock bag
- Utility knife (if necessary)
- Putty knife (if necessary)
- Small pry bar (if necessary)
- Wood shims (if necessary)
- Painter's tape
- Plastic drop cloths
- Rosin paper or canvas drop cloths
- 3" taping knife
- Premixed joint compound
- Joint compound tray
- Liquid dishwashing detergent
- 12" taping knife
- Flashlight
- Safety glasses
- Respirator
- Sanding material of choice (see page 73)
- Broom and dustpan
- Vacuum cleaner or shop vac
- Sponge
- Paintbrush and roller
- Primer
- Paint

TIME & TALENT

Skim-coating a room can take 2 to 3 days because you'll be repairing damaged areas, mudding all the walls, and sanding. But those flawless new walls will be worth it. This is something you definitely get better at with practice.

bag with their screws. If you're replacing the window and wall trim, remove the old stuff before you start (see page 103). Otherwise, mask it with painter's tape.

Move everything you can out of the room and cover what remains with plastic drop cloths. Cover your floor with rosin paper or canvas drop cloths to protect it from dropped globs of joint compound and sanding dust. If you're doing one small wall, you might be able to get by with a gallon of premixed joint compound. Otherwise you'll need the 5-gallon version.

Premixed joint compound is sold primarily for taping drywall joints. It's a little thicker than you need for a light skim coat. Thin the joint compound with a little water and stir until it reaches the consistency of frosting. Also stir in a couple drops of liquid dishwashing detergent, which prevents any bubbles from forming in the joint compound.

DOUBLE TROUBLE

If you've managed to recruit a partner to help you with this job, it's best if you work on separate walls. Sometimes two different people will end up making two slightly different textures. If these competing textures aren't on the same wall, the variations will be less obvious.

HOW TO RETEXTURE WALLS

1. Use the 3-inch taping knife to scoop some of the joint compound into the tray, and add water and liquid detergent as described at left. A joint compound tray (or some other wide and shallow container) will be easier to move around than the large bucket of joint compound. You'll also want to keep the large container covered while you work so the joint compound doesn't dry out or get any debris in it.

2. With the 12-inch taping knife, scoop some joint compound out of the tray. Start spreading it on the wall. You want to cover up the imperfections but keep the layer as thin as possible. Think of it as the second layer of frosting on a cake—you want to cover up the first layer of frosting that has all those cake crumbs in it with a thin, smooth layer.

3. Keep spreading out the joint compound until it has covered as much surface area as it can. You'll notice that the edges of the taping knife leave marks on the wall. To minimize this, don't press too hard, just barely make contact with the joint compound as you're spreading it out. Keep the blade drawn relatively flat against the surface and pull down with consistent pressure. Going back over ridges left by your tool too many times will make them worse rather than better. This is when you need to take control of yourself, stop messing with these areas, and resign yourself to sanding them later.

4. Scoop more joint compound onto your taping knife and start on the next section. When you get to an inside corner or up against a piece of trim, put the edge of the loaded taping knife into the corner vertically and pull horizontally away from the edge. This should leave a smooth line.

5. Once you've finished mudding the space, let the joint compound dry completely. This could take one or more days, depending on the room's temperature and humidity level. You can tell when it's dry because it turns from an antique white to a bright white. It will look patchy as it's drying. Leftover joint compound should be thoroughly scraped out of the pan and discarded. Wash the pan in cool water and make sure to let plenty of water run down the drain. Too much joint compound and not enough water down your drain could contribute to a clog.

6. To prepare for sanding, tape up plastic drop cloths to isolate the area. Seal all the edges with painter's tape. You can find special tape-on zippers that allow you to get in and out without having to remove the plastic. Otherwise, the painter's tape should be easy to remove and re-stick as many times as you need to. If you have any heat or air-conditioning registers in the room, be sure to cover those with plastic as well so the dust doesn't get into your ductwork.

7. Once the walls are completely dry, use a clean taping knife to scrape off any ridges. Inspect the wall for areas with too much texture or too many marks from the taping knife—basically any place you don't like. Sometimes it's hard to see these areas, so shine a flashlight at an angle to the wall to scope them out.

8. Before you start sanding, you need to get your gear on—safety glasses and a respirator are necessities. Flimsy dust masks won't protect your lungs from these fine particles. Invest in your health and buy a full respirator that will do the job. Put on a hat or scarf to protect your hair, and wear your workin' clothes. You'll look as if you're ready to enter a nuclear reactor, but fortunately this dust isn't radioactive, just messy.

9. Using one of the sanding methods described on the next page, sand the surface until you're happy with it. You'll find that it doesn't take much pressure to get the joint compound off, so start off gently and only press hard if you need to. Be prepared to do this step in one session so that you can get it over with and clean up one time rather than over and over again. If you see any small holes in the surface, or if you can still see the problems on the wall you were trying to cover up, you'll need to apply a second light coat on those portions and do steps 7 through 9 again.

10. Once all the wretched sanding is finished, get yourself cleaned up, and then start on the room. Use a damp cloth to wipe excess dust off the walls, and a broom and dustpan to sweep up as much of the debris on the floor as possible. Follow up with a vacuum. If possible, use a shop vacuum for this. Joint compound dust particles are hard on your house vacuum's motor. Finally, use a damp sponge to remove the last remnants of dust. You'll need to paint on a coat of primer to seal the joint compound before you paint it with a top coat.

sanding joint compound

When you have a lot of joint compound to sand, it makes sense to do it as quickly as possible in a way that generates minimal dust. These are the options:

SANDPAPER Fold sandpaper in quarters or use a sanding block (which is just a palm-sized block made of sandpaper). Start with 120-grit sandpaper and finish with 150 grit. This is a messy approach, but it requires the least equipment and results in a fine finish.

SCREENING Professionals often use an abrasive screen fitted on a plastic base, which can be hand-held (as shown in step 9 at left) or attached to the end of a pole. The finish is similar to what you get with sandpaper, and the job is equally messy. When using a pole sander (see page 50), you avoid having to work on a ladder.

VACUUM SANDING You can buy or rent sanders that attach to vacuums. This adds to the expense and noise, but the work goes swiftly and there's very little dust. Some systems may take practice to use well.

WET SANDING With a drywall sanding sponge (a small-cell polyurethane sponge made for this purpose), you can sand drywall mud by hand without generating dust. This is a simple and quiet solution, though it leaves the surface slightly rougher than 150-grit sandpaper does.

INSTALLING WAINSCOT

You might complain about the rusty plumbing in older homes, but you can't complain about the woodwork. One wood embellishment I always admire is wainscot. Wainscot (or wainscoting) is a series of solid wood slats that run half or three-quarters of the way up the wall. You see wainscot in older dining rooms and kitchens—presumably to spare the plaster walls from bangs and bumps when chairs are backed into them.

Traditional wainscot is constructed from pieces of bead board, which are milled wood boards measuring about ⅜ inch thick and 4 inches wide, with a tongue on one side and a groove on the other. When you push pieces of bead board together, the tongue goes into the groove to create a seamless look. Using richly grained wood and staining it a dark color gives the wainscot an Arts and Crafts feel. Painting the bead board gives it a country cottage feel.

These days you can buy plywood panels with embossed patterns that look like classic bead board. Instead of installing bead board 4 inches at a time, you can now go 4 feet at a time. The panels come in two sizes (48 by 32 inches and 48 by 96 inches) and are less expensive than individual solid pieces of bead board. Best of all, they're easier to install.

In addition to the bead-board sheets, you'll need baseboard and a cap piece to finish off the top and bottom edges. Look for preprimed kits that include all three elements. You can also find bead board made out of medium density fiberboard (MDF), which won't expand and contract the way solid wood does, making it a better choice for high-moisture areas like bathrooms, kitchens, and laundry rooms.

If you're using traditional pieces of bead board or panels, you need to install them first and then cover up the bottom with baseboard. If you're using a kit and have baseboard pieces with a groove for the bead board, install the baseboard first. For this project, MDF paneled bead-board sheets were used. If your bead board is raw wood, prime the back before installing it to prevent the wood from warping. In fact, it's much easier to do all your priming and painting before the materials go up.

STUFF YOU'LL NEED
- Small pry bar
- Scrap wood
- Tape measure
- Pencil
- 4' level
- Stud finder
- Bead-board panels
- Makeshift work table or sawhorses
- Safety glasses
- Circular saw
- Screwdriver
- Ziplock plastic bag
- Jigsaw
- Drill
- Caulk gun
- Wood construction adhesive
- Hammer
- 4d finish nails
- Nail set
- Baseboard (if necessary)
- Compound miter saw (if necessary)
- Plinth block (if necessary)
- Cap pieces
- Spackling compound or wood putty
- Caulk
- Utility knife

TIME & TALENT

The cuts make this project more complicated than most. Plus you need to feel comfortable working with a power saw. It should take about a half-day to install everything on one wall, plus time to paint.

HOW TO INSTALL WAINSCOT

1. Remove any existing baseboard with the pry bar, making sure to protect your walls with the piece of scrap wood (see page 103). Then decide how high you want the wainscot. Traditionally, it either comes up to chair-rail height (36 inches) or plate-rail height (48 inches to 60 inches). Measure up from the floor and mark the desired height on the wall. Then use a 4-foot level and pencil to draw a continuous level line across the wall(s) you'll be working on.

2. Use a stud finder to locate the studs across the wall(s). When it finds Brad Pitt, it'll beep. (Just seeing if you're paying attention.) The stud finder beeps once it reaches the corner of a stud, so make your marks a little past where it beeps. Remember to mark the wall in pencil and above the level line so you can see where the studs are after the bead board is in place.

3. Take measurements from the floor to your level line at various points along the wall(s). Floors aren't always perfectly level, so don't assume the panels will be the same height on all the walls. Cut the bead-board panels ¼ inch shorter than the shortest measurement from your floor to the level line.

4. Place a panel on your makeshift table (or sawhorses) with the part to be cut hanging off the edge. Measure and mark the area that needs to be trimmed off and, wearing safety glasses, make the cut with a circular saw (a power handsaw or jigsaw would also work).

5. If there are any electrical receptacles or light switches where you're installing the bead board, remove the covers or switch plates (store them, with their screws, in the ziplock bag). Measure down from the level line and from the side of your last panel to determine where each opening will fall. Draw the shape in place on the bead-board sheet and cut it out with a jigsaw. To cut out a shape with a jigsaw, you'll need to drill a starter hole first. Drill the hole, then put the blade of the jigsaw into that hole and start cutting from there (see page 47).

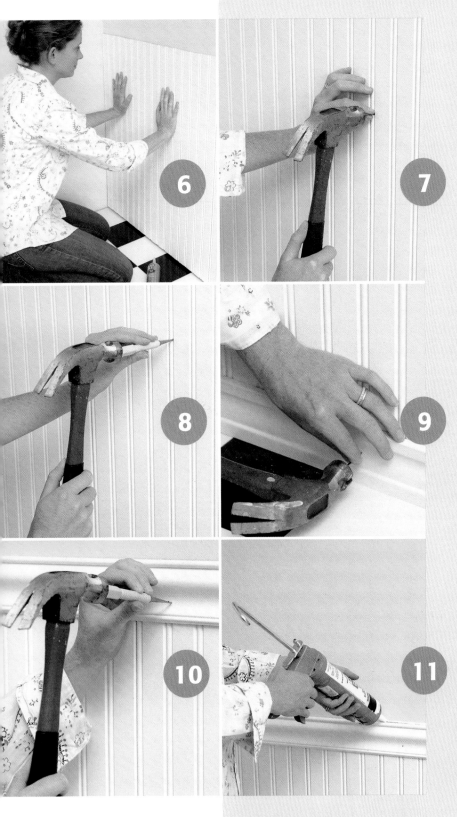

6. Start the installation in a corner of the room. Lay the first panel facedown on the floor. Load the tube of construction adhesive in the caulk gun and run a zigzag line on the back of the panel. Then pick it up and press it against the wall so it's lined up with your level line. Once it makes contact, pull it off the wall and hold it away for about 10 seconds, then press it back in place. This extra step makes the glue bond better. Double-check that this first piece is straight and level, as you'll use it to align future pieces.

7. Drive 4d finish nails through the bead board's grooves and into the wall where you've noted the studs are. Nail every 8 inches from top to bottom.

8. Once all the nails are in, countersink the nail heads with a nail set so the heads are below the surface.

9. Keep installing panels across the wall(s). When all the panels are up, install baseboard pieces to hide the gap between the floor and the bottom of the bead-board panels. You can reuse your old baseboard, which will be cut and ready for you. Or you can install new material. If you install new baseboard, either use a compound miter saw to make the corner cuts at a 45-degree angle, or use a plinth block in the corner and make straight cuts with a jigsaw or circular saw (see pages 102–104). Nail the baseboard to the studs and countersink the nails.

10. Finish off the top edges with decorative cap pieces. Cut the pieces to length, and set them in place slightly overlapping the bead-board panel. Nail through the cap piece and into the studs. Countersink the nails.

11. Fill the nail holes with spackling compound if you're painting the wainscot, or with wood putty if you plan to stain it. Run a bead (one long thin line) of caulk along the top of the cap piece and in the corners. You can get caulk in small tubes that are squeezable; otherwise you'll also need a caulk gun to get the caulk out of the tube. Use a utility knife to cut the tip off the caulk nozzle. The closer you cut to the tip, the thinner the bead of caulk will be. Smooth out the caulk with your finger or a wet paper towel.

TILING A WALL

Is the design of your kitchen or bathroom dull as dry toast? But a full remodel is too much work or too expensive? Well, there are little things you can do that'll make a big impact, such as tiling a backsplash. You could add just one row of art tiles to the top of your existing backsplash, or tile the entire area between your countertop and upper cabinets. Or, if you really want to go for the graduate level of tiling projects, do a full wall.

preparing the surface

Start with a smooth, sturdy, clean—and, ideally, straight—wall. You'll use mastic, a premixed adhesive that looks a lot like shaving cream, to stick the tiles to the wall. If you were tiling a wall that gets wet regularly (like in a shower), you'd use thinset mortar instead of mastic. You'd also be tiling over a specially prepared surface like Dura Rock, but that's another project for another time.

Mastic needs to be able to grip the wall, which it won't do if the wall is oily, dirty, or covered with glossy paint. If your wall has any of these issues, you'll have to paint on a coat of primer and let it dry completely before tiling (see pages 89–91).

You'll also want to cover up the floor or countertop with a drop cloth or pieces of rosin paper, and secure the edges with painter's tape. Setting the tiles isn't that messy, but grouting is, so you might as well protect everything from the start.

STUFF YOU'LL NEED
- Drop cloth or rosin paper
- Painter's tape
- Primer and paint supplies (if necessary)
- Tape measure
- Pencil
- Tiles
- Plastic spacers
- 4' level
- Batten board (1 x 2 cut to length with one factory cut edge)
- Drywall screws
- Drill with screw bit
- Snap cutter or wet saw
- Safety glasses
- Notched trowel
- Mastic
- Rubber mallet
- Utility knife
- Cap pieces (if necessary)
- Premixed grout with latex additive
- 3 buckets
- Margin trowel or paddle attachment for drill
- Heavy rubber gloves
- Laminated grout float
- Large sponge
- Rags
- 100% silicone caulk
- Caulk gun

TIME & TALENT

It's possible to spend an entire afternoon figuring out the perfect layout. Start fresh the next morning and set the tiles. Give them 48 hours to cure and then plan on at least 3 to 4 hours for grouting. Tiling takes patience, but it's easy once you get the hang of it.

laying out the first row

If you're not a math whiz, determining the tile layout can be challenging. You have to factor in not only the width of the tiles, but also the spaces between them, which are called "joints." Without determining a layout first, you might start in a corner with a full tile and just keep tiling merrily along until you reach the other side of the wall, where you might find that only a sliver of tile will fit.

To avoid this unsightly problem, lay out the tiles on a flat surface first to figure out how many full tiles will fit across the wall. (You'll need an area at least the width of the area you're tiling to do this.) Measure the space and draw a line on the right and left edges of the flat surface to represent the ends of your wall or the area you're tiling. Then mark the exact center (also mark this spot on the wall). Lay out a row of tiles, using plastic spacers between them so you have an accurate picture. The size of the plastic spacers indicates how large your joints will be. Adjust the whole row of tiles between the two lines that define your tiling area until you have a configuration that looks best.

Chances are, you will have room for less than a full tile at the ends. But instead of having a half-tile at only one end of the wall, split the difference and put a quarter piece of tile at both ends so it looks even. Large obstructions like windows can complicate matters, as you don't want tiny slivers of tiles around them either. Start from the center of the window and work out from both sides. Keep playing with it until you have a layout that works.

The other important issue when tiling a horizontal surface is making sure the first row of tiles is level. If the first row is crooked, the rest of the

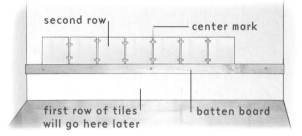

tiles will be, too. Use a 4-foot level to draw a straight line on which to set your first and second rows of tiles. You'll need to be careful not to cover the pencil lines with mastic later on.

laying out multiple rows

When you're tiling more than a few rows up, you will need the assistance of a batten board to support the tiles as the mastic hardens. You can use any straight piece of lumber with one factory-cut edge as a batten board (usually it's a 1 by 2 or 1 by 3).

Each row of tiles depends on the row beneath it to hold it up while the mastic dries. Otherwise, the tiles would slowly slide down the wall and ruin that straight and level line you worked so hard on. This is where our hero, the batten board, comes in. Screw this board into the wall studs so that its top edge is at the same height as the top edge of your

TECHNIQUE
Because floors and counters can be uneven, the first row of tiles should be set ¹/₈ to ¹/₄ inch above them. You'll fill the gap in later with caulk or a trim piece.

bottom row of tiles (see illustration at left). It seems weird, but the bottom, or first, row of tiles is the last one you'll set. The batten board provides a level and secure base for setting your starter, or second, row of tiles. It's easily removed once the mastic under the upper rows of tile has hardened (which is why it's screwed and not nailed into place). Later, when you set the bottom row of tiles, use plastic spacers to keep them propped up off the floor or counter.

Use a batten board for a backsplash if the tiles will go down to the counter. If you have a backsplash that's partially tiled and you're adding rows, you can use the existing tiles as your batten board.

You've got your layout all figured out, you've marked a level line on the wall to indicate where your first and second rows of tiles will start, and you've screwed in a batten board across the wall right under the level line for the second row of tiles. Now take a break and come back refreshed and ready to tile.

MAKING CUTS

If you're using small ceramic tiles, you can cut straight lines with a manual snap cutter. If you're using large or thick ceramic tiles that won't fit in the snap cutter, or tiles made of porcelain, stone, or terracotta, you'll need a wet saw (see page 52). You can rent one for about $40 per day. (Remember to always wear safety glasses when you're cutting tile!) If you plan to do a lot of tiling around the house, you might want to buy a wet saw for about $100. Wet saws use diamond blades to cut tiles. And if you're cutting a lot of tiles, you'll see why diamonds are indeed a girl's best friend.

HOW TO TILE A WALL

1. You're going to start at the bottom of the wall (right above the batten board, if applicable). Using a notched trowel that's the proper size for the job (the can of mastic should tell you this), scoop some mastic out of the can. Use the short, flat edge of the trowel to spread the mastic on the wall. Then comb over the mastic with the notched edge of the trowel. Spread only as much mastic as you can set tiles into in 30 minutes, and be careful not to cover your layout lines. Hold the trowel at a 45-degree angle to the wall and push the notches through the mastic with long strokes. The combing effect leaves just the right amount of air spaces in the mastic to create solid adhesion.

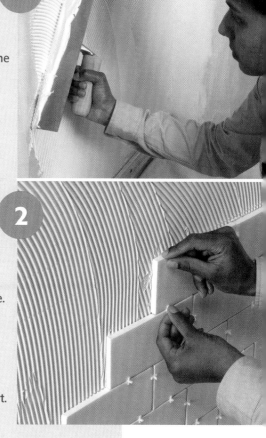

2. Press the first tile into the mastic, using your layout lines as a guide. Wiggle it a bit so you can feel if the mastic is adhering to the tile or not. If it's easy to pop off, the mastic isn't adhering. If this is happening, trowel a little mastic onto the back of the tile. This is called "back buttering." Comb out the mastic and place the tile on the wall again. Keep installing tiles a row at a time, using the plastic spacers between and below the tiles to keep them a consistent distance apart. Double-check your alignment with a level after tiling each row.

3. After you've set a few rows of tiles, lightly tap each one with the rubber mallet to make sure they're adhering and to ensure you're creating a smooth plane where no one tile protrudes farther than another. If any mastic

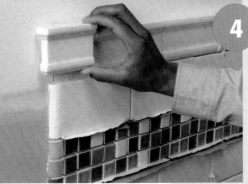

oozes up between the tiles or gets on the face of the tiles, clean it off with a damp paper towel. To remove excess mastic from the joints, use the blade of a utility knife. You don't want the joints to be filled with mastic because grout will go in there.

4. If you're tiling up to the bottom of your upper cabinets for a backsplash, you can just keep going with the field tiles (meaning the tiles that cover the main area) until you hit that point. Leave a small gap between the last row of tiles and the cabinet, and fill that in later with caulk. But if you're tiling a wall only partway up, you'll probably want to get some cap pieces that have a finished top edge so you don't see the unfinished edge of the top row of field tiles. Cap pieces can be specially decorated tiles, or "bullnose" tiles. Bullnose pieces match your chosen tile style, but have a beveled or rounded edge, which helps finish the look. Cap pieces also come with finished left and right edges if you aren't tiling all the way to the end of the wall. These are installed the same way as the field tiles.

5. After all the field tiles are set and the mastic has dried, remove the batten board (if you used one). Prepare this area with mastic and fill in that space with tiles, making sure to leave a small gap between the bottom row of tiles and the floor or counter. Set the tiles on plastic spacers to ensure a consistent gap.

grouting

Once all the tiles are set, let the mastic dry (the can will tell you how long this should take). If you laid your tile under particularly humid conditions, you'll need to give them more time to fully set. When you're ready to grout, make sure the surrounding area is well protected, as this is a wet and messy job. If you've tiled only partway up the wall and want to protect the paint, put a couple rows of painter's tape above the last row of tile. Do a final inspection on all the joints and remove any protruding mastic with the utility knife blade. Pull out the plastic spacers.

At the store, you'll find two kinds of grout—sanded and unsanded. Use unsanded grout if the space between your tiles is less than $\frac{1}{8}$ inch wide; otherwise use sanded grout. Try to buy grout that has been fortified with latex. If you can't, consider substituting the water needed to mix up the grout with liquid latex additive (you'll find it near the grout). The latex makes the grout stronger and keeps the color more consistent, but it also makes it stickier and harder to get off.

You can mix small amounts of grout by hand in a bucket using a margin trowel to stir it, but if you're grouting an area more than a few feet square, it's easier to use a power drill with a paddle attachment. If you use the attachment, straddle the bucket and secure it firmly with your feet. Otherwise, the bucket will spin like a top when you fire up the drill.

Wearing the heavy rubber gloves, mix the grout according to the directions on the bag. Pour the water or liquid latex into the large bucket first, then add the dry grout mix. If you do it the other way around, it will be really hard to make sure the liquid mixes into the grout at the bottom of the bucket. Mix until the grout is the consistency of peanut butter (smooth, not chunky). You should be able to scoop some out with your trowel without it sliding off, but it shouldn't be so dry that you can ball it up in your hand, either. Once it's mixed to the right consistency, leave it alone for 10 minutes to let it slake, or set up. Then stir it one last time and you're ready to go.

TIMING

How large an area should you grout before stopping to go back and clean up the excess? It's a tricky question. If you start sponging off the excess when the grout is still wet, you might pull it out of the joints. But if it's too dry, you'll have a hard time getting the grout off the face of the tiles, which can turn a pleasant grouting job into a living hell. If you worked quickly and the grout is still pretty wet, grout the next section before you start cleaning up. You're balancing a few things here—you have to use all the grout you mixed before it dries, but you don't want to have so large an area to clean that you can't remove the grout off the face in time.

HOW TO GROUT

1. Scoop some grout out of the bucket with the laminated grout float. Working in sections about 4 feet square, push the grout into the joints. Hold the float nearly flat and sweep it across the surface in at least two directions.

2. Once you can see that the grout has made its way into all the crevices, tilt the float up on its side and use it like a squeegee to wipe most of the grout off the tile surface. Wipe at a diagonal so the float does not take any grout out of the crevices. Let the grout sit for a few minutes until you see the beginnings of a white haze on the tile surfaces.

3. Have two buckets of water on hand for this next step. Dip the large sponge into one of the buckets, squeeze out the excess, and wipe the tiles. Your goal is to clean excess grout off the face of the tiles, while leaving the grout in the joints. Keep your sponge on the dry side. Use one bucket of water to rinse the globs of grout off your sponge, and then dunk the sponge into the cleaner bucket of water before wiping the tiles again. Continue until the tiles are clean. Repeat the process across the wall.

4. As the grout dries, you'll once again start to see a haze over the tiles. Resist the urge to keep wiping with your sponge and let the haze happen. Within a couple hours, wipe off the haze with a clean, dry rag, taking care not to disturb the drying grout.

5. Once the haze is cleaned off, you can caulk the edges. Use 100 percent silicone caulk, preferably in a color that matches your grout. Run a bead of caulk in corners, over the top row of tile, and between the bottom row of tile and the floor or counter. Use wet paper towels or your finger to smooth out the caulk.

HANGING WALLPAPER

When I was growing up, my mom was wild for wallpaper. She put up a glittery turquoise, silver, and white butterfly pattern in our bathroom. She then moved on to a tasteful fruit and flower design for the kitchen. Dad muttered under his breath while installing this particular paper. Although it was a superior design, the paper was of inferior quality. It bubbled, rippled, ripped, and wouldn't smooth out. That cheap wallpaper caused Mom and Dad to glower and growl the day it was put up. So don't buy chintzy wallpaper. You'll end up frustrated, angry, and quite possibly going to bed without speaking to yourself.

STUFF YOU'LL NEED
- Wallpaper adhesive
- Seam roller
- Sandpaper (if necessary)
- Bucket of water and ammonia (if necessary)
- Sponge
- Primer/sealer (if necessary)
- Paintbrush
- Paint roller and foam roller covers
- Plastic paint trays
- Supplies for drywall skim coat (if necessary), see pages 70–73
- Sizing (if necessary)
- Screwdriver
- Ziplock bag
- Wallpaper
- Pencil
- Step stool
- 4' or 6' level
- Tape measure
- Large work table
- Metal yardstick
- Scissors
- Smoothing brush
- Pin
- Utility knife
- Wide putty knife
- Sponge and bucket of water

If you have clean, smooth walls, you can start on the new wallpaper. Otherwise, you'll have some preparing to do.

HANGING NEW WALLPAPER OVER OLD New wallpaper can be hung over old, but it's not a great idea; it's best to remove the old paper first (see page 69). Laying new over old should only be considered if the old wallpaper is smooth, just one layer thick, and in good condition, and if the new wallpaper is a porous type. Put some wallpaper adhesive under any loose seams and flatten them with a seam roller (see page 85). Sand any nicks, rough spots, and overlapping seams. Then wash the wall with a mixture of ammonia and water and let it dry.

To see if your old paper will bleed ink through the new wallpaper, moisten a small piece of the old paper with a clean sponge. If ink comes off on the sponge, apply a primer/sealer.

PRIMING Smooth walls that are painted with a flat (not shiny), latex (water-based) paint should be good to go. Walls painted with high-gloss or oil-based paints will need a coat of primer/sealer that's designed specifically as a wallpaper undercoat. The primer/sealer helps the wallpaper adhesive stick and prevents the moisture in the

TIME & TALENT

Wallpapering is a great project for those with short attention spans because it's easy to stop and start again. A small room could take 6 hours or so if it's your first time. But the measurements are simple and the tools are inexpensive and widely available. So if you don't want to finish the project in one day, there's always mañana.

adhesive from damaging the wall. New drywall without paint will also need to be primed before hanging wallpaper. Walls with a texture will need to be smoothed out. You can sand them down or skim-coat them (see pages 70–73) before priming.

SIZING You will find cans of "sizing" near the other wallpaper materials. This gluelike solution is painted onto the wall before you hang the wallpaper, but with most modern wallpapers it's an unnecessary step. Ask a salesperson if you need sizing for your particular situation.

DESIGN Before you apply the first sheet, figure out where you want to cut off the design at the ceiling. You may want to begin with the full design at the top of the wall, or cut into it a bit. Also figure out where you want to start and end. If you're wallpapering all four walls, start behind a door so that it's less obvious if the repeating pattern doesn't join up nicely at the end.

SHORTCUT
Use the first sheet as a template and cut all your sheets at once. Otherwise, you'll have to measure the rest individually.

HOW TO HANG WALLPAPER

1. Remove all receptacle covers and switch plates and store them with their screws in the ziplock bag. Decide where you want the first sheet of wallpaper to go and mark that spot with a pencil. Next, you'll want to draw a perfectly vertical—or plumb—line to serve as an edge guide for your first piece. To make a plumb line, put the level up against the ceiling at your mark. Adjust it until the bubble is in the center, which indicates that the line is plumb, and draw a line down the wall, using the level to keep the line straight. Then use the tape measure to measure the height of the wall at the plumb line so you'll know how long to cut the wallpaper strips.

2. Roll out the wallpaper on the work table. A few inches below the top edge, find the point in the pattern that you want at the ceiling. Mark that point by drawing a line across the paper's width with a metal yardstick. Measure 2 inches up from that point and use the yardstick to draw a cutting line. From the ceiling line, measure down the equivalent of the height of the wall, add 2 inches, and draw a second cutting line. The extra 2 inches on the top and bottom of the strip will overlap the ceiling and floor and will be cut off later. Cut each strip to size.

3. Lay the first length of wallpaper facedown on your work surface. Pour some of the wallpaper adhesive into a paint tray. Use the paint roller to apply an even coat of adhesive to the back of the strip.

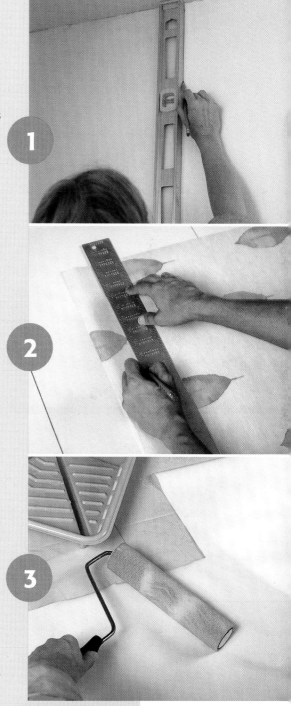

4. Take one end of the strip and loosely fold it over to the middle so the pattern side is now up and the pasted sides are touching each other. Then do the same thing with the other end, being careful not to crease the folds. This process is called "booking" and it gives the adhesive time to get sticky. Consult the directions for your wallpaper to see how long you need to let the strip book—it's usually between 5 and 15 minutes. You might want to prepare several strips at a time once you get the hang of it.

5. Unfold the top portion of the strip, allowing the rest to hang down. Hold the strip by its upper corners and carefully align the vertical edge with the plumb line you drew on the wall. Align the pattern's starting point with the ceiling.

6. Use the smoothing brush to adhere the paper at the ceiling line and to coax out any air bubbles. Start at the top of the wall and move down, and then start again at the center of the strip and move to the left and right. If you have a stubborn air bubble that won't come out, poke the center with the pin and then smooth it with the brush.

7. If your strip goes over a door or window, or meets a corner at the bottom of the wall, use scissors to cut a diagonal slit in the excess paper so it can lay flat.

8. If you've papered over a light switch or receptacle, use a utility knife to slit an X in the wallpaper over the obstruction. Carefully fold back the cut pieces and trim them so they're even with the edges of the opening.

9. When the wallpaper strip is up against window or door trim, cut off the excess with the utility knife. Hold the paper taut against the trim with the putty knife. Then move both tools together in one continuous motion along the strip. (If you lift the knife up along the way, you might tear the paper.) Trim the excess at the top where the sheet overlaps the ceiling and at the bottom of the wall along the baseboard in the same way.

10. Once all the excess is removed from the first sheet, you need to clean off the leftover adhesive on the ceiling and surrounding edges. Dip the sponge in water, wring it nearly dry, and lightly wipe off the glue.

11. Hang subsequent sheets the same way. Once you've hung about three sheets, go back and run the seam roller over the edges to make sure the seams are flat. Press lightly so you don't squeeze any adhesive out; if you do, wipe it up quickly with the sponge.

12. When you get to a corner, measure from the edge of the most recent strip to the corner in three places and then add ¼ inch to the largest measurement. Mark and trim a new wallpaper strip to this width to allow the paper to turn the corner. Hang, smooth out, and trim the strip at the corner as in previous steps.

PAINTING AND STAINING

We've all heard the expression, "That's about as exciting as watching paint dry." OK, watching paint dry is, for most of us, equivalent to discussing municipal bonds. But there's no other home improvement that can make such a wildly dramatic design change in a matter of hours. Plus, painting doesn't require the skill level of a master craftsperson, so it's something most of us can do. Best of all, it's affordable. But before you stock up on some "Golden Chalice" or "Aztec Lily" (who names these colors, anyway?), here are a few tips to make sure your brushstrokes aren't in vain.

types of paint

Oil-based paint (also called alkyd) creates a durable, easy-to-clean, water-resistant finish. It's terrific on areas that get hard use like cabinets, windows, doors, stair rails, and balusters. Oil-based paint can also give you a shiny enamel finish—the patent leather of the paint world.

Oil-based paint is more of a hassle to clean up, however, as you need a solvent like turpentine to break down the paint. It also emits something called VOCs (volatile organic compounds) that contribute to smog and air pollution. In fact, some states have very strict laws and regulations about the use of oil-based paint.

The paint industry has been quick to respond with new formulations that have many of the same benefits, but fewer VOCs. This is good news because nothing beats an oil-based paint for creating a durable, smooth, professional-looking finish. If you want to give homely wood cabinets a face-lift a Hollywood A-lister would envy, paint them with a high-quality oil-based paint (see pages 110–111).

Water-based paint (also called latex) has come a long way in matching oil based for lasting and durable finishes. The best things about water-based paints are that they clean up with water, emit very few VOCs, and are low odor. Latex paints are most commonly used for walls and ceilings.

Oil- and water-based paints come in a variety of finishes, or sheens. The higher the sheen, the more brushstrokes and flaws will be visible. But high-sheen paints also hold up better to light scrubbing, while flat paints are tough to scrub without marking the surface. Here's the shine on sheens:

FLAT Works well in large spaces such as living rooms or bedrooms. Virtually no shine to the finish, which helps when your walls are less than perfect.

EGGSHELL If you look at this finish from an angle, you'll detect a slight sheen to it. It has a slightly textured finish—hence the "eggshell" reference.

SATIN There is more shine in this finish. Often woodwork is painted with a satin finish to lend some luster.

SEMIGLOSS A shiny finish. Make sure your walls are in good shape or a lot of their flaws will be revealed.

HIGH GLOSS Very shiny finish—best for trim, molding, and cabinets.

paint quality

If you've visited a paint department lately, you're well aware of the wide range of manufacturers. Designers such as Ralph Lauren, Laura Ashley, and Martha Stewart have gotten into the game. So has Disney. It wouldn't surprise me if pop stars introduced colors like "Bubbleupchuck Pink" or "Bootylicious Blue." Paint me "jaded" for saying so.

Just because you buy a designer product, it doesn't guarantee it's the best-quality paint or that the textured finishes are user-friendly. A friend of mine butchered his walls with a "navy suede" finish that looked more like dark blue sand smeared on a wall.

If you know any professional painters, ask what brands they like to use. In fact, it's fun to listen to someone in paint-splattered coveralls pontificate with the snobbish eloquence of a wine connoisseur, "That paint has no solids! It rolls like miso soup! It's dreck, I tell you!"

Combining primary colors, even in small amounts, makes a bold statement.

The key to success is to not skimp on costs. Cheap paint isn't worth it in the long run because it doesn't give you good hideability or coverage. Also make sure you order enough paint and assume you'll need at least two coats when painting walls and ceilings. The rule of thumb is that a gallon will cover 400 square feet. That's easily two coats in your average 12-by-14-foot bedroom.

choosing colors

Like fashion, paint colors go in and out of style. In the 1970s, hip kitchens were done up in harvest gold, avocado green, and poppy red. Those color combinations were laughing stocks by the 1980s. But just like the peasant skirt and bell-bottoms, these colors have made a comeback.

I think color should be a purely personal choice. If you like "Ashley Pink" for your kitchen, go for it. If you want to paint rainbows over your headboard, knock yourself out. Choose colors you like and that make you feel good. But this wouldn't be a how-to book without some advice:

COLOR CONTINUITY It's a Design 101 precept: stick to a harmonious color palette for rooms that relate to each other. For instance, if there are views of your living room and dining room from your kitchen, don't visually break up the space with wildly varying colors. In general, use the same color value in related spaces. It permits the eye to move smoothly from one space to another.

COLOR AND PSYCHOLOGY Pastel tones, especially in cool greens and blues, have a calming effect in a room. Reds and oranges are enlivening, and yellow has a sunny, cheery effect. Purple is intense. According to mystics, it is a color that speaks to our spirituality—as opposed to red, which speaks to passion. In general, dark shades will make a room feel cozier and smaller; lighter tones will make it seem larger.

HONORING YOUR HOME'S HERITAGE The best use of color is when it's compatible with the design and style of your home. I've seen purple walls in a Victorian dining room that seemed right at home. That same color in a ranch or western-style home might seem weird. Earth tones are perfect in Arts and Crafts–style architecture, but could seem as heavy as a Wagner opera in a breezy Cape Cod cottage. Many manufacturers have done the research for you and have introduced color lines that are historical. They're worth checking out if you want to be sure you're using colors that suit your home's architecture.

COORDINATING WITH FURNITURE, FLOORS, AND OTHER FEATURES If you've just spent the equivalent of your Roth IRA on a new rug, furniture set, or art object, you'll want to make sure the walls are complementary. Not complimentary as in "Oh, rug, you have the nicest pattern I've ever seen." Complementary as in the paint colors offset the rug's colors without stealing the focus.

MATCHING EXISTING PAINT

I needed to repaint some house trim, but the only color sample I had was a pitiful sliver smaller than my pinky nail. My paint guy, Mikkael, matched it perfectly. So don't be shy about leaning on a paint-store professional—especially if you want a color that doesn't exist on any manufacturer's paint chips. A good mixer will be able to scan the color sample you provide and re-create it in paint. But don't ask the paint pros to choose your colors for you. They hate that!

Whenever possible, try to bring along a sample of your rug, pillow, accessory, or whatever when making your paint selection. And make that selection outside in broad sunlight instead of in the paint store. It makes a difference. I once selected two colors from paint chips by holding them up to some floor tile I wanted to match. But when I rechecked the colors in broad daylight, I saw that they were slightly off.

ALMOST-FREE SAMPLES Almost all manufacturers sell small paint samples that allow you to audition a color before giving it the part. You can put it on a wall and see how the color looks during daylight and at nighttime. Colors can take on an entirely different patina and personality at night. This is a good solution if you're indecisive because the samples only cost a couple of bucks. If the store doesn't carry the color you want in a sample, spring the extra few bucks and buy a quart.

preparing to paint

A paint job is only as good as the preparation that precedes it. Start by moving as much furniture as possible out of the room or into the center of it. Cover the furniture that remains with plastic. Cover the floors with canvas drop cloths; they're not as slippery underfoot as plastic ones. Remove all the switch plates and receptacle covers and keep them with their screws in a ziplock bag.

Examine your walls. Any major dings or dents should be patched (see pages 58–63). If there's dirt or grease on the walls, they should be cleaned with mild dishwashing detergent and water. The goal is to have a surface that feels smooth and dry to the touch. High-gloss surfaces should be lightly scuffed with fine-grit sandpaper to help create better adhesion.

Mask the edges of surfaces you want to protect, such as trim around doors, windows, cabinets and built-ins, the ceiling line, and baseboard. There are a lot of commercial products out there that make masking go quicker. It's worth a visit to your local home center to see if any of these would be practical for you. But I still prefer old-fashioned 1½-inch blue painter's tape. It has a water-based adhesive so it's not too gummy or sticky when it's time to remove it.

To me, masking is as important as the painting. It takes time to lay a straight tape line right up to the very edge of the surface you're painting. Even the best painters can get tired or lose enthusiasm for the job. So tape is your insurance that nothing will get slobbered on when you're "cutting in" (painting along the edges of the walls).

If you're painting a wall one color and the adjoining wall will be another color, you want to make sure the colors won't "bleed" together at the corner. Masking off one side will help, of course, but some paint may still seep under the painter's tape, resulting in a wobbly-looking line. The solution? Brush a small amount of the wall color you're trying to protect over the painter's tape first. Any seepage will then be in the right color, and the new color will be applied in a perfectly straight line.

PAINTER'S TAPE

WATCH OUT!
Painter's tape has been known to leave permanent marks on some stained wood floors and trim. So to be safe, use drop cloths or plastic sheeting on these areas.

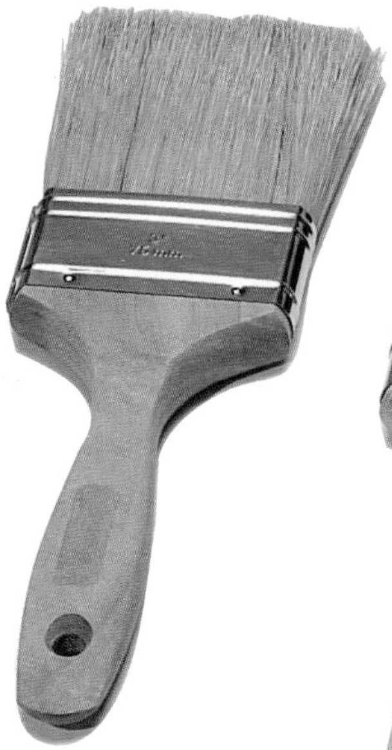

4" PAINTBRUSH

2" TRIM BRUSH

Finally, some thoughts about brushes and roller covers. Don't pull a Scrooge McDuck and buy cheap tools. Cheap brushes lose their hairs and bad roller covers shed fibers. You'll be picking out little fuzzies and having to repaint over the mars. Figure on spending around $8 to $12 for a good brush. Get acrylic bristles for latex paint jobs and natural bristles for oil-based paint. A 9-inch roller with a ⅜-inch nap roller cover works well for most applications. Read the packaging to make sure you buy a roller cover that matches the smoothness of your wall.

That sums up the preparation. Now get ready to roll…and cut in.

painting walls and ceilings

If you're going to paint over a wall that's been patched, newly built, retextured, or stained, or that has oil-based paint that you want to cover in latex, you'll need to prime it first. A recommendation for the type of primer will typically be listed on the paint can for the finish coat. Primer is white, but it can be tinted at the paint store to get closer to the color of your base coat. You don't have to be overly meticulous in applying primer, but it is your "warm-up," so apply the same principles that you would when painting your finish coat, including:

● Work from the top down. If you're repainting the ceiling and the walls, do the ceiling first.

PAINT ROLLER

STUFF YOU'LL NEED
- Plastic sheeting
- Canvas drop cloths
- Screwdriver
- Ziplock bag
- Spackling or joint compound (if necessary)
- Taping knife (if necessary)
- Dishwashing detergent, bucket of water, sponge, and rubber gloves (if necessary)
- Fine-grit sandpaper (if necessary)
- Painter's tape
- Primer (if necessary)
- 1½" to 2½" angled paintbrush
- Paint roller
- Roller covers
- Ladder
- Extension pole (if necessary)
- Paint
- Plastic cup
- Paint tray with disposable liner
- Stir sticks

• Keep a wet edge. In other words, fill in an area with paint while the edges that you cut in are still wet.

• Take your time. This isn't a race.

Ceilings can be a literal pain in the neck because it's tiring to work with your arms over your head. A lot of this stress can be relieved with an extension pole. It screws into the roller handle and permits you to paint longer, wider swaths. Otherwise, you'll be pulling a "Jack be nimble, Jack be quick" routine as you move your ladder from one spot to another. The extension pole is also good for reaching the upper portions of a wall.

TIME & TALENT

Again, preparing the room takes more time than painting it. Set aside a good portion of the day to inspect and repair walls and ceilings, and to apply painter's tape. Then you'll fly through the painting in a couple of hours.

AND ANOTHER THING ...
To remove lint from a roller cover, roll it over the sticky side of a taut piece of painter's tape a few times.

HOW TO PAINT A WALL

1. Thoroughly stir your paint to ensure it's mixed. Pour a small quantity of paint into the plastic cup. This will be your cut-in paint.

2. Dip one-third of your paintbrush into the paint. Lightly slap the brush on the inside edges of the cup so it's not overly saturated. You don't want to wipe the brush on the cup's edge.

3. Angle the brush so its bristles line up with the masked-off border and steadily draw it across the edge. As the paint starts to trail off, lightly draw the bristles away from the edge. Then reload your paintbrush and pick up where you left off.

4. Before the cut-in paint dries, you'll want to fill in the walls with the roller. Make sure you get plenty of paint on the roller, then use the dimpled shallow part of the paint tray to roll off the excess so the roller isn't dripping. Working in 4-by-4-foot sections, use a W or M pattern to roll on the wall paint. Start in a corner, close to the ceiling border, and work your way down. Make sure to overlap all the areas where you cut in with the roller.

5. Repeat the process across the wall, top to bottom. Try to maintain even pressure. If you press too hard on the roller, you can get edge marks. If this happens, just roll over them.

6. Let the paint dry completely before assessing whether or not you'll need a second coat (you most likely will to get an even finish). Once you're done painting, remove the masking tape and clean up.

painting trim and baseboard

The wood pieces that surround your windows and doors are called trim, molding, and/or the finish work. But for argument's sake, we'll just call it trim. The wood pieces along the bottom of the wall covering the gap between the wall and the floor are called baseboards. Sometimes trim or baseboard is in an unflattering color or just looks beat-up. A fresh coat of paint will restore its glory.

HOW TO PAINT TRIM

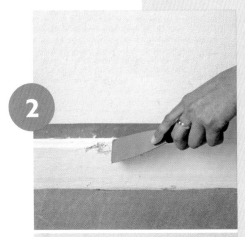

1. Start by masking off the walls around the trim or baseboard with painter's tape.

2. If there are any holes or cracks in the wood, fill them with wood putty. Use the small putty knife to press the putty into the hole and smooth it out. Once the putty has dried, sand it with fine-grit sandpaper.

3. Bare wood and incompatible paint transitions (if you're painting latex over oil-based, for example) will require a coat of primer. If the current surface is covered with high-gloss paint, sand with fine-grit sandpaper before priming to create better adhesion.

4. Use the angled sash brush to paint the top of the trim first, and then the face (or start with the top piece if you're painting door trim). Use even back-and-forth strokes to coat each piece (see step 2 on page 91 for instructions on loading the paintbrush).

5. Check the paint can for drying times. Once the first coat has thoroughly dried, lightly sand the surface with fine-grit sandpaper, wipe off the dust with a tack cloth, and paint again if needed.

TIME & TALENT

Don't cut corners and paint over dents and dings. Patch them first and your trim and baseboard will look like new. Remember to tape off surrounding areas. You'll be finished before lunch.

TECHNIQUE

To determine whether you're painting over oil-based or latex, pour rubbing alcohol on a rag and wipe it across the surface. If it's latex, the color will come off on the rag.

painting doors

Wood, hollow-core, and composite doors (these come preprimed) work well for painting. Hollow-core doors have a veneer of wood on both sides. They're used a lot because they're inexpensive. They should be sanded with 180-grit sandpaper and primed before painting. You can usually get the results you want with one coat. But putting two coats on creates a more durable finish.

If the door is solid wood and needs minor surgery as in patching or filling and sanding, it will be more practical to remove the door from the frame and lay it flat. Get some help removing the door; solid wood is heavy! If not, leave the door on its hinges. That way you can paint both sides at the same time. But be sure to wedge some rags under the door to keep it from moving while you paint.

STUFF YOU'LL NEED
- 180-grit sandpaper (if necessary)
- Primer (if necessary)
- High-quality paintbrush
- Hammer and flathead screwdriver for removing hinge pins (if necessary)
- Rags
- Small putty knife (if necessary)
- Wood putty (if necessary)
- Fine-grit sandpaper
- Painter's tape
- Drop cloths
- Satin or semi-gloss paint
- Paint tray, paint roller, and roller cover (optional)

TIME & TALENT

Painting both sides and all the edges takes longer than you'd think. Cut your time in half by using a brush on the edges and decorative details, and a roller on the rest.

HOW TO PAINT DOORS

1. Using the small putty knife, fill in any cracks or holes with wood putty. Sand smooth with fine-grit sandpaper after the repairs are dry.

2. Mask off the hinges and the hardware with painter's tape and protect the floor with drop cloths.

3. Use a high-quality paintbrush and paint that has a satin or semi-gloss finish. If the door has either raised or recessed panels, start by painting the surrounding decorative trim first.

4. Next, paint the center area. You can do this with the brush or a roller, depending on the finish you want. If the door you're painting has no detailing and the surface is smooth, it's easiest to use a lint-free roller to paint it.

5. For paneled doors, paint the stiles (vertical pieces) and rails (horizontal pieces) next, followed by the door's edges—both the hinge side and the latch side. You can also paint the edges with a roller.

painting windows

Windows come in all shapes and sizes, but most homes have casement windows that open with a crank or double-hung windows where one glass sash pulls up and over another to open the window. In general, older homes have double-hung windows. Anyone who has tried to open a stubborn double-hung and broken three fingernails in the process knows the quirks they can have. All windows take a beating from Mother Nature, so before painting a window, you'll need to assess if it needs to be repaired or replaced. For help with that, see pages 198–201.

You'll also have to make sure that the window framework will accept paint. Vinyl and aluminum windows aren't prime candidates for repainting. Certain "clad" windows probably can be painted, however. Clad means the window framework was "wrapped" with weather-resistant material at the factory. Almost all new windows are available with exterior cladding, which provides an extra line of defense against the elements. And some manufacturers have developed a new generation of fiberglass framework that's extremely durable and can be painted.

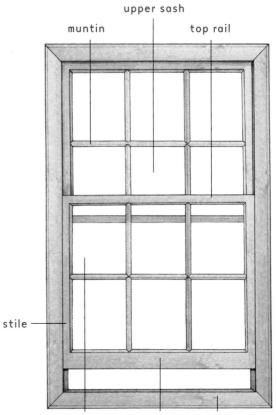

upper sash
muntin top rail
stile
lower sash bottom rail trim

TIME & TALENT

If your window has pop-out sashes, you'll be able to paint them on a flat surface, which is easier. Painting the muntins takes patience, but you'll get the hang of it. Block out about 4 hours for prep and paint.

STUFF YOU'LL NEED
- *Painter's tape*
- *Fine-grit sandpaper (if necessary)*
- *Wood putty (if necessary)*
- *Small putty knife (if necessary)*
- *Primer (if necessary)*
- *Stir stick*
- *1½" or 2" angled sash brush*
- *Paint*
- *Razor blade*

HOW TO PAINT WINDOWS

1. Protect the glass with painter's tape, but leave a tiny margin—about $1/16$ inch—unmasked. You actually want to coat the seam between the glass and the frame with a thin line of paint to help create a seal.

2. Sand any rough surfaces or areas that needed to be patched with wood putty. You'll also need to sand if the old paint is high gloss. Paint a coat of primer over any areas where you see bare wood. If you don't need to sand or patch and you're using a compatible paint (oil-based over oil- or water-based, or water-based over water-based), then you can go straight to the finish coat.

3. Stir the paint thoroughly. If the window has divided lights or wood grid work across its face, paint these pieces, called muntins, first. (Drop that word at your next cocktail party and see who knows what it means.) Using the angled sash brush, paint in a back-and-forth motion. Don't overload the brush with paint or it'll drip on the glass. Less is more.

4. After the wood elements inside the window are painted, paint the top rail.

5. Next, paint the sides, which are called stiles. Have fun with a pun like "Hey, look at me. I'm stylin' my stiles with paint!" Then paint the bottom rail.

6. The window sill is the last to be painted. If there's a wood piece underneath the sill—an apron—paint that too.

7. Once the paint is dry, pull off the tape and remove paint from the glass with the razor blade.

staining woodwork

Painted woodwork is nice. But the warmth of natural wood has its own charm. Call me Nerdy Nerdlinger, but I can get lost admiring the details in a bird's-eye maple floor, or the rustic look of knotty pine. So I'm a big advocate of showcasing wood in its natural state.

Bare wood, however, needs protection. At the very least, you'll need to seal it with polyurethane or varnish. But you can also stain it, which will enhance the grain and create richer tones. Hardwoods tend to accept stain a little better than softwoods because the grain of the wood is tight. Keep this in mind when you're buying unfinished furniture or new trim for a door or window.

JUST SO YOU KNOW ...

How do you know if you're working with a hard or soft wood? Try denting it with your fingernail. You should be able to make a dent in pine. You'll break your nail on teak.

STUFF YOU'LL NEED
- *Fine-grit sandpaper (between 180 and 220 grit)*
- *Tack cloth*
- *Rags*
- *Foam brushes*
- *Prestain conditioner (if you're using water-based stain)*
- *Stain*
- *Polyurethane*
- *Natural bristle brush*

TIME & TALENT

Staining takes a level of concentration and patience that painting does not. You'll be applying layer upon layer of stain and polyurethane, which adds up to many hours over several days with dry time. But it's worth it when you see that wood shine!

HOW TO STAIN WOOD

1. Wood accepts stain better if the grain is raised. So use the fine-grit sandpaper to lightly sand the surface smooth. Wipe off the dust with the tack cloth or a clean cotton rag.

2. If you're using water-based stain (totally up to you, but the water-based stuff doesn't stink like oil-based and cleans up with water), use a foam brush to apply prestain conditioner first. This step is especially important on softer woods like birch, pine, or even maple. The conditioner will help the stain from looking blotchy. If you're using oil-based stain, you can skip this step.

3. Use a clean foam brush to apply a generous amount of stain. Be sure to use water-based stain if you used water-based prestain conditioner.

4. Use a rag that has been saturated with the same stain to wipe off the excess. Wipe with the grain. If the color isn't dark enough, you can apply a second coat once the first coat is dry.

5. Once you're happy with the color and the wood has dried, apply a coat of oil- or water-based (your choice) polyurethane with a foam brush. When the polyurethane has dried, lightly sand the surface.

6. Brush on another coat of polyurethane with the natural bristle brush. The bristle brush has less of a tendency to form small bubbles in the surface, which you don't want on your finish coat. When it's dry, check out your finish in bright light. You might see some spots you missed. If so, lightly sand and give it another coat.

cleaning up

Leftover paint should be poured back into its can. Use the brush to get every last drop out of the roller tray or bucket. Lightly hammer the can's top so it's sealed. Use permanent marker to note the paint's sheen on the lid, as well as where it was used. Tape the paint chip to the can, noting which color was used. This will save you headaches if you have to buy more.

If you don't plan to reuse the paint, look for a local charity or school that you can donate it to. Oil-based paint can never be thrown in the trash, as it's considered hazardous waste; you'll need to bring it to a trash-collection agency that accepts hazardous materials. Latex paint can be thrown away in your regular household trash, but only if it's dry. If you have a good amount left over, pour in some kitty litter and stir until the liquid is gone, then throw the mixture away.

Wipe off excess paint from the paintbrush on a paper towel and then, if you used water-based paint, thoroughly rinse the brush in cool running water. Use your fingers to massage the paint out of the bristles. Squeeze the bristles in a back-and-forth motion to clear out the paint. Or use a paint comb to brush through the bristles. Once the water runs clear, blot the paintbrush on a clean rag. Store brushes in their original packaging when dry. Latex-paint roller covers can be washed in cool water, but they take time and patience to clean. They're relatively inexpensive, so you could just let the covers dry out and throw them away. Roller tray liners should be allowed to dry out and then you can throw them away.

Brushes that have been used with oil-based paints must be cleaned with a solvent such as paint thinner or turpentine. These substances are flammable and can't be poured down drains. Instead, pour enough turpentine into a clear glass jar to cover all the bristles, and put the paintbrush in. Using a back-and-forth movement, press as much paint as possible out of the brush. Lift out the brush and wipe it on a clean rag. Repeat the process until the paint bristles are clean. Once they are, rinse them with mild detergent and warm water and let dry.

Leftover paint thinner or turpentine should be capped and stored in a ventilated space away from any combustible sources such as a furnace or water heater. In a few days, the paint solids should sink to the bottom of the jar, leaving the clear solvent on top. Carefully pour that back into the original container and store. Let the paint solids on the bottom of the jar dry out and then you can throw the jar away.

WATCH OUT!
NEVER store solvent-soaked rags in a closed container. Let them dry on a clothes-line outdoors and then wash separately in cold water with detergent.

HANGING HEAVY OBJECTS

So, you've just spent $300 to custom-frame a cherished family photo and want to hang it in a place of honor. You sure as shootin' don't want it crashing to the ground. When hanging anything over a few pounds, you can't just hammer a nail into the wall and hope for the best—you need to nail into a stud. If there is no stud where you need one, use one of the many other types of fasteners available to secure the item.

nails

A quick trip to the fasteners aisle at the hardware store will show there are many different nails for different purposes. A common nail is generally used for rough construction. It has an extra-thick shank (the long part) and a broad head. Drywall nails have a thinner shank and a larger, slightly cupped head. There are also nails with ribbed shanks that grip better; these are often used when nailing something against gravity, like drywall to ceiling joists. Finish nails have teeny-tiny heads because they're designed to be countersunk, meaning the head sits slightly below the surface of the wall. Nails with different coatings, like "hot-dipped galvanized," are used when the nail might come in contact with moisture; the coating stops the metal from rusting. Tiny pin nails are best used for arts and crafts projects and for temporarily hanging paper holiday decorations on the wall.

screws

A nail can sometimes pop out of a wall when the structure shifts, whereas a screw will hold firm. This is why it's always better to screw drywall into studs rather than nail it (although many builders use nails for this purpose because nails are cheaper). Screws are easier to remove later if you're hanging something temporarily, plus you don't have to worry about hammering your fingers when you use them.

Drywall screws are usually black and come in many sizes. Galvanized deck screws are longer, have a coarser thread (the ridges on the shank), and are suitable for wet areas. You can use deck screws on projects other than building a deck; they are often used for attaching cabinets to wall studs, for example. Finish-head screws have small heads that can be countersunk and are designed for some types of finish carpentry. Lag screws (also called lag bolts) are hard-core fasteners designed to bear a lot of weight. They have a square or hexagonal head that needs to be secured with a wrench or a ratchet and socket.

SHOPPER'S TIP When buying screws or nails for a specific task, visit a store that permits you to pick your own quantity. I mean seriously, do you really need a box of 500 drywall screws? It's not as good as picking out and bagging your own candy, but saving money is always sweet.

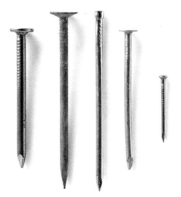

LEFT TO RIGHT: COMMON NAIL, DRYWALL NAIL, FINISH NAIL, HOT-DIPPED GALVANIZED NAIL, PIN NAIL

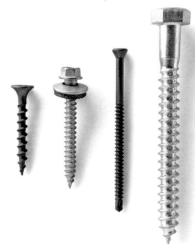

LEFT TO RIGHT: DRYWALL SCREW, GALVANIZED DECK SCREW AND WASHER, FINISH-HEAD SCREW, LAG SCREW

specialty wall fasteners

Now that you know about the different categories of nails and screws, it's time to discover the world of specialty wall fasteners. Use these to hang heavy pictures, art, or shelves when no part of the object spans a wall stud. When you can hit a stud, that's all the strength you'll need. When you can't, wall fasteners like toggle bolts and threaded drywall anchors will disperse the weight for you or grab onto the back side of the drywall after you drive them into the wall. Wall fasteners are rated by how much weight they can hold. Get an idea of how heavy the object you're hanging is, and then buy the wall fastener that says it can carry more than that weight.

Wide, horizontal pieces hang better from two fasteners. Use a level to space the hooks or bolts 6 to 10 inches apart.

PICTURE HOOKS

PICTURE HOOKS While not high-tech, a picture hook can often get the job done. Put the tiny nail through the opening on the metal hook and nail it into the wall so the hook is facing up. Picture hooks are also rated in pounds, so buy the right hook for what you're hanging.

THREADED DRYWALL ANCHORS These anchors have deep threaded shafts and they don't need predrilled pilot holes. Easy to install and remove, they can be used to hang relatively heavy objects in drywall. Make sure you buy them in the right size to match the depth of your wall; they come in $\frac{1}{2}$-inch and $\frac{5}{8}$-inch lengths.

THREADED DRYWALL ANCHORS

TOGGLE BOLT Toggle bolts come in different sizes and should be used when hanging something from the ceiling, or to hang a particularly heavy wall object. This screw has a toggle (looks like metal "wings") on the shaft that flips out, holding it securely to the back side of the drywall. Be sure you put the toggle on the bolt correctly—the flat part should be facing you as you put it in the wall. Drill a pilot hole that's big enough for the toggle to fit through when its "wings" are folded flat and then slip the bolt through the hook or object you're hanging before driving it into the wall. If you put the bolt in the wall first and the toggle activates, the only way to unscrew the bolt is to lose the toggle (it will fall into the wall cavity, which is no big deal). As you screw in the bolt, you need to pull it toward you so that the toggle can catch onto the back of the drywall or plaster; don't fasten toggle bolts too tightly or you'll actually weaken the grip.

THREADED DRYWALL TOGGLE BOLT Threaded bolts with clamping mechanisms that flip out after you drive them into the wall, threaded drywall toggle bolts can hold heavy items with ease. The clamping mechanism sits flush with the bolt, so you only need to predrill a hole that's wide enough for the shaft. Insert the bolt with a screwdriver or drill, and then press and turn the bolt until you see that it's flush with the wall and that the arrows on the head are parallel to the wall stud. Tighten the screw to engage the clamp.

MOLLY BOLT Don't ask me why a "Molly" bolt instead of a "Karen" or "June" bolt. Mollies are also called spreading anchors. This bolt has an anchor that collapses as you screw the bolt into it, grabbing onto the wall from the inside. Molly bolts come in different sizes. Some need pilot holes (those with a pointed end do not), but they all have the spreading anchor. The plastic shank stays in the wall if you need to remove the bolt.

THREADED DRYWALL
TOGGLE BOLT

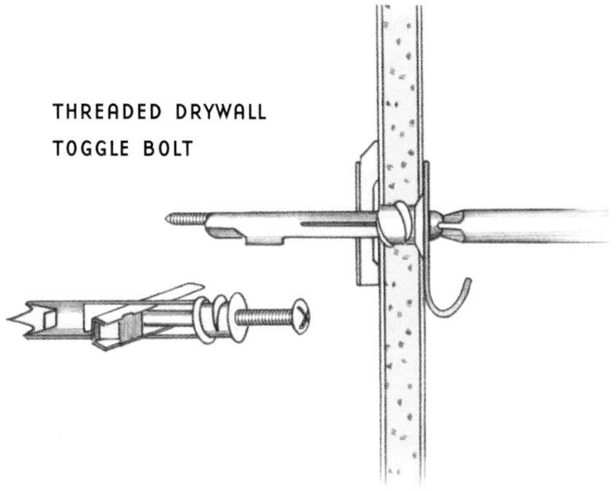

TOGGLE BOLT

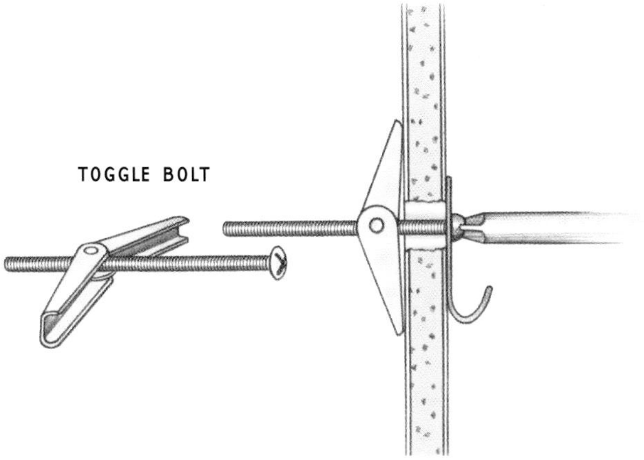

MOLLY BOLT

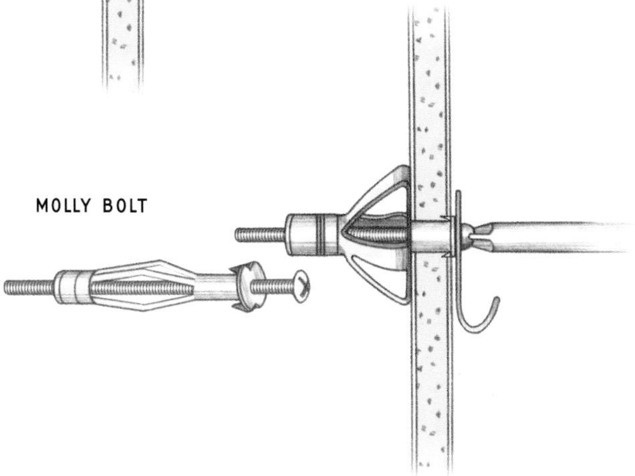

FINDING THE STUDS

The easiest way to find a stud is to use an electronic device called a stud finder (and no, they don't make these to find a man). This device will beep or flash when it passes over a wall stud or ceiling joist, but some also beep when going over other objects in the wall, like pipes. For this reason, it's good to double-check. Slide the stud finder across the wall and mark the spot where it beeps with a pencil. Then keep going across the wall until it beeps a couple more times. Studs are generally placed 16 inches or 24 inches apart from center to center (a builder would describe this as "16 on center" or "24 on center"). Measure the distances between where the device beeped each time and see if they match this description. Also knock on the wall with your fist. When you knock on a stud, it should sound solid, not hollow. Stud finders don't work on lath and plaster walls; you'll need to drive a small test nail just above the baseboard in various spots until you hit something solid.

INSTALLING BASEBOARD

Baseboard is trim that runs along the bottom of your walls, sitting right above the floor. It could be a simple trim with flat edges, it might have a decorative profile, or it could be a series of trim pieces that sit as much as 5 inches high.

If your current baseboard is beat-up, chintzy-looking, or simply nonexistent, it's not tough to install new baseboard. Normally you'd need to deal with mitered (angled) joints where two corner pieces meet. But by using special corner blocks, you can avoid these tricky cuts altogether. Simply install the blocks in the corners first, and fill the spaces between them with lengths of baseboard cut blunt (straight) on the ends.

It's much easier to paint or stain baseboard before you install it. Always prime bare wood before painting, and for trim, it's important to also prime the back so termites and other wood-boring critters don't get a sniff of that fresh wood and come looking for dinner. ("Hey gang, look what we got here! Number two grade oak! Let's eat!") Priming the back also helps keep the wood from warping.

You can buy preprimed pieces of trim, which is a time-saver. Before painting, lightly sand the surface with 180- to 220-grit sandpaper to get off any rough spots. Wipe off the dust with a clean rag, and then paint with a good-quality brush. After the pieces are installed, you can go around and fill nail holes with spackling compound and touch up those spots with more paint. Use satin or semigloss paint; it cleans more easily than flat. If you plan to stain the trim, you'll need to buy stain-grade hardwood, which costs more than paint-grade trim. You can stain it, seal it, install it, and then touch up nail holes with wood putty and polyurethane.

Usually, baseboard comes in 16-foot pieces. For walls that measure less than 16 feet, you will be able to use full pieces. For longer walls, you'll need to join two pieces of baseboard somewhere along the wall. Try to pick a place that will fall behind a piece of furniture. You can join the two pieces together at 90-degree angles and fill in the joint with caulk, or make a 45-degree angle with a compound miter saw (see pages 107–109).

TIME & TALENT

With the easy-to-use corner blocks, cutting and installation will be a snap. It may take several days to prime and paint the pieces (with drying time), but you should be able to install baseboard in a small room within a couple of hours.

HOW TO INSTALL BASEBOARD

1. Remove the old baseboard, if you have any. If it looks as if some-one painted the wall and the baseboard all at once, leaving one fused to the other, use the utility knife to cut through the paint. Then slip something thin and wide like a putty knife into the narrow gap you've just cut, and gently wedge a wood shim behind the blade. This shim will protect the wall; if you don't use one, you may poke through the wall. Remove the putty knife and slide the small pry bar in front of the shim. Pull it toward you to widen the gap. As you do this, you'll be loosening nails that are holding the baseboard in place. Continue along the wall until you can pull the trim off the wall.

2. Drill pilot holes into the outside corner blocks about 1 inch from the top and 1 inch from the bottom. You may need to clamp them to a piece of scrap wood on the work table to hold them steady. Use a drill bit that's the same diameter as the finish nails you're using for this project. Drill from the back side of the block and make sure the pilot hole goes all the way through the front side.

3. Hold the outside corner block in position, making sure it's flat on the floor and flush against both walls. Drive a finish nail into each hole. To avoid hitting the wood, leave ¼ inch of the nail sticking out, and then sink the nail heads below the surface with the nail set.

4. Pilot holes for the inside corner blocks can be drilled with the blocks in place. Hold an inside corner block in position and drill two pilot holes through each face of the block about 1 inch from the top and bottom. Drive finish nails into the holes and countersink the nail heads with the nail set. Your walls may not be perfectly square, so it's wise to check the angle of the corner blocks before cutting a straight length of baseboard to fit between them. Hold the handle of the bevel gauge against the floor and adjust the blade so it rests flush against the inside corner block. Then adjust the angle of your miter saw to the angle set on the bevel gauge.

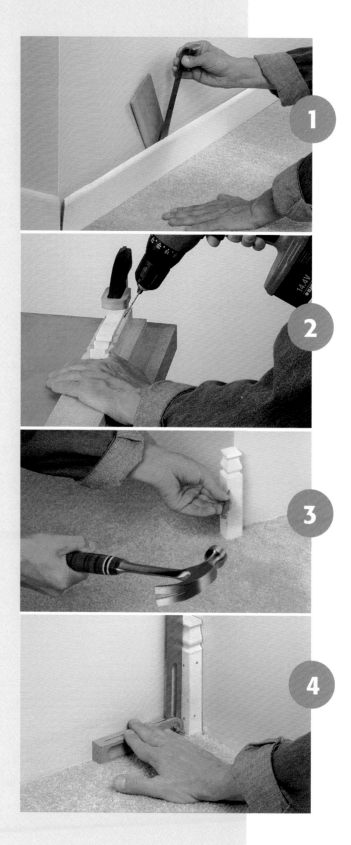

5. Measure the distance between the inside and outside corner blocks. Transfer those measurements to a straight length of baseboard. It's safest to make the cut marks a little farther apart than you think you need. Then you can make a cut that's close, dry-fit it in place (i.e., don't nail it yet), and know for sure how much extra needs to be cut off. You can always cut more, but if you cut too much, you've wasted a piece. Lay the baseboard face up on the miter saw, align your cutting mark with the blade, and make the cut. (You could also use a power handsaw or circular saw.) Dry-fit the piece of molding, and cut again if necessary.

6. With the stud finder, locate the wall studs between the corner blocks. Mark them with small pieces of painter's tape. Then nail the molding in place along the wall, driving two finishing nails into each wall stud. Countersink the nails with the nail set.

7. Fill the gap between the top of the baseboard and the wall with latex caulk. Conceal the nail heads with spackling compound (or wood putty if you're staining), sand smooth, and touch up with paint (or polyurethane for stained wood).

WATCH OUT!
If you cut a little too short and there's a slight gap, fill it with sandable wood putty. For gaps larger than 1/8 inch, cut a new piece. Try not to swear while doing this.

INSTALLING CROWN MOLDING

Even the name has a regal ring to it. Crown molding is trim that creates a decorative element where the walls and ceiling meet. Adding crown molding to a room gives it instant architectural character. It's also useful for hiding cracks and other unsightly problems.

Standard styles of crown molding can be purchased from home improvement centers and millwork shops. Millwork shops can also custom-design crown molding to match existing molding you have in your home.

Crown sits at an angle from wall to ceiling, and comes together at an angle in the corners. Some people make the corner cuts with a coping saw, which is pretty complicated. But if you use a compound miter saw to make the cuts, it's straightforward once you get the hang of it.

Compound miter saws can be purchased for about $100 or rented by the day. Be sure to read the user's guide that comes with the saw (you can also find PDF files of user's guides online). The user's guide will walk you through the process of installing crown molding and give

you the proper saw settings for cutting inside and outside corners. You can't do the job without that information.

The project shown here is in a square room with 12-foot-long walls. Crown typically comes in 16-foot-long sections, so a whole piece could be used for each wall. If you're doing a larger room, you may need to join two pieces together. Make that connection with 45-degree angled cuts and glue the two pieces together. Then nail them in place. If you have any outside corners in your project, consult the compound miter saw user's guide, which will give you the correct angle and bevel settings.

If you don't get the cuts exactly right or your wall isn't straight and the corners just won't come together perfectly, you can fill the gap with sandable wood filler and paint over it, and no one will know the difference. Caulk will provide similar coverage at the top and bottom of the crown molding where it meets the ceiling and wall. Gaps up to $3/16$ inch are normal and can be hidden with caulk.

STUFF YOU'LL NEED

- Stud finder
- Painter's tape
- Two ladders and a helper
- Compound miter saw
- 1 x 1 lumber or precut triangular wood pieces
- Tape measure
- Crown molding
- Pencil
- Drill with bits
- Hammer
- Finish nails
- Nail set
- Sandable wood filler
- Small putty knife
- Cotton rag
- Fine-grit sandpaper
- Spackling compound or wood putty
- Latex caulk
- Caulk gun
- Paint or stain and polyurethane
- Paintbrush

TIME & TALENT

The cuts seem intimidating, but as long as you remember whether you're cutting a left or right inside corner, you should be OK. The rest is just paint and muscle. Plan on working about 1 full day to get the crown installed in one room, plus time to paint and touch up.

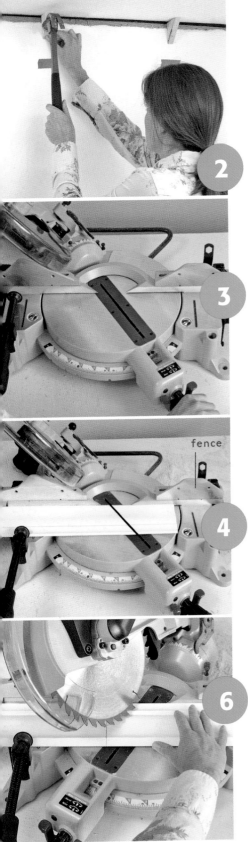

HOW TO INSTALL CROWN MOLDING

1. Go around the room with the stud finder and mark each wall stud with a piece of painter's tape, placing the tape just below the area the crown will cover.

2. Installing small wood blocks where the wall and ceiling meet gives you something solid to nail the crown into. You can either cut 1-by-1 lumber into 3-inch-long blocks, or buy precut wood triangles and nail one into each stud. Use the tape from step 1 to guide you on the placement of each block so you're sure to hit a stud. Also nail one block into each corner. Now you'll be able to nail into the center of the molding rather than at the top and bottom, where the contours of the crown can leave you little room.

3. Prepare the saw for a left-side, inside-corner cut (see step 10 photo) by setting the miter table at the bottom of the saw to the right at 31.62 degrees. Set the bevel angle (the top of the saw that tilts left and right) to 33.85 degrees. Tighten down both settings.

4. Stand facing a corner of the room. The wall on your left will need a length of crown with a left-side inside-corner cut, and the wall on your right will need a length of crown with a right-side inside-corner cut. First measure the wall on your left. Then take a length of crown that's several inches longer than that first wall over to the compound miter saw that you set up in step 3. Place the piece of crown on the saw table faceup with the top edge (the edge that will touch the ceiling) against the fence. You'll be making this cut on the *right* side of the length of crown, even though it's the cut for the *left* side. Don't let that

confuse you. Cut the piece (it will look like the left side of a V).

5. Now you'll cut the other end of the same piece of molding. This will be a right-side inside-corner cut (see the step 10 photo). It sounds confusing, because you're cutting what will be the left side of the length of crown. Measure from the side you've already cut (start your tape measure at the bottom of the V) out to the length of the wall that you determined in step 4. Add a little slack and then mark the spot with a pencil on the piece of crown. It's better to make this cut a little long and shave it down than to cut it too short and have wasted the entire piece.

6. Take this piece back to the compound miter saw and this time lay the bottom edge of the molding against the fence. Move the miter table to the left at 31.62 degrees, and keep the bevel angle where it was at 33.85 degrees. Tighten down the settings. Align the piece of crown under the blade so that the blade will hit just past your cut mark. You're cutting off the excess on the right side of the saw again, and this cut will look like the right side of a V.

TECHNIQUE
Practice cutting left and right inside corners with small scrap pieces to see how they fit together before cutting a piece of molding.

7. Now that both ends are cut, lift the crown into place. If it's too long, go back to the saw and shave off a little more. You want the bottom "point" of each side to fit snugly where the two walls meet. Once you've got the piece cut to the right length, have your helper hold it in place while you drill pilot holes through the crown into the underlying wood blocks. (The painter's tape is your guide for the block locations.) Then drill pilot holes about 1 inch in from each end. Set the crown down and gather your hammer and nails.

8. Lift the piece back into position, and while your helper holds it in place, drive finish nails through the pilot holes. Work your way across the piece. Stop hammering right before you get the nail flush to the surface—you don't want to accidentally bang up your beautiful crown molding. Besides, it's good to keep the pieces a little loose so you can adjust them when you're trying to match up with neighboring pieces in each corner. Later, you can go back and countersink the nails with the nail set.

9. Now that you have your first piece up, you'll have something to match your next piece to. Measure from the bottom tip of the adjoining piece of crown across the next wall. Remember to set up the saw correctly for the right- and left-side cuts (review steps 3 and 6). Also remember to cut each piece a little long first and test in place before making the final cut.

10. Once the second piece is cut, hold it in place and try to get the edge of the second piece and the edge of the first piece to meet flush. Sometimes you can't, no matter how hard you try, but other times it works beautifully. Just get it as close

as you can. Then follow steps 7 and 8 to drill the pilot holes and drive the nails.

11. Continue with the third wall. The fourth wall will be the hardest, because your cuts will have to conform to the crown at both ends. Just get it as close as you can.

12. Once all the pieces are up, go back and countersink the nails.

13. If there are gaps between pieces in the corners, fill them with sandable wood filler. Apply it with the small putty knife, and then smooth it out with a damp rag. Once dry, sand until smooth.

14. Fill nail holes with spackling compound or wood putty, let it dry, and sand any high spots.

15. Caulk the top and bottom edges, ideally with the same color as the paint or stain you've used for the crown. If you painted the pieces before installing them, clean off any smudge marks with the rag. Then touch up the paint over the nail holes and in the corners. The paint will hide all sins, leaving you with clean and seamless crown molding. If you stained the trim, buy wood filler in the same color and apply a small amount in the nail holes. Once dry, dab the areas with a little stain, and once that's dry, coat the area with more polyurethane. Congratulate yourself—this is a challenging job!

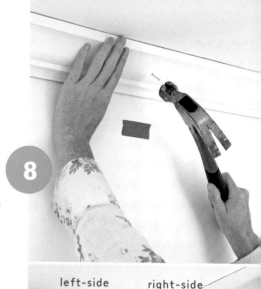

left-side inside corner   right-side inside corner

GIVING YOUR CABINETS A FACE-LIFT

I once bought a house whose kitchen was darker than a Chekhov play. The cabinets were dirty brown. The wallpaper was faded and spotted with grease. I knew I had to lighten up that space before I moved in a single dish. So I painted the cabinets—instant transformation!

Many of us have cabinets in good condition, but the finish is cringe-inducing. Fortunately, there's an easy, albeit time-consuming, fix that doesn't involve taking a sledgehammer to the room. You can paint the cabinets any color you like and top them off with new hardware.

STUFF YOU'LL NEED
- Screwdriver or drill
- Ziplock bags, pencil, and paper
- Work tables or sawhorses
- Rubber gloves
- Trisodium phosphate cleaner (TSP)
- Bucket of water
- Sponge
- Wood putty (if necessary)
- Small putty knife (if necessary)
- 150-grit sandpaper
- Vacuum
- Cotton rags
- Painter's tape
- Drop cloths
- Primer/sealer
- 4" or 6" paint roller with foam roller cover and paint tray, or spray gun
- Paintbrush (if necessary)
- Plastic sheeting and scrap wood (if using spray gun)
- Paint
- 220-grit wet/dry sandpaper

TIME & TALENT

You'll need to remove the items from your cabinets and set up a work area for painting doors and drawers. Your kitchen will be unusable during this time, so you'll want to work as quickly as possible. But depending on how large your kitchen is, it may take you a couple of days just to apply the first coat. Set aside at least four days, including drying time.

painting cabinets

Before you get too excited, you need to make sure your cabinets are paintable. Solid wood, wood veneer, and metal cabinets take paint well, but laminate and melamine finishes do not. If this is what you have, there is still a way to give them a face-lift, but it's best done by a professional. Look in the yellow pages for cabinet resurfacing companies. They will sell you new doors and drawer fronts, and put a veneer (a thin outer layer of higher-quality wood) over your current cabinet frames and sides.

GET THE RIGHT MATERIALS You need high-quality paint for this project. The last thing you want is to invest this much time and effort only to have your paint peel a couple of months later. Satin or semigloss paint is the most scrubbable, but you should choose a finish you like.

Using a paintbrush will leave visible marks, which may or may not bother you. A spray gun will create the cleanest finish. If you decide to rent one for this project, practice on some scrap wood first and make sure you cover all the surfaces you don't want to paint with plastic sheeting. The microscopic overspray will get all over the room. The quickest and easiest way to paint cabinets is with a foam roller, which leaves a very light pattern on the surface. Use a 4-inch or 6-inch roller to paint the frames and doors.

HOW TO PAINT CABINETS

1. Take out any items from your cabinets that you want to protect from dust or paint. Remove all the hardware with a screwdriver or drill. If you're reusing the hinges or pulls, store them in ziplock bags with a note indicating where each set came from. Set up some tables or sawhorses in an open area with good ventilation and bring all your doors and drawers to that location. This will be painting headquarters for the doors and drawers.

2. Wearing rubber gloves, thoroughly clean the surfaces you're going to paint with a trisodium phosphate solution (follow the instructions on the box), which will slightly etch the surface. Rinse thoroughly with a wrung-out sponge and allow the surfaces to dry. If you're going to install new hardware that won't use the same screw holes, fill in the old holes with wood putty. Once dry, lightly sand the surfaces with 150-grit sandpaper and then vacuum to remove the dust. Wipe any residual dust off with a slightly damp cloth. Then mask the surfaces around the cabinet boxes with painter's tape and cover the floors and counters with drop cloths.

3. Start with a coat of primer/sealer. If you're painting the cabinets a color other than white, ask the paint store to tint the primer to match your top coat. That way, you might be able to get by with just one finish coat. Otherwise you'll most likely need two coats of paint over the white primer. You can choose to paint only the faces of the cabinet boxes, as shown, or the interior as well. Use a brush if you paint the interiors.

4. Paint one side of the doors and the edges. While that side dries, paint the drawer faces; then paint the other side of the doors and edges. Allow the surfaces to dry overnight, and then lightly sand everything you painted with 220-grit wet/dry sandpaper. Vacuum the surfaces, wipe them with a cloth, and apply a second coat.

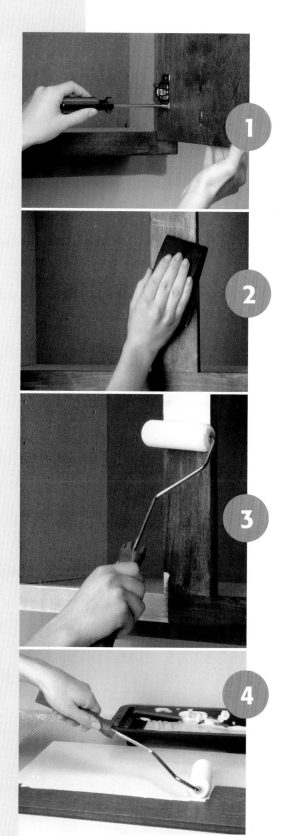

replacing hinges and pulls

The easiest thing to do is buy new hardware that's the same size as the old. That way, it's a simple switch-a-roo from old to new. Otherwise you'll need to get jiggy with it—fill in the old holes and drill new ones.

STUFF YOU'LL NEED
- Tape measure
- Drawer pull jig (if necessary)
- Pencil
- Drill and bits to fit cabinet hardware
- Screwdriver
- New pulls and hinges

TIME & TALENT

If you're using existing holes, this won't take more than an hour. Creating consistently spaced holes with the jig adds to the time and labor.

HOW TO REPLACE PULLS AND HINGES

1. A jig is a template that ensures the holes you are drilling are consistent and evenly placed. Measure to find the center of the drawer face, and put the center of the jig on that mark. Then use a pencil to mark the spot(s) the jig indicates for your style of pull. It will have holes for pulls of various widths.

2. Drill pilot holes before screwing the drawer pulls into place from the inside.

3. To install new hinges, lay the door facedown on a sturdy work surface. The top hinge should go one hinge-length down from the top of the door (or the top of the lipped section of the door, if there is a lip). Put the hinge in place on the back of the door, and mark the holes with a pencil. Do the same for the bottom hinge.

4. Use the drill to make pilot holes where you've made your marks, then screw the hinges to the door.

5. Position the door on the cabinet so that it will open in the right direction. Line it up so it's centered over the opening. Then line up the hinges over the cabinet frame, mark the holes with the pencil, and drill pilot holes. Screw in the top hinge first and then the bottom one.

EASY UPGRADES: KNOBS, HINGES, AND PLATES

Some homes are functional plain Janes with no discernible architectural style. Others may have suffered a bad remodel that stripped them of their character. No worries. Here's a subtle enhancement you can get a handle on.

replacing doorknobs and hinges

Many older homes have beautiful solid-wood doors, but the hardware and hinges can look dowdy and dull. You can find some well-made interior doorknobs and hinges at home centers and hardware stores. There are also many specialty hardware stores on the Internet that sell reproductions of period doorknobs, so be sure to search online. Measure the thickness of your door and buy new knobs that will fit. Choose a style and finish that you want to carry throughout your home. Finish choices include polished brass, chrome, satin nickel, brass, and antique bronze. For bedrooms and bathrooms, buy doorknobs with privacy locks. Look for interior door hinges in the same finish, and make sure your replacements are the same size and shape as your current hinges.

PICKING NEW HINGES To make sure you buy a replacement hinge that will fit the cutout in the door, put a piece of paper over one of your current door hinges and trace the outline with a pencil. Be sure to mark the screw locations, too. Take this sketch with you to the store. This way you can choose hinges that fit your doors without having to dismantle them.

If you can't find a hinge that matches, or you prefer a finish that doesn't match your existing

style, you'll have to do a little extra work to make the new hinge fit. For example, the new hinge may have curved edges instead of pointed. Use a wood chisel to remove wood if the new hinge is larger than the old. If the new hinge is smaller, fill in the remaining area with sandable wood putty and paint over it.

STUFF YOU'LL NEED
- Pencil and paper
- Flat-head screwdriver
- Nail (if necessary)
- New doorknob
- Sheet or towel
- Hammer
- New hinges with matching screws
- Chisel (if necessary)
- Wood shim or thin book

TIME & TALENT

You'll need a helper to get the door off if you're replacing the hinges as well as the knob. Some knobs are just downright stubborn and tough to remove. Follow the detailed instructions that come with the new knob, and this should be an open-and-shut case in a half-hour.

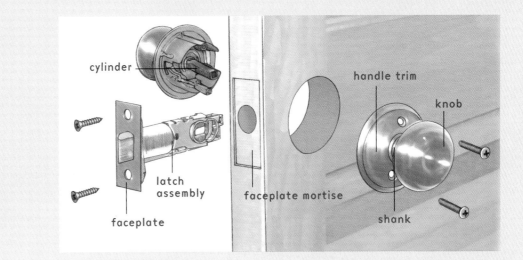

cylinder

latch
assembly

faceplate

faceplate mortise

handle trim

knob

shank

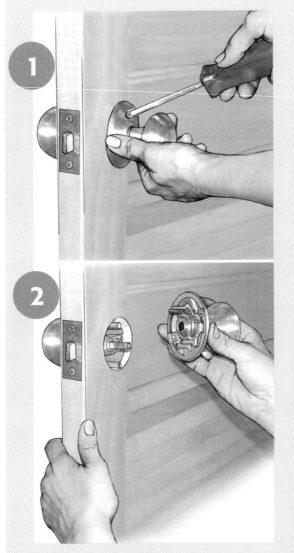

HOW TO REPLACE A DOORKNOB

1. To take out the existing knob, remove screws from the handle trim. If there are none, look for a small slot in the shank (the area between the knob and the handle trim). Push the tip of a small screwdriver or nail into the slot; this should release the knob so you can pull it out.

2. Unscrew and remove the handle trim if it was separate from the knob. Pull on the knob on the other side of the door to remove the cylinder. Unscrew and remove the faceplate and latch assembly.

3. Insert and screw on the new latch assembly and faceplate. Hold the knob that's attached to the long cylinder and slide it through the latch assembly. Screw the handle trim on. Insert the other knob and screw on its handle trim.

4. To replace the hinges, you'll need to remove the door, which can be heavy. Enlist a helper for this job. If you want to protect your floors, slide a sheet or towel underneath the door. While one person holds the door steady, the other can remove the hinge pins. Place the end of a flat-head screwdriver under the head of the hinge pin and hit the screwdriver with a hammer to lift the pin out of the hinge (see page 207). Once all the pins are out, with one person on each side, lift the door off the hinges and onto the floor. Once on the floor, slide the door to the nearest wall to lean against (the sheet makes this easy). Then unscrew the hinges that are attached to the door and the door frame.

5. If you bought the right-sized hinge replacements, they should fit perfectly in the current cutouts. Use the matching screws to screw one side of the hinge to the door. If your hinge doesn't come with matching screws, you'll need to buy screws (with the appropriate finish if you can). Bring the old screws to the store for sizing. Screw the other side of the hinge into the door frame.

6. Move the door back into position at a 90-degree angle to the door frame. Put a wood shim or a thin book under the side of the door closest to the jamb to lift it up into position while your helper holds the door steady. Then both of you can adjust the door until the two sides of the hinge interlock. Quickly drop the hinge pins in place. Once each pin is in place, hammer them all the way down.

replacing receptacle and switch plates

Do you have old, dingy, cracked, or just plain ugly receptacle and switch plates? Well, you don't have to! If you attend any arts and crafts shows, chances are you'll see some fancy switch and receptacle plates made from copper or wood, mirrored, or ceramic. You can also find unique plates in specialty stores and on the Internet in a range of styles and colors.

Sometimes the price can really add up if you include every switch and receptacle you have. If you start to go over budget, just select a few choice places where you'll get the most bang for your buck, and replace the rest with clean plastic plates. Remember, you can always take these specialty covers with you when you move.

Make sure the new plates will fit in the same spot as the old ones, and that there are enough openings for multiple receptacles and switches. Then just unscrew the old ones and screw on the new.

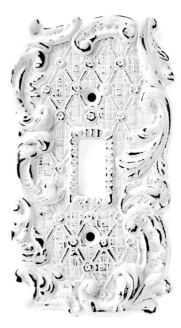

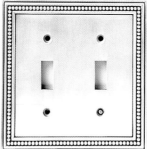

chapter 5

FLOORS

BACK IN THE 1970s, my sister dated a guy who had the ultimate bachelor pad. He hired some swingin' designer to do up the place in chrome, glass, and geometric foil wallpaper. The real design highlight, however, was the carpet. Acres and acres of royal blue shag covered the living room like some wild, exotic sea grass.

I loved how it felt—soft, padded, and warm. I also recognized its practicality; the pile was so deep, it hid dirt. By the same token, you wouldn't want to drop anything valuable in it because it'd take a metal detector to find it.

There was one bad thing about shag carpeting—it was high maintenance. Not unlike teenagers who spend hours moussing their hair to get that casual-unkempt look, shag had to be combed and preened. It even came with its own rake so you could fluff up the matted fibers.

As a fad, shag lasted about as long as pet rocks. In fact, you don't see shag in many homes anymore. If you do, the homeowner is probably planning to pull it out. In this chapter, we'll show you how to do that and more as we explore the wide world of floors.

WOOD

It's hard to believe, but there was a time when wall-to-wall carpeting had snob appeal. In the 1960s, people actually bragged about covering their "plain wood floors" with it. But I think that was just temporary design insanity. Today's homeowners are pulling up old carpeting, hoping there's wood flooring underneath.

OAK

MAHOGANY

BRAZILIAN CHERRY

MAPLE

AMERICAN CHERRY

Wood flooring is available in solid planks that can be stained and sealed, or as prefinished laminated planks (also called laminate or engineered flooring). Solid planks are typically ¾ inch thick and between 1½ and 3¼ inches wide. They fit together in a tongue-and-groove fashion, kind of like a Tupperware bowl and its lid.

Engineered wood floors have a wood veneer top, and a layered core of plywood and/or high-density fiberboard. They're called "prefinished," because they've already been stained and/or sealed with polyurethane.

A wood's hardness is rated on something called the Janka scale. The higher the number, the harder the wood. Hardwoods are more durable and less likely to dent when you drop something on them. But some people prefer softwoods because the nicks and dents give the floor that trendy "distressed" look. You can also buy prefinished "antiqued" wood planks that have been beat up for you.

The most common hardwood floors in older American homes are maple, red oak, white oak, birch, and Douglas fir. But recently, the wood-flooring market has exploded with more exotic options. You can literally go from ash to zebrawood with your hardwood floor choices.

maintenance and repairs

Most hardwood floors installed or refinished from the mid-1960s on are sealed with polyurethane. It protects the wood and provides the shine. So when you clean your wood floor, use products that are compatible with the poly finish. Vinegar and water can compromise the finish over time; multipurpose cleaners can dull the shine; oil-based soapy products can leave a residue; and plain water can warp. The best way to clean your hardwood floor is to vacuum, sweep, or dry-mop the dirt and follow up with a spray-on hardwood-floor cleaner.

If the finish has worn down completely and you see patches of bare wood, or if you want to change the color, you should consider having the floor professionally refinished. The sanding equipment spreads a lot of dust, and the polyurethane sealer stinks (although you can usually pay extra for water-based sealer that's not as smelly). If you have all the wood floors throughout your house refinished, you'll have to clear the rooms and move out for a week or so. It's a hassle, but the results are worth it.

With proper care, hardwood floors can last hundreds of years. Of course, they're prone to the vagaries of old age. Here are some techniques for dealing with squeaks, gaps, cracks, and stains.

FIXING SQUEAKS Floors and wood stair treads are secured into a plywood or plank underlayment (also called a subfloor), and the underlying joists, which are the horizontal framing members that support the floor. Joists provide the structural muscle for a floor. Over time, the fasteners that hold the finished floor to the subfloor can lose their grip. Wood rubs against wood, and you get squeaks that sound as if they came out of a haunted house. Squeaks can also be caused by the uneven settling of your house.

STUFF YOU'LL NEED
- Drill and bits
- Tape
- 1½" finish-head screws
- Wood putty
- Small putty knife
- Staining and sealing supplies

TIME & TALENT

Pinpointing the squeak is the hard part. Resecuring the plank to the framing underneath it only takes a few minutes. Make sure you've found or concocted a mixture of colored wood putty to match your floor before you start this project.

HOW TO FIX FLOOR AND STAIR SQUEAKS

1. Locating the squeak's source will bring out the Nancy Drew in you. If you can't access the area underneath the floor, the repairs will have to be made on top. In that case, walk across the offending squeak many times to pinpoint its location. You'll know you've found it when you step on one particular area and get a squeak every time. Mark the spot with a penny or whatever's handy.

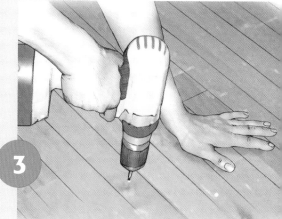

2. Using a wood-boring drill bit just slightly smaller than the diameter of the finish screw you plan to use, drill 1½-inch-deep pilot holes through the face of the floorboard. Use a small piece of tape to mark the bit at 1½ inches so you'll know when to stop drilling.

3. Drive the screw through the floorboard, making sure the screw head sinks below the surface of the wood.

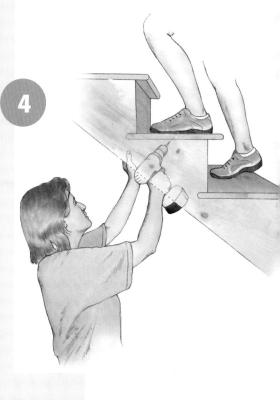

4. On stairs, you might be able to fix the problem from underneath if the area under your stairs is exposed. Have a friend walk up and down the stairs to help locate the most offending squeaks. Drive screws up through the framing and into the treads where the squeak is located. Be sure to use a length of screw that won't penetrate the top side.

5. When all the squeaks are quieted, cover up the countersunk screws with wood putty that matches your floor color. Follow the steps on page 121 to finish the putty areas.

REMOVING STAINS Lots of things can mar the good looks of your hardwood floor. One of the biggest offenders—and nearly impossible to get out—are pet stains. Floor refinishers shrug and say "Let's hope for the best" when presented with a stubborn pet stain. Often it penetrates so deeply into the grain, it can't be sanded away.

Other stains, however, aren't so hopeless. With scuff marks and waxy types of stains, take a gentle hardwood-floor cleaner and a clean white rag and simply buff them out. To avoid milky white water stains from houseplants, they should be placed on pedestals or nonporous trays.

If you catch the water stain right away, you might be able to get it out with an iron (yes, an iron). Turn the iron to a medium-high setting, such as for cottons. Once it heats up, place a clean white rag over the stain and iron over it. If you see a little steam rising, that's a good thing: it means you're evaporating the moisture trapped underneath the finish coat. Remove the rag and check out your results once the floor cools down.

Other stains require more time and elbow grease. Getting good results are a little iffy, so try your technique in an unobtrusive area first.

STUFF YOU'LL NEED
- *80-, 180-, and 220-grit sandpaper*
- *Vacuum cleaner or shop-vac*
- *Tack cloth*
- *Foam brushes*
- *Stain*
- *Stir stick*
- *Polyurethane*
- *Natural-bristle brush*

TIME & TALENT

The tricky part is matching the new stain to the old, since ultraviolet rays and time change the patina of wood. The stain probably won't be a perfect match, but you can get it close. This shouldn't take more than 30 minutes, plus drying time.

POOR WOMAN'S REFINISHING

Sometimes all your hardwood floors need is a face-lift to restore shine and luster. You can do this yourself with commercially available all-in-one kits. In three steps—and a little over an hour—you will thoroughly dry-mop the floor, follow up with hardwood cleaner, then apply a light coat of refinisher. The floor actually gets another layer of protection and looks terrific—all for under $20. Or call in a professional to rescreen the floor, which involves sanding the surface with fine sandpaper and applying a polyurethane sealant. This process usually costs less than half what refinishing does, because it doesn't involve sanding down to bare wood and restaining.

HOW TO SAND OUT A STAIN

1. Sand the stained area with 80-grit sandpaper until the stain is removed. If it isn't gone already, sanding will remove the polyurethane finish so you'll be down to bare wood.

2. Vacuum up the sawdust and resand using 180-grit sandpaper. Clean up that sawdust and follow up with a tack cloth.

3. Use a foam brush to apply some wood stain (see pages 96–97). Wipe off the excess with a stain-soaked rag and repeat if the color isn't dark enough. When you're satisfied with the color and the stain is dry, move on to the next step.

4. Coat your repair with polyurethane. Remember that polyurethane comes in a variety of sheens, so pick the one that looks most like what's on your floor now. Stir the polyurethane to ensure its ingredients are blended and use a foam brush to lightly coat the area. Feather it out at the edges. You want to blend with the existing finish—laying it on too thick near the transition area will make the repair obvious.

5. Once the polyurethane is dry (wait at least 24 hours), sand the area with the 220-grit sandpaper. Use a tack cloth to clean up the dust. Apply your final coat of polyurethane with the natural-bristle brush.

SCRATCHES AND CRACKS Cracks and warps are pretty common with older wood floors. Wood expands and contracts depending on how much humidity it's exposed to, so a little movement is natural. But sometimes wide cracks form, particularly where one board meets another. You can try filling these in with wood putty that matches your floor color.

Often scratches are superficial and are on the polyurethane finish only. Again it behooves you to try buffing these out with gentle cleaner and a soft cotton rag. Deep scratches that cut right into the bare wood need to be sealed. Here's where your fine-motor skills come into play. Make sure the scratch is free of debris, clean, and dry. Use a small paintbrush (or even a clean eyeliner brush that you don't want anymore) and lightly apply polyurethane in the crack. Try to keep the application localized to the indentation and don't overlap onto the edges.

If large portions of the floor have holes, or there are several cracked floorboards, you'll want to hire a professional to patch in some replacement flooring. The pro will remove the damaged section, lay new boards, and finish them. I've seen refinishers do this with such skill that you'd never know where the patch is.

LAMINATE

Just as Kleenex has become synonymous with tissues, Pergo has come to represent laminate floors. Pergo is the Swedish manufacturer that jumpstarted the laminate-flooring trend, but American manufacturers quickly responded with their own laminates. This category of flooring keeps growing because laminates are guaranteed not to fade, stain, or wear through for 20 to 30 years.

Laminate is a close cousin to melamine, which is familiar to most of us as shelving sold at home centers. Laminate flooring is made of a high-density wood core topped with a decorative pattern. When you examine a wood-grain laminate, for example, you're actually seeing a high-resolution photographic image. Sometimes you have to look long and hard to see if a floor surface is stone or wood, or if it's a laminate imitator.

The image or design is coated with a tough-as-nails finish that gives laminate its durability. Some finishes are so durable that a smoldering cigarette could be dropped on them and not burn the surface. But don't try that experiment. Even if the floor can handle it, smoking is bad for you! The point is that with their built-in durability, laminates—especially the newer generation of high-pressure laminates—aren't prone to damage.

maintaining and repairing laminate

Most laminate floors are not nailed into the subfloor; they're either glued directly to it, glued together, or interlocked in a tongue-and-groove–like system. When laminate planks or tiles snap together and form one cohesive unit, it's called a floating floor. With this construction, removing a damaged piece of laminate and replacing it isn't easy. You have to use a circular saw to precisely cut out the damaged section and glue in a replacement. Sorry, but making a perfectly straight plunge cut isn't part of the Beginning Power Tools curriculum.

If you have a badly damaged piece of laminate, call a professional to fix it. Check the manufacturer's warranty; your repair job might be free.

Finally, make sure you hold up your end of the warranty by maintaining the floor with the right cleaning products. It's OK to damp-mop, but a gentle, nonsoapy cleanser applied with a soft pad is best.

TILE

I recently moved into a house where both bathrooms were carpeted. Now I know some people like the warmth and comfort of bathroom carpet. But I fixate on all the hidden dirt, hair, and dander that never quite get sucked into the vacuum. I envision a giant mold and bacteria party as all that organic matter feeds on the bathroom moisture and turns that carpet into an orgy of skankiness. So I couldn't wait to pull up the carpet and lay down clean, pristine, sanitary tile.

PORCELAIN TILE

As a flooring and building material, tile has been around for thousands of years. These days there are more choices than ever: there are metal tiles, glass tiles, tiles made from recycled glass, art tiles, ceramic and porcelain tiles, handmade terra-cotta tiles, marble, limestone, granite, onyx…well, OK…you get the idea.

CERAMIC TILE Most of us are familiar with ceramic tile. It's made of clay fired at a high temperature and glazed with color, pattern, and even texture. It's popular in kitchens and baths because glazed ceramic tile is nonporous, meaning it resists staining and water absorption. Textured glazes can also give ceramic tile a nonslip surface.

Ceramic tiles come in just about every size, shape, and color imaginable. Whether it's a 1-inch mosaic, or a 16-by-16-inch jumbo floor tile, the sizes, shapes, and colors give tile infinite design possibilities.

PORCELAIN TILE Porcelain tile looks a lot like ceramic tile, but the similarities end there. Porcelain is Goliath-like in its strength. Believe it or not, this tile has 30 percent more strength than granite.

It won't crack if exposed to frost, and is extremely stain and water resistant. As a result, it's a great surface for high-traffic, high-moisture spaces like kitchens and baths, as well as for outdoor applications.

Porcelain tile is so tough, it has to be cut on a wet saw. A snap cutter will wimp out like a 98-pound weakling.

CERAMIC TILE

TUMBLED MARBLE

POLISHED MARBLE

GRANITE

TERRA-COTTA AND SALTILLO TILES

Imagine sipping a margarita on a terrace in Mexico and you've conjured up a picture of earthy terra-cotta or saltillo tiles. These thick, heavy tiles take on the clay color from whence they originated. As a result, the earthy coloration runs throughout the entire body of these tiles. In fact, *terra cotta* is Italian for "baked earth."

Saltillos (saul-TEE-yos) are terra-cotta tiles made in Saltillo, Mexico, and they range in color from yellow to deep orange. Often, these tiles are handmade, which results in uneven surfaces and other imperfections. But that's part of the charm. My friend Jean has saltillo tile in her entryway; one tile has a dog's paw print embedded in it.

Terra-cotta and saltillo tiles are extremely porous and require sealing before you install them. Don't skip this important step or that margarita will soak right in and stain.

POLISHED STONE TILE If it's good enough for kings, it's good enough for your palace. With its intricate veining and wide palette of colors, marble has long been associated with wealth, luxury, and beauty. It is, however, prone to scratching, so it's not the most durable surface for high-traffic areas. Travertine is mottled and veined, with small pits in its surface. Like marble, it's "soft"—if you can say such a thing about a stone. Its coloration is warm beige. Granite, on the other hand, is plenty tough. It's available in many colors, which appear as speckles and flecks rather than veins.

Polished tile is slippery, so you may not want to use it in areas where there's a lot of contact with water (unless you use mosaic stone tiles, in which case the many grout lines should keep you standing upright).

All natural stones absorb moisture. Even on highly polished surfaces where you can't see the pits or the pores, they're there. As a result, all natural stone, regardless of its finish, needs to be sealed.

ROUGH STONE TILE The dark coloration and rough, cleft face of slate make it instantly identifiable. It's used in entryways, baths, and even kitchens because it's durable and nonslip. Limestone lends a rustic character because the tiles come in large, thick slabs, but it is the most porous of all the stone tiles. Unpolished marble looks very different from the polished version. It has the variation of color, but loses a lot of the veining.

SALTILLO

installing underlayment for a tile floor

With floors, what goes under the surface is just as important as the material on top of it. Tile needs a cement-based underlayment. If you're tiling over a clean cement slab, congratulations! Feel free to skip this section. Relax. Make a sandwich. Have some tea. Then head straight for page 127. But chances are, you'll be tiling over a plywood sub-floor. That plywood needs to be completely covered with cement backer board.

Cement backer board is available at most home centers. It comes in 3-by-5-foot sheets that weigh about 50 pounds apiece, so you'll want to enlist help and a sturdy truck when picking up this material. In most cases, backer board that's ½ inch thick will be adequate for your underlayment.

Some considerations before laying a tile floor: The tile's thickness, plus the mortar, plus the backer board can add up to as much as 1 inch in height. Consider how that height will impact adjoining floors. Will you need a special sloped transition strip between the two floor types? Will doors still operate easily with the addition of new tile? If none of this poses a problem, you're good to go.

If you like jigsaw puzzles, you'll enjoy determining the layout for your backer board. The goal is to lay as many full-size sheets as you can with minimal seams. To maximize sturdiness, lay the backer board in the same direction as the floor joists. (You can tell which direction the joists run because there will be a line of fasteners on the subfloor.)

Figure on dry-fitting and cutting all the sheets before any of them are installed. Backer board is attached to the subfloor over a layer of thin-set mortar, and then the sheets are screwed to the subfloor. Trust me, you don't want your mortar sitting around drying while you figure out how the next piece is going to fit.

STUFF YOU'LL NEED
- Stud finder
- Chalk line
- Cement backer-board sheets
- Tape measure
- Pencil
- Drywall square
- Utility knife with fresh blade or circular saw with diamond blade
- Broom and dustpan
- Disposable gloves
- ¼" notched trowel
- Premixed thin-set mortar with latex additive
- Level
- Backer board screws and appropriate screw bit
- Drill
- Scissors
- Fiberglass mesh tape

HOW TO INSTALL UNDERLAYMENT

1. Use a stud finder to locate the floor joists, and snap a chalk line (see page 127) over each joist to mark its location. Plan your installation so that none of the backer-board seams will fall over a joist.

2. Do a rough layout of backer-board sheets so that they are staggered—like you see in a brick pattern. Leave a ¼-inch gap at the walls, and ⅛ inch between neighboring sheets.

3. Chances are you'll have to cut some of the backer-board sheets to fit your pattern. Take your measurements and mark them at the top and bottom of each sheet.

TIME & TALENT

Give yourself half a day to take your measurements and gather all the right materials. Figure it'll take you a day to complete the underlayment.

4. Place the drywall square on the two marks. Holding it firmly, use the utility knife to score along the line. Score it a couple of times. Make sure the blade is fully penetrating the material.

5. Kneel on the backer board with your knees at the cut line, and lift the edge up until the piece snaps. It won't sever completely—just halfway. Use the utility knife to finish the cut on the back side of the seam.

6. Once all the pieces are cut and dry-fit, you're ready to install. Make sure you sweep up any residual debris that's on the plywood subfloor.

7. Put on disposable gloves. Working in sections, use the notched trowel to spread the mortar on the subfloor. Make sure you apply enough mortar to accommodate a whole piece.

8. Carefully lay the backer board into the mortar bed. Use a level on top of the piece to see if it's sitting flat. Check in each direction and in several places. If the sheet sits level, you can screw it into place. If it's overly low in one corner, you might have to shore it up with more mortar.

9. Screw the sheet into the subfloor using the backer-board screws. Make sure that the screw heads are countersunk. The manufacturer of the backer board will recommend how far apart the screws should be. Generally, it'll range between 4 and 6 inches. Yep, it's a lot of screwing.

10. Once all the pieces are secured, you'll need to tape up the seams. Use scissors to cut fiberglass mesh tape to size and secure the pieces over the seams with mortar, using the flat end of your notched trowel. Mortar is gloppy and gloopy, but try to skim over the seams as smoothly as possible.

11. Let the mortar dry before tiling. This will take between 24 and 48 hours.

SHORTCUT

If you have a circular saw, you can cut the backer board more easily with that. Or buy a special lightweight backer board that cuts just like drywall.

tiling a floor

If this is your first time tiling, I'm going to encourage you to keep the job simple. Don't plan to lay tiles on the diagonal, or use multiple tile sizes in a random pattern. This is a bit of an experiment to test your technique—and your fortitude. So go with a simple pattern where all the grout lines and tiles are designed to match up evenly.

Not to sound like a broken record—or a skipping CD—but planning the layout is key. In general, you want to use full-size tiles in the most visible, obvious part of the room. That usually means your cut pieces will be relegated to the sides (walls) of the space.

STUFF YOU'LL NEED

- Vacuum or broom and dustpan
- Tape measure
- Pencil
- Chalk line
- Tiles
- Spacers
- Batten board (1 x 2 cut to length with one factory-cut edge)
- Cement screws
- Drill and screw bit
- Disposable gloves
- Knee pads
- Safety glasses
- Premixed thin-set mortar with latex additive
- Margin trowel
- Notched trowel (size depends on size of tile)
- Level
- Rubber mallet
- Wax pencil
- Wet saw or snap cutter
- Utility knife
- Clean rag
- Grout saw
- Materials for grouting (see page 77)

HOW TO USE A CHALK LINE

A chalk line is a long chalk-coated piece of string that's released and retracted kind of like a line in a fishing reel (only you don't cast it …). To use it properly, stretch the string between the two measurements and set it flat on the surface. Make sure it's pulled taut and then grab the string from directly overhead—the 12:00 position—and let go quickly, which is referred to as "snapping." Don't pull the string off to the side when you snap it or your line won't be accurate.

TIME & TALENT

It depends on your space. If you have a lot of obstacles, such as cabinets or irregular walls, you'll be spending a lot of time on cuts. If it's a straightforward job in a small space, tile setting can be completed in a matter of hours.

HOW TO TILE A FLOOR

1. Make sure the underlayment and work area is clean and free of debris.

2. Find and mark the center of the room. To do this, measure the width and length of the room and divide those numbers in half. Mark the midpoint of each of the four walls.

3. Snap two chalk lines (see page 127) connecting the midpoints. Where the chalk lines intersect is the center of your room. This intersection represents where your first four tiles will be laid—maybe!

4. Now comes the design part. Line up the tile edges against the lines of your intersection, and dry-fit an entire row of tile, including the spacers, all the way across the room. If life were a fairy tale, the entire row would fit perfectly; no cuts required. But you probably will end up with cut tiles at the edges. Adjust your layout so the cut tiles on each end of the row will be about the same width. This may mean shifting your perfectly marked center either to the right or left. Measure the distance those tiles had to shift, then snap a new chalk line. This will now be your new starting point for setting the tiles.

5. Take the batten board and line it up with your new chalk line. Temporarily screw the batten board into the underlayment using the drill. This is your cheater board. By butting the tops of all your tiles against it, your first row will be even.

6. Put on the disposable gloves. Working in manageable 3-by-3-foot sections, spread mortar over the underlayment. You can use a notched trowel for this, but I like to use a margin trowel to dump mortar on my work area. Then comb it out with the notched trowel. Hold the trowel at a 45-degree angle to the floor and comb the mortar with swoops and curves. Comb away any major globs.

7. Once a section is completely combed out, set the tile in the mortar. Press it into place with a slight jiggling motion. Adjust the edges so they're aligned with your chalk lines.

WATCH OUT!
Strap on your knee pads; you're going to need them. Wear safety glasses when making cuts.

8. Set the neighboring tile in the same manner. Use spacers along all the tile edges. This will keep the tiles aligned and will give you consistent grout lines.

9. While setting the tiles, keep checking with the level to make sure the tile surfaces are even with each other. If one is sitting too high, gently tap it down with the rubber mallet. You don't want one errant tile sitting higher than the others. That's a toe-stubber in the making!

10. When it's time to cut tiles, measure from the edge of the closest tile to the wall. Factor in the grout line (or spacer) and transfer the measurements to a tile. Mark the top and bottom and draw a line joining the two points with a wax pencil. Then make your cut.

11. If you're lucky, you're making cuts on a wet saw (see page 52). If you don't have a wet saw and your tiles are small enough and weak enough to be cut with a snap cutter, line up your cut line underneath the blade of the snap cutter. Score it a couple times, then press down on the handle and make the snap. The tile should cut cleanly in two.

12. If your mortar doesn't extend all the way to the wall, you'll need to "butter" the backs of cut tiles. Apply and comb out the mortar on the back of the tile piece just as you would on the floor. The cut edge should go against the wall; the clean edge goes next to its neighboring tile.

13. As you tile, mortar will ooze out between the grout lines, or joints. Use the blade of a utility knife to clean out these joints. Mortar that gets on the face of the tile should be wiped off with a rag.

14. Once all the tile has been set, let it dry overnight before walking on it. Before you grout, you'll have a little cleanup work to do. Remove the spacers. Inspect all the joints between the tiles. If there's dry mortar that has oozed up level with the tile surface, it needs to be removed. A hand-held grout saw will do this easily. Simply pull the serrated edge of the grout saw along the joints. Vacuum up all the debris and you're ready to grout (see pages 80–81).

VINYL

Like laminate, vinyl flooring is a "man-made" product. And as with laminate, the resilient-flooring industry has introduced designs in vinyl that emulate natural materials like slate, wood, and marble.

Many of us associate vinyl flooring with the pliable sheet vinyl we grew up with in our baths, kitchens, and laundry rooms. The new breed of vinyl definitely isn't from your mother's generation, however. In fact, one manufacturer of luxury vinyl features a three-dimensional, chrome-colored pattern that's so hip, it looks as if it dropped in from *The Matrix* movie set.

Vinyl flooring is divalike in its underlayment requirements; the underlying surface for vinyl tiles and sheet vinyl has to be smooth as glass or you'll see imperfections in the finished floor surface. This typically means installing a ¼-inch high-quality plywood that's secured every 4 inches over the subfloor. Fastener heads need to be countersunk and patched.

Another way to create a smooth vinyl underlayment is to use a pour-on embossing leveler. It removes any ridges, bumps, or impressions by creating a new skin over the surface. Either way, the preparation and installation of an entire vinyl floor is a mid- to advanced-level home improvement project.

replacing a vinyl tile

Like many floor surfaces, vinyl will get superficial scratches over time. The more rigid styles can chip. Repairing a damaged section is relatively easy with vinyl tiles because you're simply swapping out the damaged tile for a new one.

STUFF YOU'LL NEED
- Blow dryer
- Putty knife
- 4" wallpaper scraper or single-edged razor blade
- Disposable plastic gloves
- Replacement tile
- Vinyl floor adhesive (follow tile manufacturer's recommendation)
- V-notched trowel
- Soft cotton rag
- Mineral spirits or denatured alcohol
- Painter's tape

TIME & TALENT

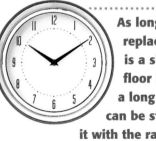

As long as you have a replacement tile, this is a slam dunk. If the floor has been in place a long time, the glue can be stubborn. Keep at it with the razor blade. It'll eventually come off.

HOW TO REPLACE A VINYL TILE

1. Vinyl floors are secured with adhesive, so the first step is to use the blow dryer to heat the tile and soften the adhesive underneath it.

2. Use the putty knife to pry under the tile. It should come off easily. If it breaks into pieces, warm up the glue again and use the wallpaper scraper to pry up the remnants.

3. Use the razor blade or wallpaper scraper to clean the surface of residual glue. Easy does it if you're using a razor!

4. Put on the plastic gloves, then lay the replacement tile facedown and spread some vinyl flooring adhesive onto its back. Use the notched trowel to evenly comb and distribute it, making sure you have enough at the edges.

5. Flip the tile over and carefully press it in place. Be sure to press it firmly along all the edges.

6. If any excess adhesive has squeezed out between the joints, clean it off with the soft cotton rag and mineral spirits or denatured alcohol. Demarcate the repair area with painter's tape and stay off it for a day while the adhesive dries.

131

LINOLEUM

Think back to the floors in your grade school and you're probably remembering linoleum. Thanks to its durability and affordability, linoleum has suffered from a bit of a bad design rap. It seemed "old-fashioned" or "too industrial" or "that is so-o-o 10th-grade chemistry class!"

Indeed, linoleum has been around for more than a hundred years. But there are a lot of good reasons it's endured and is now making a comeback. Environmentalists like linoleum because it's made from renewable resources (linseed oil, cork dust, wood, and other natural materials) and is naturally biodegradable. Kitchen designers like it because it's antibacterial, water resistant, and available in a wide range of styles. Pet-lovers like it because it's easy to clean and resistant to scratching. Hey, what's not to like? It could be time to jump on the linoleum bandwagon.

Like vinyl, linoleum is available in sheets or as tiles and is glued onto the subfloor. If you need to replace a tile, follow the steps for replacing a vinyl tile on pages 130–131.

CORK

It seems bizarre that the very material that bottles your bubbly can be manufactured into a flooring material. Cork flooring has a lot of attractive qualities: it's nonallergenic, it's soft and warm underfoot, it has insulating value, it lasts for decades, and it's environmentally sustainable. Plus it's pretty. Cork's natural coloring ranges from buff beige to deep cocoa, but some manufacturers offer it in a rainbow of color choices.

Cork comes from the cork oak tree that grows in Mediterranean regions. It's the bark that's harvested, so the tree doesn't have to be cut down. The bark regrows and is ready for harvest every nine years or so, making it as environmentally minded as a Green Party candidate.

As a construction material, cork was widely used in the early part of the 20th century. Frank Lloyd Wright even used it in Fallingwater, his home in Pennsylvania.

Cork is available in plank or tile form and can go over a concrete or plywood subfloor. It installs as a floating or a glue-down floor. It's not the best flooring choice for areas with high moisture content.

MAINTAINING CORK FLOORS It's important to protect cork from permanent indentations, so make sure to use furniture leg protectors, castors, or chair pads. Keep the surface swept free of grit and dirt so the finish doesn't scratch. Spills and excess water should be wiped up immediately. If you have a cork floor that is overly scuffed, it can be buffed and refinished. This procedure is best left to a flooring professional, however.

MOISTURE AND FLOORING

Some spaces, especially below-grade basements, are so naturally humid that certain floor coverings won't perform well. Have a professional check damp rooms with a hygrometer if this is a concern. Or do your own test: set an empty glass upside down on the floor and leave it for 24 hours. If any condensation or moisture forms on the glass, use a floor covering that can handle humid conditions, such as ceramic tile.

BAMBOO

Like cork and linoleum, bamboo is an environmentally friendly product. Although it looks like an engineered wood floor, bamboo is technically a grass—one that acts like it's hopped-up on caffeine, it grows so fast. Bamboo can grow between 12 and 18 inches a day. Because of this, bamboo gets kudos from environmentalists as a sustainable building material.

VERTICAL BAMBOO

HORIZONTAL BAMBOO

Although bamboo is "green," its coloring ranges from a pale tan natural shade to a carbonized medium brown. You can also buy unfinished bamboo and stain it any color you like. The grain is distinctive because it shows the striations of the bamboo canes. It's a subtle but sophisticated look.

Bamboo is also strong. In the Far East, it is used as a building material for homes and other structures. There's even a 250-yard bridge in China that rests entirely on bamboo cables. As a floor covering, bamboo rates 1380 on the Janka scale (see page 118), which makes it comparable to white oak and maple.

Bamboo is available as a nail-down, glue-down, or floating floor. If you're considering bamboo as a flooring material, do your research regarding manufacturers. I've seen planks so precisely milled they could win the Miss Bamboo Floor beauty contest. I've also seen planks that are bowed, cupped, and poorly laminated. Make sure the manufacturer provides a warranty with the finish, and that the ends and sides butt tightly together. Take this to heart lest you get bamboo-zled.

REPAIRS AND MAINTENANCE Like the engineered wood products, most bamboo flooring comes prefinished. But that factory-applied finish can be compromised. I should know! A dining room chair that lost its leg protector left a nasty gouge in the bamboo floor in my house.

The repair techniques for bamboo are the same as for a wood floor (see Scratches and Cracks, page 121). Use matching wood putty for the small holes and cracks, and sand down and reapply polyurethane on the bigger gouges.

Bamboo should be swept free of dirt, grit, and debris on a regular basis. Cleaning should be done with a gentle spray-on hardwood floor cleaner that has neither soap nor wax in its ingredients.

CARPET

It seems only appropriate that a chapter that began with carpet should end with it. Sure, sexy new floor coverings have been given the spotlight of late (can you say Brazilian cherry?). But carpet is still a popular floor covering for bedrooms and other living spaces. There are countless colors, styles, and designs to choose from. It's a soft, warm, quiet surface, and it's affordable.

CUT PILE Here's where you'll find the luxurious velvet or plush types of carpet often used in bedrooms—the types that show every footprint or vacuum line. Frieze (pronounced frih-zay) is a cut pile with a perm. The fibers are twisted, which gives the floor covering a kinky or curled appearance.

LOOP PILE This is a good-wearing carpet where the fibers are woven in a continuous loop. Berber is considered a level-loop pile (all the loops are the same height) and is distinguished by large loops constructed with olefin and/or nylon—fibers that are extremely stain resistant. A multiloop pile has loops at different heights that create texture and pattern.

CUT AND LOOP PILE As the name implies, this is a combination of the two styles.

Almost all carpets these days are made of synthetic fibers, typically nylon or polyester. There are also wool carpets that are more costly than their synthetic cousins. Wool is beautiful, but as a floor-covering professional told me, "Don't use it in a high-moisture room. It'll smell like wet dog."

Loop pile carpet is a smart choice for a baby's room, where spills are likely to happen.

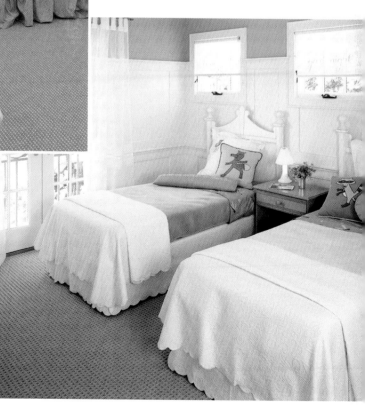

Warm wool carpet is soft and inviting—who needs socks when your feet can nestle into this?

removing old carpet

Carpet is economical, especially if you can pick up a remnant. I carpeted a bedroom with a high-quality cut-pile remnant for about $300—including the labor. If you're looking for a quick, inexpensive room face-lift, you can't beat new paint and carpeting. Do hire a professional for the new carpet installation. They have special equipment to stretch the carpet tight to the walls, and it's back-breaking work. But you can save a few bucks on the installation price by tearing out the old carpet yourself.

STUFF YOU'LL NEED
- Knee pads
- Work gloves
- Pliers
- Utility knife with fresh blade
- Twine or packing tape
- Drywall knife (if necessary)
- Solvent (if necessary)
- Hammer
- Pry bar
- Safety glasses
- Cardboard box

TIME & TALENT

Old carpet can be removed in a matter of hours. A key consideration is the proper disposal of the old carpet. Check with your local waste hauler to see what its policies are. Most haulers will take carpet off your hands for a nominal fee.

HOW TO REMOVE CARPET

1. Clear the room of all its furnishings, and put on your knee pads and gloves.

2. Carpet is held in place with spiked tack strips that are secured around the perimeter of the room. Starting in a corner, use pliers to pry a piece from the tack strip. Once you get a corner free, the rest should release pretty easily. Be careful! Tack strips are like an instrument of torture with their upside-down nails.

3. As you pull up the carpet, use the utility knife to cut it into manageable sections that are 2 to 3 feet wide and about 6 feet long. Each section should be rolled up as tightly as possible and bound with twine or tape. This makes it easier and more lightweight to move.

4. If you're recarpeting the space, inspect the pad. If it's in good shape, leave it alone. Leave the tack strips in place too.

5. If you're using a different floor covering, or reclaiming the hardwood floors underneath, you'll need to get rid of the pad and tack strips. Pads are typically stapled or glued down. Again, cut the pad in sections (without cutting into the wood floors underneath if you're resurrecting them), roll it up, bind it, and haul it away. Leftover staples can be removed with pliers. Glue will have to be either scraped off (use a drywall knife or anything with a flat edge and a handle) or removed with a solvent.

6. To remove tack strips, use the hammer and pry bar to get underneath the strip and loosen it. Remember to put on safety glasses first! Because of all the sharp edges, dispose of tack strips in a cardboard box.

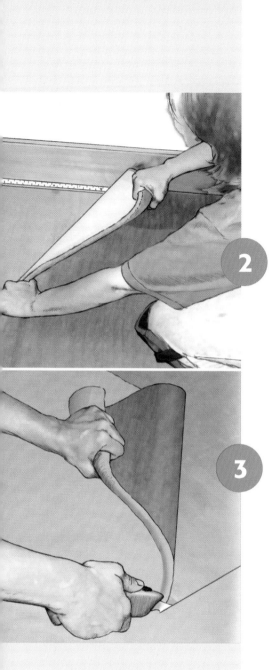

maintaining carpets and removing stains

Carpet professionals will always recommend a professional cleaning for carpets with stains and ground-in dirt. Even though commercially available cleaners will remove a stain, the pros say that the fibers can be compromised, leaving them more prone to future stains.

That may be true, but what happens when you spill a half-gallon of paint? Or the dog just, uh, rejected his dinner? My tried-and-true trick has been three simple ingredients: club soda (sparkling water also works), baking soda, and lots and lots of clean white rags. You pour on the water, add the baking soda and blot, blot, blot 'til that stain comes out. Of course, the key to successfully removing any stain is getting it out before it's had time to set.

There are a number of other remedies for spills and stains. For candle wax, pick off as much as you can by hand once the wax has dried. Then put a warm iron over a white paper towel so that the wax "melts" and is absorbed by the towel. For permanent ink, use alcohol-based hair spray and a clean white rag to blot it up. For pet urine, use disposable diapers to fully absorb the moisture, then follow up with baking soda.

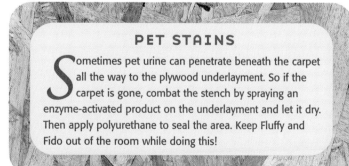

PET STAINS

Sometimes pet urine can penetrate beneath the carpet all the way to the plywood underlayment. So if the carpet is gone, combat the stench by spraying an enzyme-activated product on the underlayment and let it dry. Then apply polyurethane to seal the area. Keep Fluffy and Fido out of the room while doing this!

chapter 6

PLUMBING

DAVE FREDERIXON IS A PLUMBER you can trust. He has the kind eyes of a Labrador and the demeanor of a Boy Scout. Dave, a Mr. Rooter Plumbing franchise owner in Minnesota, and I have had a couple of opportunities to work together and talk shop. Because I never got past second-grade potty humor, I like to ask him about what he's found in clogged toilets (besides the obvious). You'd be surprised at the kinds of things people pitch down the loo, like pork chops, bras, panties, toothbrushes, dental floss, potato peelings, jewelry, bottles of hair dye, combs, dolls, rubber balls, deodorant, cauliflower, apples, and lots and lots of toys. There's something about the now-you-see-it-now-you-don't flush mechanism that fascinates some kids. "I was lucky," Dave says, with a shrug of his shoulders. "My kids never liked to play with the toilet."

The toilet is just one fixture whose depths we'll plumb in this chapter. Stand by as we supply you with information that won't be a waste of your time. And by the end of this chapter, you might even mildly appreciate the puns you just read.

PLUMBING OVERVIEW

OK, if you didn't read Chapter 1, stop here. Go no further. Do not land on Boardwalk. Do not collect $200. It'll take you all of 5 minutes to skim over the plumbing basics on pages 12–14. So go ahead. We'll wait. (Insert *Jeopardy!* theme song here.)

Although designing and installing an entire plumbing system isn't easy, the logic of plumbing is simple: What comes in must flow out. Plumbing is all about supply and waste. The major concerns you'll have will be with leaks, which can affect supply and waste lines, and clogs, which affect waste lines only.

Clogs are the worst. Very often we think it's some big dramatic event that led to the clog—like a Lhasa Apso sliding down the drain during a kitchen sink bath. But usually it's a slow-growing collection of grease, food, hair, and soap residue that's at the root of a clog. Clogs especially like to collect at bends and curves in the pipes where they can affix to something. Some of them are so deep into the system only a professional can root them out.

CLOSET AUGER

COPPER FITTINGS

common plumbing terms

ABS This is short for acrylonitrile-butadiene-styrene (and thank goodness—'cuz that's a mouthful). It's rigid plastic pipe (often black) that's used for drain/waste/vent lines.

BALL COCK Commonly found in the toilet tank, this is a valve that controls water flow from the water supply line. When the toilet is flushed, the float ball drops down and opens the ball cock, releasing water into the tank and bowl. When the tank is finally refilled—and quiet—the ball cock shuts off.

CLEANOUT An access point for a drain line or trap. It looks like a plug and unscrews.

CLOSET AUGER Your best friend as a toilet tool. This is a flexible rod with a curved end that is designed to slip into the trap of a toilet and remove clogs.

PREVENTING CLOGS THE NATURAL WAY

There are several gentle biological drain treatments on the market that feed on grease and soap. If you can get past any squeamishness at the thought of actual microscopic organisms feasting on your pipe waste, it's worth the relatively high price of the treatment. Pour the product of your choice down your drains once a month and buy a little peace of mind.

COCK Another term for a valve or faucet. Seriously.

COUPLING A fitting that links two lengths of pipe in a straight run.

DRAIN People who complain all the time and do nothing to change their situation. Uh…I mean a pipe that carries away waterborne waste.

DWV Short for drain/waste/vent lines, which comprise the outgoing elements of a plumbing system.

ESCUTCHEON A decorative metal flange or trim piece used beneath a faucet handle.

FITTING Any pipe part used to join sections of pipe. Many are named for their shapes, like an "elbow" or a "T" fitting.

FIXTURE Anything that provides a supply of water or disposes of it—a faucet or tub, for example.

FLOAT BALL The floating ball that connects to the ball-cock valve inside a toilet tank.

GPF Gallons per flush. Current law mandates that new toilets use only 1.6 gpf. Older toilets typically use between 3.5 and 3.7 gpf.

GALVANIZED Refers to the zinc coating put over a product to protect it from corrosion.

GASKET The rubber equivalent to a washer, creating a watertight seal between joints.

MAIN The primary pipe for either the supply or drain systems. All other pipes branch out from the mains.

O-RING A close cousin to a gasket, this is a round rubber washer used to create a watertight seal, primarily in faucets.

OVERFLOW TUBE A vertical tube, located in the toilet tank, that directs excess water into the bowl instead of letting the tank fill up and overflow. It's an insurance policy against a failing ball cock.

PITCH The downward slope of a drain and the ability to sing on key.

PVC Short for polyvinyl chloride, this rigid, white plastic pipe is used in irrigation systems and for waste and vent lines.

ROUGH-IN Installation of supply and DWV lines for future fixtures. Think of it as "pipes-in-waiting."

GALVANIZED FITTINGS

PVC FITTINGS

ABS

SHUTOFF VALVE

SHUTOFF VALVE This valve enables you to shut off water to specific fixtures and to the whole house. There should be shutoff valves underneath every fixture in the house, but that's not always the case. Shutoff valves can have different handle styles—two are shown on this page.

SOIL STACK (ALSO CALLED A WASTE STACK) The star player in the DWV system, this is a large vertical pipe that vents sewer gas out through the roof and also carries waste to the sewer line.

SUPPLY SYSTEM The network of hot- and cold-water lines that feeds fixtures and water-using appliances.

TRAP A short, curved section of waste pipe located underneath a fixture. The trap's curve pockets a small quantity of water that prevents

sewer gases from entering the room. P-traps are under tubs and sinks; S-traps are in toilets.

VALVE A device that regulates the flow of water. When you turn a faucet on, you're opening a valve.

VALVE SEAT The nonmoving part of a valve. Water flow comes to a halt when the movable part of the valve contacts the seat.

VENT PIPE A pipe that allows gas to escape from plumbing stacks. Vents also allow air into the drain system.

WASTE Everything that flushes down the drain lines, including your morning toothpaste and coffee remnants.

SHUTOFF VALVE

TRAP

TOILETS

There's nothing glamorous about the toilet. Even in toilet-cleaning commercials, the women look exasperated. They throw up their rubber-gloved hands in hopelessness while their eyes plead, "Get me out of here! I'd rather be cast in a Volvo commercial."

But look on the bright side. You really start to appreciate your toilet when you consider the alternatives—like an outhouse or a porta-potty. So pay your respects to the lowly toilet, it's your friend. Now let's see what makes your friend tick.

Every time you flush the toilet, a configuration of chains and rods opens up the flapper (also called a tank stopper), which is a rubber stopper at the bottom of the tank. Opening the flapper allows the fresh, clean tank water to pour into the bowl and gravity helps push the bowl contents down the drain. When the tank has emptied as much water as is needed, the flapper reseats itself, and a pressure-sensing valve sends the signal to refill the tank. The tank water comes from a supply pipe in your wall, and travels up through a tank-fill tube. As the tank refills with water, the float ball slowly rises. When it hits its mark, the valve gets the signal that enough water has been sent and all is quiet on the toilet front. Your toilet is now ready to do its duty again.

Most problems and malfunctions occur in the tank, so that's where your repairs will likely be. Remember, the tank brings in fresh water so you don't have to be grossed out reaching in there and making adjustments. The parts may be old, corroded, and worn out, but the water's clean.

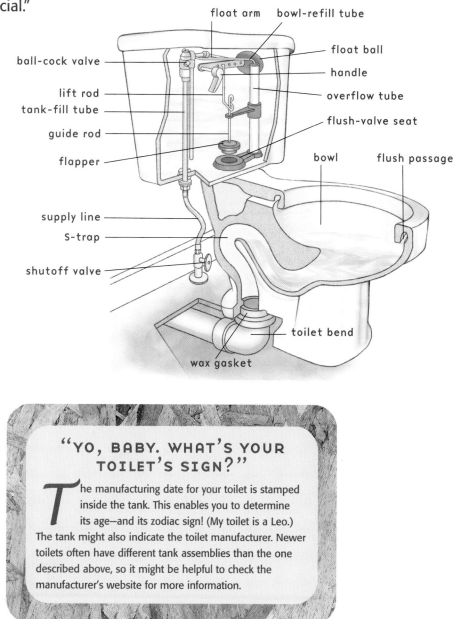

float arm bowl-refill tube
ball-cock valve
float ball
handle
lift rod
tank-fill tube
overflow tube
guide rod
flush-valve seat
flapper
bowl flush passage
supply line
S-trap
shutoff valve
toilet bend
wax gasket

"YO, BABY. WHAT'S YOUR TOILET'S SIGN?"

The manufacturing date for your toilet is stamped inside the tank. This enables you to determine its age—and its zodiac sign! (My toilet is a Leo.) The tank might also indicate the toilet manufacturer. Newer toilets often have different tank assemblies than the one described above, so it might be helpful to check the manufacturer's website for more information.

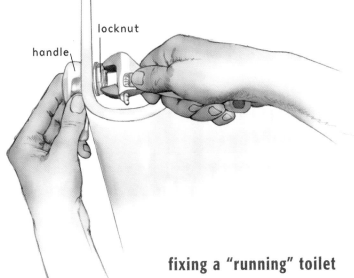

fixing a "running" toilet

There can be all manner of malfunctions at the root of the proverbial "running" toilet, so start with the simplest solution—the handle. If jiggling it stops the running, you may only need to adjust the handle. Tighten the locknut that attaches the assembly to the tank by turning it counterclockwise with an adjustable wrench (as shown above). If that doesn't work, replace the handle.

Another easy fix lies in the float ball. This ball is tied into the valve mechanism that triggers the inflow of fresh water. Its ideal position is to be half-covered with water. If it isn't, gently bend the float-ball arm to "reset" its level (as shown at left). If this doesn't solve the problem, turn off the water supply to the toilet and flush it. This will enable you to check the float ball and see if it's full of water. If it is, unscrew it, bring it to the hardware store, buy a new one, and install it.

Another cause for a running toilet is a flapper that isn't seating properly. Think of how tight the seal is when you recork a bottle of wine. If the cork was misaligned, wine could spill out. The flapper works on the same principle. But before you start messing around with it, try this test:

Squeeze a few drops of food coloring into the tank. Check your bowl 5 minutes later. If you see that the food coloring has colored the water in the bowl, your flapper's watertight seal ain't so watertight.

The flapper sits on top of a flush-valve seat (as shown below). Close the shutoff valve (see page 143), and flush the toilet to empty the tank. Then flush the toilet again and observe how the flapper sits on the valve seat. It might be that the guide rod and chain are misaligned and steering the flapper off course. Adjust them until they're centered over the flapper.

Sometimes this area can build up with mineral deposits. Use steel wool to gently scour off any buildup on the flapper or the valve seat. If the flapper feels worn and out of shape, remove and replace it.

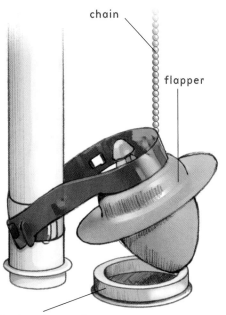

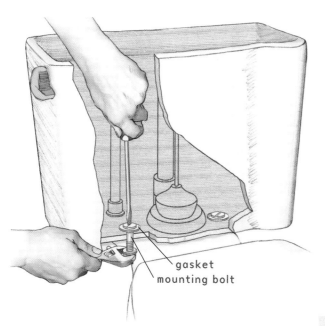

gasket
mounting bolt

REPLACING A TOILET SUPPLY LINE

Another culprit of leaks is the supply line. Sometimes the slender tubing that connects the cold-water supply line to the toilet corrodes or becomes compromised. If there's water dripping from that area, or the floor underneath it is wet, take action! You'll want to replace it with a braided stainless-steel supply line. Even if your old one just looks old and crusty, it's good preventive maintenance to replace it.

STUFF YOU'LL NEED
· Sponge
· Bucket
· Two adjustable wrenches
· WD-40, oil, or similar lubricant
  (if necessary)
· Tape measure
· Braided stainless-steel supply line

fixing a leaky toilet

Toilet leaks can be insidious. I once had a toilet quietly and sneakily leak from the supply line overnight. By the next morning, the ceiling below it was like a giant wet diaper. So, this is not a problem you want to ignore.

Like all fixes, determining the cause can be more frustrating than the fix. Adding to the confusion is the normal condensation that happens with pipes and fixtures in hot, humid weather.

Sometimes leaks occur in the area where the tank is connected to the bowl. Mounting bolts link the two components. Use an adjustable wrench to tighten the bolt underneath the tank while you hold the bolt in place with a screwdriver from inside the tank (as shown above). If that doesn't do the trick, the gaskets might be worn out and will need to be replaced.

TIME & TALENT

Replacing the toilet's supply line involves a trip to a hardware store and less than an hour of labor—if all goes well.

HOW TO REPLACE A SUPPLY LINE

1. Close the shutoff valve located on the supply line. If there isn't a shutoff valve, curse the previous owner, and shut down the water to the whole house (see pages 12–13).

2. Flush the toilet to get the tank as empty as possible. You may have to use a sponge and bucket to sop up the residual tank water.

supply
line

shutoff
valve

1

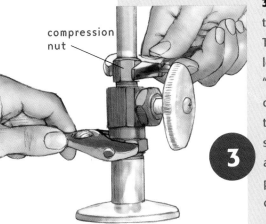

compression nut

3. Use one adjustable wrench to lock onto the shutoff valve and keep it from moving. Then use the second wrench to gently loosen the compression nut. Remember, "lefty loosey, righty tighty." This can be a delicate operation because you don't want to break off the valve. If the connections seem stuck and stubborn, try lubricating the area with WD-40 or oil. Disconnect the supply line at the tank too. Use the bucket to catch any remaining water.

3

4. Measure the distance from the shutoff valve to the area under the tank where the supply line feeds in. When you buy your braided stainless-steel supply line, use this distance, plus another inch or two for slop. Bring the old tubing and connectors to the hardware store so you can make sure the replacement will fit.

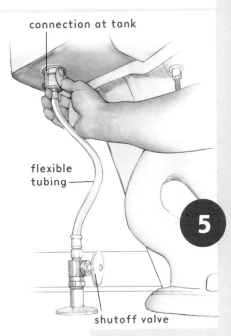

connection at tank

flexible tubing

shutoff valve

5. Connect the new flexible tubing at the tank and supply areas. Loosely make the connection with your fingers, then use the two-wrench approach to stabilize that valve. Be sure your connections are tight!

5

6. Turn the water back on and check for leaks.

LEAKING AROUND THE TOILET BASE

Uh-oh. You've got ring around the toilet! Yes, toilets can leak at the base. A wax ring underneath the bowl creates a watertight connection between the bowl and the waste pipe. Naturally, years of sitting on the bowl can wear out that wax ring. Plus, the material degrades over time. If you notice that your tile grout appears moist near the bowl, or the floor feels damp, this might be why.

The repair is cheap; new wax rings aren't more than a couple of bucks. But it means draining and disassembling the entire toilet, replacing the wax ring, and reassembling everything. Frankly, this is probably one for a professional. For one thing, the bowl is heavy. Once the ring is replaced, positioning it over the closet bolts and lining it up over the drain is tricky. Also, once you start disassembling bolts and fasteners, more often than not you find that they should be replaced too. A plumber will have everything on hand and can handle the job quickly and efficiently.

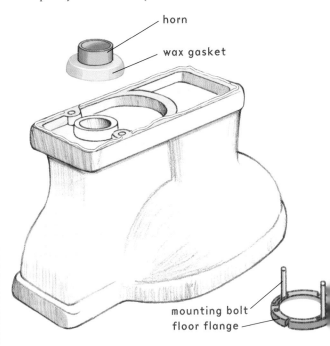

horn

wax gasket

mounting bolt

floor flange

SWEATING TOILETS Do you think if a toilet "runs" too much, it works up a "sweat"? Haw-haw-haw! Just a little third-grade humor for you. "Sweating" refers to the condensation that forms on the toilet when the weather warms up and gets humid. After all, it's cold water in the toilet. You only have to look at the condensation on a glass of iced tea on a sultry summer day to understand what's happening with your porcelain throne.

You do want to make sure that your tank is just sweating and not actually leaking. So put a few drops of food coloring in the tank. About an hour later, take a tissue and dab the mounting bolts underneath the tank. If the wet area has coloration, you've got a leak. You'll likely need to replace the gaskets on those bolts in the tank (see top illustration, page 145).

If it's not a leak, you can remedy a sweating toilet with an insulated tank liner. Buy one, drain and dry the tank, and follow the instructions to secure the liner. Or you can buy a tank cover. It's a cheap solution, but tank covers aren't very stylin.' I think my grandma had one in powder blue fuzzy nylon. Not my style, but she must have liked it.

You can also have a plumber replumb your supply line so that hot water mixes in with the cold. But before spending the bucks to do this, consider whether or not the sweating is really a problem. If it's constant, and the drips are ruining the floor, then you'll need to address it. If it only happens a few days a year and doesn't seem to be dripping profusely, you can probably live with it.

fixing a clogged toilet

My Scandinavian cousins have a word to describe really gross stuff; they call it "ishy." Not only is a backed-up toilet ishy, unclogging it ranks right up there in the Top 10 Grossest Home-Improvement Tasks. If this happens to you, a) you have my sympathy; b) turn the water supply off!; and c) put on your rubber gloves and adopt a can-do attitude. You'll need it.

Sometimes, as we saw in the beginning of this chapter, things can accidentally fall into the toilet and cause a clog. If that's the case, try reaching down into the drain (with your gloves on, of course) and see if you can fish it out. You hate to ask your kids to do something like this, but the truth is, their hands are smaller. They might be able to get at it better than you.

Clogs with other causes at their root can be handled by following the steps on the next page.

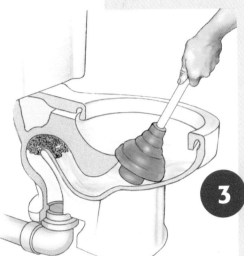

closet auger

If you're lucky, you can dispose of this matter in 15 minutes.

HOW TO UNCLOG A TOILET

1. Turn off the water supply at the shutoff valve, and the overflow will subside. With gloved hands, use the small bucket to bail water out of the toilet until it's about half full.

2. Center the toilet plunger firmly over the drain hole. Make sure you use a toilet plunger and not a regular sink plunger. A toilet plunger has a cone-shaped cup that's designed to snugly fit into the toilet's drain hole.

3. Press firmly up and down on the plunger a number of times. The pressure should free the clog. If it does, use the bucket to pour some water into the toilet until it's half full and plunge again—just to be good and sure.

4. If the plunger didn't do the trick, try the closet auger. This is a snake specifically designed to fit the contours of a toilet. Don't use any other types of augers, as they can damage the toilet. Pull the snake back in the tube as far as it will go. Then feed the curved tip into the opening.

5. Crank the auger in a clockwise direction. When it tightens, reverse the direction counterclockwise. Proceed in this manner, going back and forth, until the auger has gone as far as it can go—which is about 3 feet.

6. Once you're satisfied the clog is cleared, turn the water back on and flush the toilet several times to make sure all is clear on the toilet drain front. Clean the area with disinfectant and bask in the satisfaction that you saved yourself a plumbing call.

WHAT AN HONEST PLUMBER WOULD TELL YOU

*I*t's easy to laugh about some of the bizarre things plumbers have found in clogged toilets. What's not so readily talked about are the—ahem!—singularly female items that get flushed down the john. Don't do it. Feminine hygiene products can jam up drain lines. It may be less convenient for you, but your drainpipes will be better off for it.

old vs. new toilets: the debate

Low-flush toilets, also known as water-saving toilets, were mandated for new construction during the 1990s. These toilets use 1.6 gpf (gallons per flush), versus older toilets, which can use between 3.5 and 3.7 gpf. But there are still die-hards who swear by their old toilets. They're not adopting environmental consciousness quietly. So let's address this issue like a *Crossfire* debate:

CONSERVATIVE: "Balderdash, bunk, and hooey! These so-called low-flush, water-saving toilets stink."

LIBERAL: "No, what stinks is that so many people think fresh water is an endless resource…"

CONSERVATIVE (interrupting): "It is in Seattle! It rains all the time there."

LIBERAL: "Seattle, Schmee-attle. We need to conserve water any way and anywhere we can. The average American family can save up to $100 on its water bill and roughly 6,000 gallons of water annually with low-flush toilets. Besides, it's the law now."

CONSERVATIVE: "I don't remember voting for that."

LIBERAL: "You were probably out golfing with lobbyists."

CONSERVATIVE: "Let's stick to the issue. I hear you have to flush twice just to get a clean bowl with these low-flush johns. Do you call that water-saving?"

LIBERAL: "That was a problem in some early models. Manufacturers have addressed those complaints. The designs have improved and now you can even get dual-flush toilets."

CONSERVATIVE: "Dual-flush?!"

LIBERAL: "They've been in Europe and Australia for years. One flush button is for liquid waste and uses less than a gallon. The other button is for, well, solid waste and uses the mandated 1.6 gpf."

CONSERVATIVE: "Hmm. Dual-flush. And they have those in Australia? Do you think Nicole Kidman and Russell Crowe are familiar with this technology?"

LIBERAL: "I'd guess so."

CONSERVATIVE: "Well, who doesn't like Nicole Kidman and Russell Crowe?"

LIBERAL: "They're both terrific actors!"

CONSERVATIVE: "Maybe we're not so far apart on this low-flush toilet issue as we think."

LIBERAL: "I agree. Lunch?"

CONSERVATIVE: "Sure."

LIBERAL: "You're buying…"

FIXING A LEAKY SINK FAUCET

A leaking faucet can keep you up at night, as well as waste gallons of water in no time. And it's not the type of thing you can just ignore. It will only get worse. You can either take this leak as a sign that you should buy a new faucet, or try to fix the old one. Give it a shot yourself before you call a plumber. You may be able to save some money.

There are four types of faucets: compression, ceramic disc, rotating ball, and cartridge. The illustrations and instructions on the following pages show standard scenarios and parts, but yours might be slightly different. Have a towel spread out on the counter and organize each piece in the order you removed it. Then follow that same order when you put things back and you should be OK.

If the faucet still leaks after you've replaced the suspect parts, try tightening the connections with more force. If that doesn't do the trick, it could be that the outer housing is cracked and you'll need to break down and buy a new faucet.

STUFF YOU'LL NEED
- Flat-head and Phillips screwdrivers
- Crescent wrench and valve-seat wrench (for compression faucet)
- Utility knife
- Ziplock plastic bag
- Heat-proof plumber's grease
- Allen wrench and needle-nose pliers (for rotating-ball faucet)
- Replacement faucet kit (for cartridge, rotating-ball faucets)
- Distilled white vinegar (for ceramic-disc faucet)

TIME & TALENT

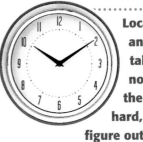

Locating the problem and then fixing it could take an entire afternoon, including trips to the store. But it's not hard, as long as you can figure out what each piece is.

WATCH OUT!
Remember to close the shutoff valve and open the faucet before starting any faucet repair project.

compression faucets

When compression faucets leak, it's usually because the seat washer needs to be replaced. Other than making sure you get everything back in the right order, this isn't hard to do. To find out which handle is the problem, turn off the shutoff valves one at a time to see which one stops the drip. Once you've found it, keep the shutoff valve off and turn on the faucet to drain it.

HOW TO FIX A
COMPRESSION FAUCET

1. Remove the handle by pulling straight up. If the handle won't come off, there may be a screw holding it in place. Look for a decorative cap (it might have an H or a C on it), and pry it off with a screwdriver to find the screw that's holding the handle in place.

2. Use the crescent wrench to loosen the packing nut.

3. Unscrew the stem from the packing nut. Remove the seat washer from the stem and cut off the O-ring with the utility knife. Put them in the ziplock bag to take with you to the hardware store for replacements.

4. While you're at it, go ahead and replace the valve seat too. You'll need a valve-seat wrench to get it out (on some models, the valve seat doesn't come out, so if that looks to be the case for yours, let's hope the new seat washer and O-ring do the trick).

5. Coat the new pieces with heatproof plumber's grease and reassemble. If the new seat washer is beveled, face the beveled side up and the flat side down against the valve seat.

6. Once the components are reassembled, turn on the shutoff valve and then turn on the faucet very slowly. You should be leak free!

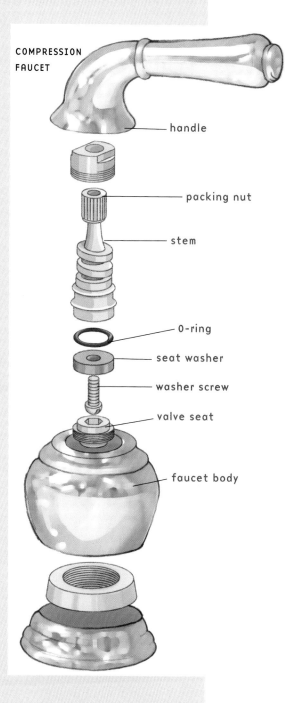

COMPRESSION FAUCET

handle

packing nut

stem

O-ring

seat washer

washer screw

valve seat

faucet body

rotating-ball faucets

These types of faucets have lots of little parts and it can be difficult to determine which one is failing and causing the leak. You can get a replacement kit for about $10 and avoid having to figure out which piece goes where.

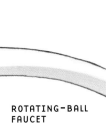

ROTATING-BALL
FAUCET

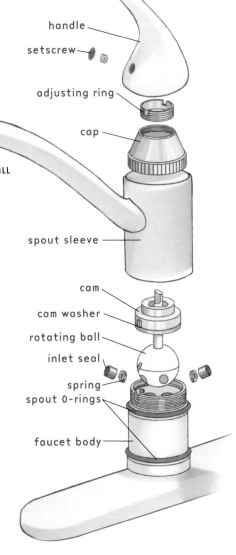

handle
setscrew
adjusting ring
cap
spout sleeve
cam
cam washer
rotating ball
inlet seal
spring
spout O-rings
faucet body

HOW TO FIX A ROTATING-BALL FAUCET

1. Remove the faucet handle by loosening the setscrew with an Allen wrench. Then remove the cap and spout sleeve. Using the tool included in the faucet-repair kit, loosen the cam and lift it out, along with the cam washer and rotating ball.

2. Use the needle-nose pliers to reach into the faucet body and remove the inlet seals and springs.

3. Cut off the spout O-rings with the utility knife, grease up the new ones with heat-proof plumber's grease, and roll them into place.

4. Install the new kit using the instructions that came with it.

5. Turn on the shutoff valve and then turn on the faucet very slowly, checking for leaks.

ceramic-disc faucets

Today's ceramic-disk faucets are virtually maintenance and drip free. But if you have an old model, it's possible that the disk assembly has a problem. Try cleaning the debris off, as described on the next page. If that doesn't work, you will need to replace the entire ceramic disk assembly, which will cost about $25.

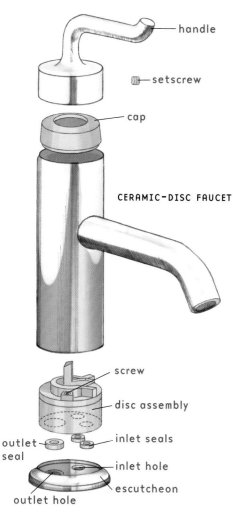

handle

setscrew

cap

CERAMIC-DISC FAUCET

screw

disc assembly

outlet seal

inlet seals

inlet hole

outlet hole

escutcheon

1. To repair a dripping spout or a leak at the base, push the faucet handle back until you can see the setscrew. Unscrew it and lift off the handle.

2. Remove the cap and then the disk assembly by loosening the two screws that hold it to the escutcheon.

3. On the bottom of the disc assembly is a set of two inlet seals and an outlet seal. Use the tip of a small flat-head screwdriver to take each seal out.

4. Clean the disk assembly and inlet holes with distilled white vinegar, and then rinse with water.

5. Install new seals and reassemble the faucet. Then turn on the shutoff valve and turn on the faucet very slowly. If you aren't leak free, replace the entire disc assembly.

cartridge faucets

As with rotating-ball faucets, you should buy a replacement kit for the entire cartridge assembly.

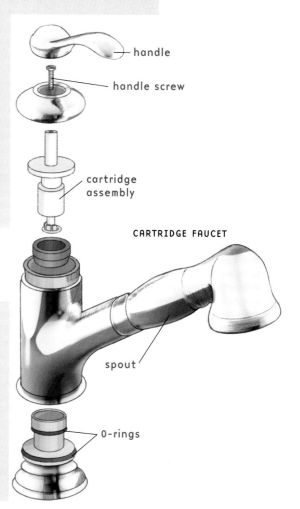

handle

handle screw

cartridge assembly

CARTRIDGE FAUCET

spout

O-rings

HOW TO FIX A CARTRIDGE FAUCET

1. Remove the handle, handle screw, and cartridge assembly.

2. Remove the spout and use a utility knife to cut off the old O-rings. Grease up the new O-rings with heat-proof plumber's grease and roll them into place. Reassemble the faucet using the instructions on the kit.

3. Turn on the shutoff valve and then turn on the faucet very slowly.

UNCLOGGING SINK DRAINS

A clogged drain always seems to happen at the worst time, such as when you're expecting visitors in an hour. The drain intuitively knows when it's going to be the biggest hassle for you. So, tune in to your drains. Pay attention to any warning signs. If the sink isn't draining with its usual gusto, investigate the situation sooner rather than later, and you might avoid the clog altogether.

In the kitchen, try not to put large amounts of food down the drain, even if you have a garbage disposal. Particularly if you live in a house with old pipes, rice and other easily compacted foods, or waste such as coffee grounds and grease, can create a whopper of a clog. It's always best to scrape food into the trash before rinsing dishes.

In the bathroom, hair is the usual suspect. If you shed as much as a Persian cat, put a hair catcher in your sink, tub, and shower. And while it is a gross job, you could put cleaning out your pop-up stopper on a regular maintenance schedule. If you remove the hair and gunk attached to it with a gloved hand a few times a year, you might avoid bathroom-sink clogs. Another idea is to pour a solution of equal parts baking soda and vinegar down bathroom drains to break down soap and hair clogs. Do this every couple of months, let it fizz, and then pour hot water down the drain to clear it.

THE POWER OF WATER If your sink is draining slowly or not at all, try pouring scalding hot water down the drain and wait a few minutes to see what happens. Quite often, this pushes the obstruction out of the way.

BRING OUT THE PLUNGER Sometimes a clog needs to be bullied out of the way with a little force. This is where the sink plunger comes in. Please don't be cheap (and gross) and use your toilet plunger for this job. Toilet plungers have a cone-shaped cup at the bottom; sink plungers do not (see page 54). So spend a few bucks for the second plunger that should be used exclusively for sink and tub clogs.

CHEMICAL CLOG DISSOLVERS

There are two schools of thought on chemical liquid clog dissolvers. Some say you should use one whenever you have a clog and try other solutions only if it doesn't work. Others say never to use it in any circumstance because it's too hard on your pipes. I lean toward the second school. These products are caustic, so you need to protect your hands and eyes when using them. A one-time application might not hurt your drainpipes, but what about repeated use? And what about environmental considerations once this stuff hits the city water-treatment plant? You'll just have to decide whether you want to "pour it on" or "root it out."

HOW TO PLUNGE A CLOGGED SINK

1. With gloved hands, remove the drain stopper (if you have one). Then stuff the wet rag in the over-flow vent. Usually it's located opposite the faucet and hard to see unless you turn your head upside down and look under the countertop rim. If your vent has more than one hole, cut the rag into pieces and stuff one in each.

2. Put some petroleum jelly on the rim of the plunger and insert it into the sink at an angle to trap as little air as possible inside. Center the plunger over the drain hole. If the standing water doesn't cover the cup of the plunger, add more water until it does. Plunge quickly and forcefully about 15 times. Repeat once or twice. If it doesn't work, move on to cleaning out your P-trap.

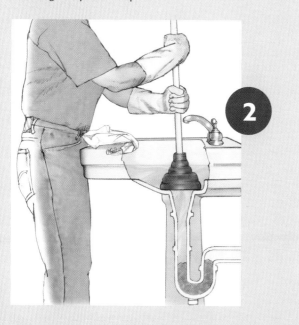

REMOVING THE P-TRAP If hot water and the plunger didn't work, you can try removing the P-trap, which is that U-shaped pipe directly under your sink. Sometimes things get caught inside the curved part of the pipe, so you can disassemble it and dig out the obstruction. To do this, you'll need to clear out all the lotions and potions under your sink (you know you've been meaning to do it anyway). Once you have access, grab a bucket and get to work!

TIME & TALENT

About an hour. It can take some muscle to tighten the slip nuts enough so they don't leak. If you don't have good hand strength, you may need to enlist some help.

HOW TO REMOVE A P-TRAP

1. Don those rubber gloves. If there's a cleanout plug at the base of your P-trap, position the bucket underneath the pipe and remove the plug with the wrench (if not, proceed to step 2). Water may come spilling out, so be prepared. If no water comes out, stick a piece of wire into the hole and fish around for an obstruction. No luck? Looks as if you have to remove the P-trap.

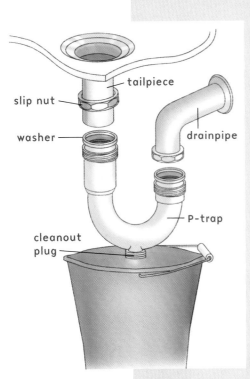

slip nut

tailpiece

washer

drainpipe

P-trap

cleanout plug

2. Use the wrench or a pair of slip-joint pliers to loosen the slip nuts that attach the P-trap to the sink's tailpiece and the drainpipe sticking out from the wall, or coming up through the floor. If you have pretty brass or copper drainpipes, you can tape the jaws of the wrench to avoid scratching the finish. On metal drainpipes, the loosened slip nuts can be pushed out of the way and the washers removed; for PVC pipes, the slip nuts and washers should both be removed.

3. Hold the P-trap over your bucket and empty out the contents with your hand or the piece of wire. You can also knock it against the side of the bucket a few times to dislodge the contents.

4. Reassemble the P-trap. If you need to replace the washers or slip nuts, take the P-trap to the store with you so that you can get the right sizes. To help prevent leaks, wrap some plumber's tape around the threaded parts of the P-trap before putting the washers and slip nuts back on. Test the system for leaks before putting your lotions and potions back under the sink.

USING AN AUGER If none of these other remedies worked, the clog may be deeper in the bowels of the drain system. So if you're feeling plucky and lucky, try one more approach before calling a plumber. Buy a drain auger (also called a snake, but it's a different type than the one used on toilet clogs on page 148). The auger will feed through your sink drain and push the obstruction forward. You might not be able to reach and break through the clog with an auger, but it's sure worth a shot.

For bathroom sinks, remove the pop-up stopper and sink strainer. Insert the auger into the drain opening and twist it through the trap. This will take some patience—keep turning the auger clockwise as you push forward. You might get hung up on some turns and joints—just keep trying to advance the auger. Once the head of the auger won't go forward any more, you've reached the obstruction. The auger has a hook on the end, so pull it back a bit to dislodge some of the clog. Then push the rest through the pipe. Once the clog has been broken up, pull the auger out slowly and have a bucket ready to catch debris. Then flush the drain with hot water.

Kitchen sinks without a disposal can be augered the same way, but those with a disposal are more complicated. First, be sure to turn off electricity to the disposal. If the disposal's drainpipe (the pipe leading into the wall) is clogged, you'll need to disassemble the trap and thread an auger into the drainpipe. If both basins of a double sink with a garbage disposal clog, snake down the one without the disposal. If only the basin with the disposal is clogged, you will have to remove the P-trap to dislodge the blockage. Good luck!

TUBS AND SHOWERS

Usually you'll know when your tub is about to have a problem because you're showering in 2 inches of standing water, or it takes 20 minutes for the tub to drain. Act quickly to avoid a larger problem.

If your tub surprises you and backs up unexpectedly or muck starts coming up the drain into the tub, check to see if other fixtures are affected. If so, you have a problem with the main sewer drain and need to call a plumber.

types of tub drains

Before you start any repair, determine whether you have a pop-up or a plunger drain. A pop-up drain has a metal stopper that raises and lowers when you move the lever on the overflow plate. A plunger drain has a strainer over the drain, and you can't see the mechanism that closes the drain when you move the lever up and down.

clearing clogs

If water drains but takes its sweet time, you might have hair wrapped around the tub stopper. Remove the stopper and attached rocker arm by pulling the stopper straight up. Clean off any hair or gunk wrapped around it. Wear rubber gloves and use needle-nose pliers to do the dirty work for you.

For plunger drains, turn the strainer counterclockwise to remove it and shine a flashlight down the pipe. If you see hair, dig it out with a piece of wire or needle-nose pliers. If you still have a problem, remove the overflow plate assembly. Clean off any hair wrapped around its components. When none of these do the trick, you can try plunging the drain or augering the P-trap.

PLUNGING THE DRAIN Remove either the stopper or the strainer and put a wet rag in the overflow hole so water won't come shooting out at your face. Fill the tub with a few inches of water and put your special plunger that's used only on sinks and tubs over the drain hole. Plunge quickly about 10 times. If that didn't get things moving, move on to the auger.

POP-UP DRAIN

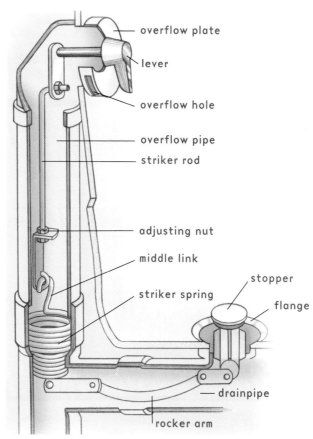

overflow plate
lever
overflow hole
overflow pipe
striker rod
adjusting nut
middle link
stopper
flange
striker spring
drainpipe
rocker arm

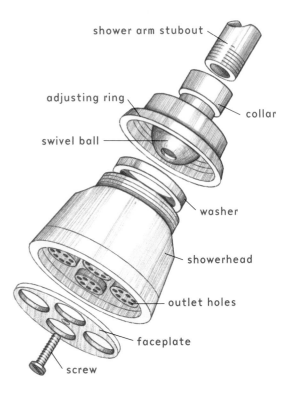

shower arm stubout

adjusting ring

collar

swivel ball

washer

showerhead

outlet holes

faceplate

screw

CLEARING A TUB'S P-TRAP If you have a pop-up drain assembly, remove the stopper and rocker arm. Unscrew and remove the overflow plate (see page 157) and pull out the assembly. Then feed a drain auger down through the overflow pipe (not through the drainpipe) and into the P-trap, turning clockwise as you go. If you can push the obstruction through, it was probably soap. If not, it's hair and you need to try to hook it onto the end of the auger and pull it through the drain. This isn't a pleasant fishing expedition and you might need to do this several times to get it all out. When you're finished, reinstall the stopper and overflow plate and run hot water down the drain for 10 minutes.

CLEARING A SHOWER'S P-TRAP Remove the strainer on the shower drain and thread a drain auger down the drain (as shown below) until you feel an obstruction. Push it through the drain (or pull it back out if you think it's hair) and then run hot water for 10 minutes.

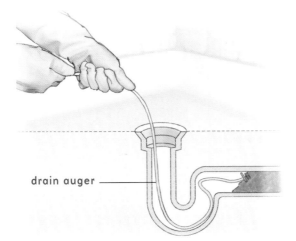

drain auger

maintaining your showerhead

If your showerhead is dripping or the spray has changed from wonderful to wimpy, you'll need to remove the showerhead and investigate. Sometimes mineral deposits make their way into your water-supply pipes, get caught in the showerhead nozzles, and block the flow of water.

Remove the showerhead following the directions in step 1 on page 159. Once the showerhead is off, look to see if there are any mineral deposits caught behind the head. Put a paper towel on a sturdy surface and slam the showerhead on top of it, facing up, to dislodge the deposits. Or pick them out with tweezers. Once they're all out, reattach the showerhead to the stubout (see steps 2 and 3 on page 159).

For leaks that appear to be coming from the showerhead, remove the showerhead and check out the washer. If it looks beat up, bring it to a

"YIKES! WHO FLUSHED THE TOILET?"

If this is a familiar line in your house while someone's in the shower, you need a scald-free shower and tub valve. There are two types of scald-free valves. The pressure-balancing types automatically adjust the mix of hot and cold water when there's a rapid change in the line (when someone turns on the washing machine, for example). Thermostatic types kick in when the water coming through to the fixture no longer reflects a preset temperature.

Most building codes require these valves for new construction. Even if you aren't planning to do a major bathroom remodel, consider hiring a plumber to install one. It's not just the inconvenience of being hit with unexpected hot or cold water—if there are children or elderly people in the house, it can be downright dangerous.

hardware store and get a new one that's the same size. Put the new washer in place over the showerhead, followed by the swivel ball, adjusting ring, and collar. Wrap plumber's tape around the stubout threads, and screw on the showerhead tightly.

installing a new showerhead

Walk into any home improvement center or plumbing fixture store and you'll find an array of showerhead choices—some that are big enough to cover half your shower with waterfall-like streams. Beyond the size of the heads, there are models that offer various settings and levels of pressure. So pick one you like and get to work!

TIME & TALENT

As long as your old showerhead isn't rusted on, this shouldn't take more than 10 minutes.

HOW TO REPLACE A SHOWERHEAD

1. Use an adjustable wrench to unscrew the collar of the old showerhead from the shower arm stubout. Make sure the stubout doesn't start to turn! It could break off from the water supply pipe, and then you'll be in a big mess.

2. Once the old showerhead is off, wrap plumber's tape around the end of the stubout. Three passes should do it. Make sure you don't tape past the threaded area.

3. Tighten down the collar of the new showerhead with the adjustable wrench. Wrap the ends of the wrench with painter's tape first so you don't scratch the finish on the showerhead.

fixing a leaky tub faucet

Troubleshooting a leaking bathtub faucet is time-consuming and takes some muscle, but you should be able to fix it without calling a plumber if you have the time to spend on the project. If you have an access panel with shutoff valves for the tub (many times these are located in an adjoining closet or hallway), go for it. Turn those valves off. Otherwise, shut off the water to the whole house just to see if you can figure out what's wrong. If you start the project and get stuck, you'll need to call a plumber to bail you out. Have a number handy for one that makes same-day appointments.

The instructions here are for tubs that have separate hot and cold handles and a third handle that diverts the water up to the showerhead. (For tub/shower combos that have one handle rather than three, remove the handle and escutcheon as described here and then replace the entire cartridge assembly.) If the leaking water is hot, you'll want to focus on the hot-water handle; if it's cold, then fix the cold-water handle.

Before delving into this repair, check online to see if you can find detailed instructions for disassembling your particular faucet. If you can't see a manufacturer's name, then you're outta luck and will have to feel your way along with these generic instructions.

STUFF YOU'LL NEED
- Towel
- Flat-head screwdriver
- Rag
- Adjustable wrench
- Pliers (if necessary)
- Painter's tape (optional)
- Socket wrench
- Old toothbrush (if necessary)
- Lubricating spray (if necessary)
- Seat wrench
- Ziplock bag
- Plumber's tape

TIME & TALENT

Start in the morning after everyone has showered, as this will take a good part of the day, including at least one trip to the hardware store. Remember that if you have to shut off water to the whole house, no sinks or toilets will be working while you fix this.

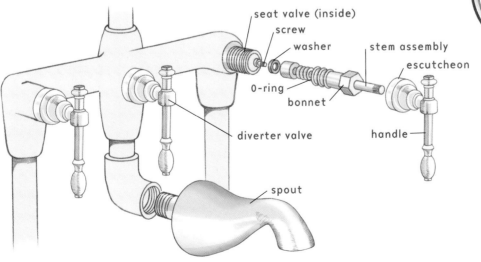

seat valve (inside)
screw
washer
O-ring
bonnet
diverter valve
stem assembly
escutcheon
handle
spout

160

HOW TO FIX A LEAKY TUB FAUCET

1. You've already turned off the water (either by turning off the shutoff valve to the tub or to the whole house), so now open a few faucets in the house to drain the pipes. Put a towel over the drain so you don't drop any parts down there.

2. The handles might be attached with a screw that's under a decorative cap piece (which usually has H or C on it). Pry off the cap with a flat-head screwdriver, and then remove the screw that's underneath. The handle should pull off (place a rag around it to get a better grip). Then remove the trim piece, called an escutcheon, if there is one. You might have to use an adjustable wrench or pliers to remove it. Wrap the jaws of the tool with painter's tape or put a rag around it to protect the finish.

3. Now you'll see the inner workings of the handle, called the stem assembly. Use the adjustable wrench to loosen the arm of the stem assembly right where it meets the seat valve. Note: If your stem assembly is mostly behind the tile wall, your choices are to chip away the tile to get a better grip with your wrench, or stop and call a professional.

4. Use a socket wrench to remove the stem assembly from the seat valve. Once it's off, check it out and see if it looks corroded or damaged. If it does, replace the piece. If you want to keep it, take this opportunity to clean the stem assembly with an old toothbrush.

5. At the end of the stem, there's a washer held on by a screw. Remove the screw and inspect the washer (if it won't come off, try some lubricating spray). Try to keep the washer intact so you can bring it to the store to get a replacement. You could just replace the washer and be done with it, but it might only be a temporary fix if you don't go on to replace the seat valve. So, this is your chance to bail out if you've had enough, or you can keep going.

6. Next is the seat valve. This is the nonmoving part of the valve. You'll need a special tool called a seat wrench to remove it. Put the wrench into the seat valve and turn counterclockwise. If it's really hard to remove and the wrench starts to strip the threaded part that holds the seat valve to the main water pipes behind the wall, stop and call a plumber.

AND ANOTHER THING ...
If you want to replace the spout, wrap the jaws of the adjustable wrench with painter's tape, then grasp the spout opening with the wrench and turn counterclockwise.

7. If you've successfully removed the seat valve, take it, the washer, and possibly the stem piece in the ziplock bag to the store and get new ones that are the same size. While you're there, consider getting new handles as well.

8. Put all the parts back in the opposite order that you took them off. Wrap the end of the new seat valve with plumber's tape before installing it. Finally, put on the new handles, then slowly turn on the water and test for leaks. Congratulations if you've pulled this off. It's a big job.

WASHING MACHINES AND DISHWASHERS

They sit quietly in the laundry room and under the kitchen counter, doing their jobs in complete anonymity...until something goes wrong. Then these unobtrusive machines become your worst nightmare, spewing water and belching suds all over the floor, and if you don't catch it quickly, throughout the entire house. How can you prevent such a catastrophe? With a little preventive maintenance.

Washing machine leaks can happen where the hoses meet up with the supply pipes in the wall, or the hoses themselves can fail. In this case, water can gush from the hoses, and if it's the hot-water line there's the added danger of scalding. All those Diligent Dianas out there who remember to close the supply-line valves when the machine isn't in use are doing all they can to prevent their hoses from bursting. But most of us don't bother with this extra step each time we unload our clothes, which is why people have invented devices that do it for you. Look online for these products, which open the valves when the machine is turned on, and close them when it is turned off. Or look into water-leak detectors (see page 25 for more information).

While we're talking washing machines, remember that your clothes dryer needs some occasional attention as well. See pages 30–31 to find out what you should be doing and when.

STUFF YOU'LL NEED
- Bucket
- Towel
- Replacement drain hose (if necessary)
- Adjustable pliers
- Small bristle brush
- Two braided stainless-steel supply lines
- Plumber's tape (if necessary)

TIME & TALENT

This should only take an hour or so, including a trip to the store to get the new hoses.

replacing rubber hoses

If the rubber hoses that came with your washing machine are more than 5 years old, you should replace them with steel-jacketed hoses that won't burst. Here's how.

HOW TO REPLACE RUBBER HOSES ON A WASHING MACHINE

1. There should be shutoff valves on the water supply pipes that feed your washing machine. If there aren't, you'll need to shut off water to the entire house (see pages 12–13).

2. Unplug the washing machine. Pull the drain hose out of the drainpipe so you can move the machine to get better access to the back. Have the bucket nearby and shake any excess water from the drain hose into it. If the drain hose seems brittle or you see any cracks, take it to the store and get a new one.

3. Put down the bucket or use a towel to absorb any excess water where the drain hoses meet up with the hot- and cold-water pipes. Use adjustable pliers to remove the hoses from the supply pipes. The bucket should catch any drips, but also shake the hoses into the bucket to remove any accumulated water. Then remove the hoses where they are attached to the machine itself. (If there's so much corrosion around the connections that you can't get them off, you'll need to call an appliance repairperson.)

4. At the back of the washing machine where the supply hoses attach, there are small filters that keep any sediment in the water line out of the machine. If you don't see them there, check the insides of the supply hoses where they connect to the water pipes. Use a small bristle brush to clean off any buildup.

5. Screw the hose fittings at the ends of the new supply hoses onto the machine with your fingers and then tighten with the pliers. Do the same with the water-supply side, making sure that you attach the hot-water hose to the hot-water valve, and the cold-water hose to the cold-water valve.

6. Turn the water back on and then slowly open the valves and check for leaks. If there are any, try wrapping the threaded part of the water-supply pipes with plumber's tape and then reattach the supply lines.

7. Move the machine back into place, plug it in, and put the old drain hose (or the new one, if you decided to replace it) back into the drainpipe.

leveling your washing machine

Does your washing machine shake when it's running, or even shimmy a little out of place from time to time? Does it have more moves than Madonna? That means the machine isn't level. It's not exactly good for the appliance to shake that much; appliances aren't meant to dance. Plus, fixing it will make the machine quieter.

Get down on the floor and look for the stubby legs at the front of the washing machine. The legs can be adjusted to the proper height and a locknut keeps them from moving. Loosen the locknut of the leg that's not touching the floor, extend it down, and then lock it in place again. Keep the legs as close to the floor as you can to reduce vibration. (If your machine's legs won't move by hand, check the owner's manual to find out how to move them.)

Some machines have legs that you can also adjust in the back, but most have self-adjusting rear legs. When you tilt the machine forward, the rear legs spring into action and automatically adjust when you set the machine back down.

cleaning your washing machine

Yes, that's right. The machine that cleans other things also needs to be cleaned from time to time. Just put a little dish detergent on a damp rag and wipe the inside of the drum to remove dirt and water deposits. You can also pour two cups of lemon juice or vinegar into the machine and run it empty with hot water to clean the drum. Then run the machine empty again with hot water to remove any last remnants. While you're at it, remove the soap dispenser and clean it with some hot water and detergent in the sink.

Some machines have lint traps that need to be cleaned out occasionally, while others send lint down the drain after each cycle. Check your owner's manual to see if lint collects in the center agitator, near the top of the tub, or someplace else so you can clean it out.

maintaining your dishwasher

New dishwashers are great. They're quiet, energy efficient, and virtually maintenance free. If you're limping along with an old machine, you really ought to think about replacing it. But, until that time comes, here are some common problems with old machines and tips on how to fix them.

CLEANING THE FILTER Some older dishwashers have filters that need to be cleaned out regularly (new ones clean themselves). Check the owner's manual to see if yours has one and how to find and clean it.

SLOW LEAKS Small amounts of water around the front of your machine may indicate a faulty gasket around the door. Shine a flashlight on it to see if it has any cracks. If it does, or if it looks brittle, remove it and take a sample to the store to get one the same size. Soak the new gasket in warm water so it's pliable enough to install in the groove.

If the gasket looks fine, it could be that the door isn't closing properly. Adjust the latch by loosening the screw that holds it to the cabinet, pushing the latch in a little, and tightening the screw.

Leaking can also occur when the machine isn't level. Open the door and put a small level on the bottom edge. If it's tilting slightly to one side or from front to back, use the leveling feet under the machine to adjust it until it's level. The feet may be behind a panel if you don't see them.

DIRTY DISHES When dishes aren't coming out as clean as they used to, inspect the spray arm at the base cabinet interior. Its holes can get clogged with mineral deposits or food. Unscrew it and soak it in a solution of warm water and white vinegar until the clogs are loosened. Then clean them out with a small pointed object.

It could also be that your water isn't hot enough. Stick a thermometer into the hot water that comes out of your kitchen sink. If it's below 120 degrees, that might be why your dishes aren't getting clean. You can increase the water temperature to the whole house using the thermostat on your water heater, but don't set it higher than 120 degrees or you might get burned.

WATER WON'T DRAIN There may be a clog in the drain line that connects your dishwasher to your garbage disposal. If you feel confident of your plumbing skills, remove the line, clean it out, and reattach it before running the machine again.

RUST STAINS If the coating on your dishwasher racks is coming off, there could be rust on the metal that is getting on your dishes. Buy plastic coating replacement material or use a marine-grade sealant to cover any exposed metal.

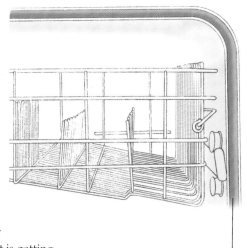

gasket in dishwasher

TRY THIS BEFORE CALLING THE REPAIR PERSON

Sometimes you think an appliance has a major problem that only a professional can fix, but if you'd done a little investigative work before picking up the phone, you could have saved yourself the time and money. One such issue is when a washing machine fills slowly. It's probably not a major plumbing problem, but that your supply hose is kinked or the intake filters are clogged. See the instructions for changing the supply hoses on a washing machine to find out where the filters are and how to clean them (see page 163). If the screens have hardened mineral deposits on them, you may need to remove and soak them overnight in white vinegar. Machines that won't fill at all probably have a faulty inlet valve, in which case a plumber will be needed. Sorry!

GARBAGE DISPOSALS

We've all gotten so used to being able to throw food down our kitchen sink drain that when the means of chopping up our scraps into little pieces goes haywire, so do we.

Before we get into fixing it, let's talk about how you got here. Have you been misusing your garbage disposal? You know what I mean—pouring grease into the sink when no one is looking, filling up the entire sink with stringy spinach and celery stalks before bothering to turn the disposal on?

For those who don't know, you can't put grease, coffee grounds, potato peelings, or anything else into the disposal that, when pulverized, could turn into a sticky paste or solid mass that will clog your drain. Make it a general rule to scrape dirty plates into the trash, and only rinse what won't easily come off (assuming it's safe) down the drain. There are two problems you want to avoid: clogging the mechanism of the garbage disposal, and clogging the drainpipe once the food has passed through the disposal.

disposal maintenance

Ever walk past the kitchen sink and get a whiff of some foul stench that stops you dead in your tracks? It's only natural that the garbage disposal will start to stink worse than road kill if you don't clean it. Luckily, you don't have to buy any special cleaner or toxic chemical to pour down the drain—in fact, you want to avoid these altogether. Just periodically feed the disposal a nice meal of ice cubes. For dessert, put coarsely chopped citrus peel down the drain, add cold water, and turn on the disposal. That's the winning recipe to make it smell better.

If you don't have any citrus, try combining about 6 tablespoons of baking soda with $\frac{1}{4}$ cup of vinegar and pour the solution down the drain with the disposal shut off. Once it's done foaming, rinse it down the drain. Then, every time you use the disposal, run a little cold water with no waste through the system afterward to flush out any remnants.

REPAIR IF YOU HEAR A HUMMING SOUND

The workings of a garbage disposal consist of a wheel that throws food into a shredder, which then flushes small bits of food into the drainpipe. If the disposal won't turn on when you flip the switch but you can hear a humming sound, something is probably stuck in the wheel.

WATCH OUT!
Never put your hand down the disposal, even when trying to remove an obstruction and the power is turned off. It's too risky! Use tongs to pick things up if you have to.

TIME & TALENT

Takes just a few minutes of troubleshooting, unless you have an electrical problem (see right).

HOW TO FIX A STUCK GARBAGE DISPOSAL

1. Shut off the main circuit that powers the disposal. Then try the switch to make sure it's powered off, and put the switch in the "off" position.

2. Use a flashlight to look into the disposal and see if you can find the obstruction. If you can, pry it out with tongs. If not, you need to manually turn the wheel. This can be done two ways. Look under the sink and see if your disposal has a hole in the bottom that accepts an Allen wrench (sometimes this comes with the appliance). If so, use the Allen wrench to manually turn the wheel back and forth until it moves freely. Or you can use the handle of a broom from above. Stick the handle into the disposal and push back and forth until you feel the wheel move freely.

3. Turn the main circuit back on. Then reach under the disposal and press the reset button. Turn on the water and flip the switch on and off a few times quickly to spin the wheel and wash whatever had been stuck down the drain.

REPAIR IF YOU DON'T HEAR A HUMMING SOUND If you flip the switch and the disposal won't turn on and doesn't make any humming sounds, it's probably an electrical problem.

Turn the electrical switch off. Then press the red reset button on the disposal. If it still doesn't turn on, check to see if the circuit breaker has tripped in the main electrical service panel. If the circuit breaker is flipped off, push it back on and try the disposal again. If that doesn't work, or if the breaker wasn't flipped off, then there's either a problem with the switch or with the machine. Try replacing the switch (see pages 179–180), and then the disposal.

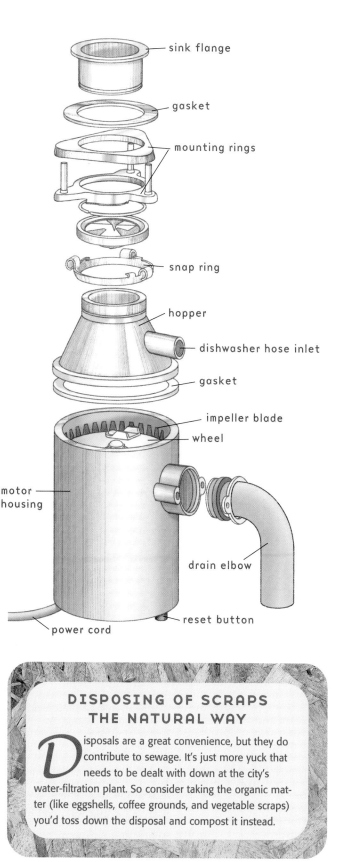

sink flange

gasket

mounting rings

snap ring

hopper

dishwasher hose inlet

gasket

impeller blade

wheel

motor housing

drain elbow

power cord

reset button

DISPOSING OF SCRAPS THE NATURAL WAY

Disposals are a great convenience, but they do contribute to sewage. It's just more yuck that needs to be dealt with down at the city's water-filtration plant. So consider taking the organic matter (like eggshells, coffee grounds, and vegetable scraps) you'd toss down the disposal and compost it instead.

WATER HEATERS

Pity the poor water heater. It's awkward, squat, round, and plain. It'd never win a Miss Appliance Beauty Contest. But when you think of all the delights it delivers, such as a luxurious hot bath, you can get downright sentimental about a water heater.

Most homes are equipped with storage-type water heaters that use either electricity or gas to heat the water. Gas water heaters have a gas burner underneath them, a flue that travels up and outdoors to vent fumes, and a pilot light—that always seems to go out at inopportune moments. Electric water heaters simply plug in and don't require ventilation. On the energy costs scorecard, electric water heaters cost more to operate than gas water heaters. But with gas prices fluctuating and supplies dwindling, this may not be the case forever.

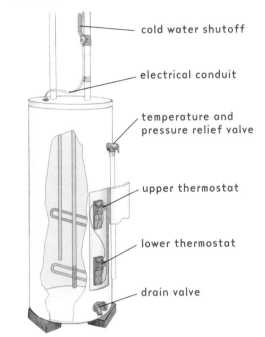

- cold water shutoff
- electrical conduit
- temperature and pressure relief valve
- upper thermostat
- lower thermostat
- drain valve

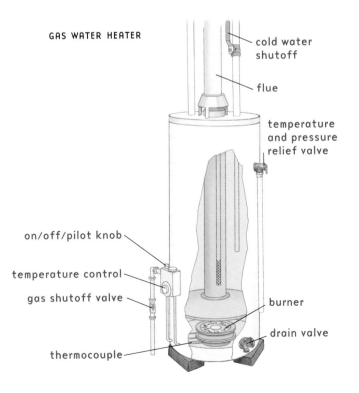

GAS WATER HEATER

- cold water shutoff
- flue
- temperature and pressure relief valve
- on/off/pilot knob
- temperature control
- gas shutoff valve
- burner
- drain valve
- thermocouple

Here's how a water heater works: A cold-water pipe feeds the water heater, where the water is warmed by gas or electric heating elements. The heated water then comes out another pipe and is directed to fixtures and appliances all over the house. You can pretty much gauge which faucet is farthest from the water heater because the hot water takes forever to get there.

Your water heater is busy; it's sending hot water to various appliances and each sink, tub, and shower in the house. So it pays to give it some care and attention. Because water heaters use gas or electricity, you need to be extremely careful working with them. Get familiar with the directions for how to relight the pilot. You might even want to print them on a piece of paper and tape them to the water heater.

maintaining a water heater

Like the furnace, this is not something you will repair yourself. But there are things you can do to keep your water heater functioning efficiently.

CHECK THE BURNER If you have a gas water heater, check out the burner when it's on. You can usually spy on it by removing a cover plate. The flames should look more blue than orange, which means there's a good fuel-to-air ratio. Make sure the vent is unobstructed and drafting upwards.

CHECK THE VALVES Once a year, give the valves a test drive to make sure they're working. The top valve is a pressure-relief valve. It's got a scary name but its function is all about safety. If too much pressure should build in the tank, this valve is designed to open up and relieve the pressure. To make sure it works, put a bucket underneath the attached pipe and gently pull up on the toggle. Hot water should flow out of the pipe.

DRAIN THE TANK The valve on the bottom of the tank is designed to let you drain water that's hanging around in the bottom of the tank. Why? There's usually some sediment that settles at the tank's bottom. Older water heaters in particular tend to have gunk on the bottom, and it needs to

be removed both for the longevity of the water heater, and the state of the water coming into your home.

Follow the instructions that came with your water heater. If you have an electric water heater, unplug it and make sure the plug won't come in contact with water. If you have a gas water heater, turn the burner down to its lowest setting. (It isn't necessary to extinguish the pilot unless you're draining the whole tank.) Next, scout the area and see if there's a drain nearby. If there isn't, you'll have to drain the water into a bucket. Most drain valves are threaded, so you should be able to attach a garden hose. Connect the hose and direct the end toward the drain or into the bucket. Gently open the valve. Let the water run for about 5 minutes and turn it off. If you drained the water into a bucket, see what the water quality is like. If it's seriously cloudy or rusty, you might want to consider a new water heater.

JUST SO YOU KNOW ...
Many local utilities offer rebates or incentives for buying eligible energy-saving appliances, such as water heaters. Check it out before you buy.

NEW WATER HEATERS

Almost all appliances have beefed up their energy efficiency in the last several years. So if your water heater is 15 to 20 years old, it pays to invest in a new one. Some home centers will handle the whole transaction—removal and disposal of the old one, delivery and installation of the new one—for about $600 to $700. Be sure to check with your city's building department to see if you need a permit to install a new water heater.

PREVENTING FROZEN PIPES

Not so fast, southerners! I saw you glance at this headline and almost skim right past it. The truth is, freezing pipes can be a problem in southern homes, too. Granted, it's a rare and wretched day when temperatures plummet down to the teens and twenties in Dixie. But when it does get that cold, your pipes are vulnerable to freezing. That's because the plumbing supply lines in southern homes are often located in unheated and noninsulated spaces.

All northerners are well aware of the horrors caused by pipes that freeze and burst. Inevitably it's happened to folks we know—usually while they're defrosting on a winter vacation somewhere down south. Pipes that freeze and burst are a nasty and expensive problem. Luckily it's a problem that can be avoided.

For starters, any time you northerners go on vacation during the winter, shut down your house water supply. Then open up the valves and drain the system. What causes frozen pipes to burst is the buildup of water pressure. If no water is coming into the house, there's nothing in the pipes to freeze. So make sure you take care of that important step while turning down the water heater and thermostat, not to mention simultaneously packing your bags, dealing with pet care, and finding someone to pick up your mail. (You know how multitasking goes before you head out of town... .)

Here are some other preventive measures that both northern and southern homeowners can use.

INSULATING VULNERABLE PIPES Head to your main water-supply line and start tracking pipe runs. Are there supply lines in unheated or uninsulated areas like the attic, garage, or crawl space? These are your first candidates for insulated pipe sleeves. These sleeves are made of foam, rubber, or fiberglass and easily fit over the pipes. The ends should butt tightly together and be sealed with aluminum tape. An added benefit to insulating hot-water pipes is that you'll save a little on your energy bill.

WEATHER STRIPPING AND CAULKING
Check the weather stripping around doors and windows. Can you feel a draft? If so, seal the areas with weather-stripping materials. Check around the house exterior for service entry points and where your dryer vents to the outdoors. Recaulk all the areas that have gaps or cracks. (For more information on exterior caulking, see pages 218–219.)

WHEN ALL ELSE FAILS OK, so the really cold snap has hit, you've done nothing to protect your pipes, and you're leaving town for the weekend in 5 minutes. At the very least, open up the sink cabinet doors so the warm air can circulate around the pipes. Then turn on a faucet and let a tiny trickle of

INSULATING PIPE SLEEVE
AND ALUMINUM TAPE

water come from the tap. Even a steady drip can keep a pipe from freezing while you're gone.

thawing a frozen pipe

A dead giveaway for a frozen pipe is when you open the tap—and nothing comes out. Either the pipe is frozen, or you were negligent in paying the water bill. Do your best to track down the frozen portion of the pipe. It's probably in the most underinsulated part of your house. With any luck, it's accessible. If it hasn't burst, thank your lucky stars and patiently thaw it out.

Turn off your main water supply. Then open the tap on the sink closest to where the frozen pipe is located (remember it's the built-up water pressure that causes pipes to burst). The water needs a place to release once you've successfully thawed the pipe and your sink is a safe place for that.

Wrap a heating pad around the frozen section of pipe and turn it on. Check it every 15 minutes or so to see if the pipe is warming up. You can use a heating pad by itself, or in tandem with a blow dryer. Simply sweep the blow dryer across the affected section. Make yourself comfortable, grab some coffee. You might be here awhile. The key in using the heating pad and blow dryer is to slo-o-o-wly thaw the pipe. NEVER use a torch to defrost a pipe. The more gradual the thaw, the better chance you have of it not bursting.

OUTDOOR FAUCETS

Before cold weather hits, disconnect hoses from outdoor faucets and store them. Turn off the water supply that feeds the outdoor faucets. Ideally, there is a shutoff valve for them indoors. Once the valves are closed, open up the outdoor taps and drain them dry.

Some homes are equipped with freeze-free or frost-free outdoor faucets. These have sensors that detect changes in the air and water temperatures for freeze protection. Even though the freeze protection is "built in," it's still a good idea to disconnect the hoses and store them indoors when cold weather hits. This should prevent any potential freezing water damage (and it's better for the hoses, too).

chapter 7

ELECTRICAL

....

BEING SOLELY RESPONSIBLE for maintaining a home can feel overwhelming at times. Between mortgage payments, repairs, housecleaning, yard work, and keeping up with neighbors, kids, and pets, you can feel like an overloaded circuit. One more thing goes wrong with the house—and zap!—your emotional breaker trips.

But the more you understand your home and face its challenges head-on, the faster you'll go from overwhelmed to empowered. Case in point? The first home I owned was a newly constructed townhouse. There was nothing to repair, so my tool collection was pretty paltry; all I had was a hammer, tape measure, and a key chain–size Swiss Army knife.

One evening I decided to install a new ceiling fixture in my bedroom. With the bed as my step-ladder, I used the miniature scissors on the Swiss Army knife to strip the sheathing around the wires. With the knife's tiny screwdriver, I secured the mounting plate to the ceiling. After much frustration, sweat, and cursing, the job was finished.

You won't be using a Swiss Army knife for any of the projects in this chapter, but you'll feel just as empowered doing your own electrical work as I did that day.

UNDERSTANDING YOUR ELECTRICAL SYSTEM

VOLTAGE TESTER

When you flip on a light, you're probably not giving much thought to where the power for that light comes from. Power lines carry electricity to a meter located outside your house, which monitors the amount of energy you use each month. Wires from the meter lead to the main service panel (housing the circuit breakers or fuses), which can be outside or inside the house or garage. This panel is where you'll find the main switch that can shut off power to the entire house.

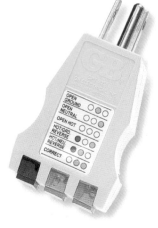

CIRCUIT TESTER

Wires from each circuit breaker or fuse in the main service panel branch off through the house. Each grouping of wires is referred to as a circuit. These circuits provide the power to your fixtures and receptacles (see pages 18–19).

Electrical systems are rated for the maximum amount of current (measured in amperes) they can carry, which is called the service rating. The minimum service rating of most new homes today is 100 amps. But your service rating could be as low as 40 amps if your house is old, or as high as 400 amps if you have lots of high-tech equipment. You can determine your service rating by looking at the main service panel. The number will be stamped on the main fuse or circuit breaker. Why should you care? Because if you do a major remodel and need circuits for new appliances, a hot tub, or steam shower, the electrician will ask what your service rating is. Sometimes, if you're already close to being maxed out, you can't just add a new circuit; you'll need to have an electrician upgrade your entire service panel, which can cost around $2,000.

read this before you touch anything!

As you probably realize, doing your own electrical work can be a risky proposition. If you don't know what you're doing, you could get shocked (or worse!) or start a fire. The projects in this chapter can all be accomplished by beginners, but even so, you must use extreme caution at all times. The most important, number one rule is to *make sure the power is off before doing any electrical work.* Not just think it's off, not just turn off the switch for that fixture, but turn the power for that circuit OFF at the main service panel.

Your indispensable tools for this chapter are electrical testing devices. There are many products that can be used for the same purpose—to check whether a receptacle or wires have power. A voltage tester has one or two probes that you touch bare wires or terminals with. If the tester lights up, the wires are hot (electrical current runs through them). A circuit tester plugs into a receptacle and different lights tell you a range of things, including if the receptacle is grounded or wired correctly.

Whenever you need to touch the main service panel, make sure the ground you're standing on is completely dry. Use one hand to touch the panel. Your other hand should be empty and at your side because there's less of a chance of getting shocked if only one hand is touching the panel. Scared yet? Still with me? OK, read on.

fuses and circuit breakers

Inside your main service panel, you will find either round fuses or circuit breakers that look like toggle switches. Both fuses and circuit breakers guard electrical systems from damage that can be caused by too much current. If wires are ever forced to carry more current than they can handle safely, a circuit breaker will "trip" (switch itself off) or a fuse will blow, and power will be lost on that circuit. A blown fuse has to be replaced, but a tripped circuit can be switched back to the "on" position. If this is happening frequently, however, you're putting too much demand on that particular circuit or the whole system. Have an electrician come and troubleshoot it for you. But before you call someone out, see if you can figure out under what circumstances the fuse blows or breaker trips (for example, does it only happen when both the space heater and the hair dryer are on?).

SHUTTING OFF A CIRCUIT BREAKER It works like a light switch. Simply flip the circuit breaker to the "off" position when you want to kill power to that circuit. Flip it back "on" when you want to restore power.

CIRCUIT BREAKERS

SHUTTING OFF A FUSE If your fuse has a handle, pull it toward you and then remove the fuse from its mounting clips with your fingers or a tool called a fuse puller. If your fuses don't have handles, they are the screw-in type. Grab the rim of the fuse with your fingers and unscrew it by turning counterclockwise. If a fuse has blown, the metal wire or strip visible behind the glass will appear to be broken. If you need to replace a blown fuse, buy a replacement with the same amperage rating. Just screw the new one into place.

FUSES

grounding

You've probably heard people say "that receptacle is grounded" and thought "What did it do wrong?" But actually, in electrical terms, grounding is a good thing. This safety feature provides excess current with an un-interrupted metal pathway into the ground, rather than into you or your $1,000 computer. Power surges are rare, and your system may

sheathing

insulation

neutral wire

grounding wire

hot wire

never experience one, but if it does, grounding can save your life. If you don't know whether your receptacles are grounded, buy a circuit tester, plug it into the receptacle, and it will tell you.

common electrical terms

AMPERE (OR AMP) This is the tape measure for electricity. An amp describes the amount of current that flows past a given point in one second.

CIRCUIT Two or more wires providing a path for electrical current to flow from the source and back. A circuit is also like an "electrical neighborhood" in your house. Big electricity guzzlers like clothes dryers often require their own circuit.

CIRCUIT BREAKER The switch in the main service panel that cuts off the flow of electricity to that circuit.

CURRENT Just as a river's flow is measured in miles per hour, current represents the movement or flow of electrons through a conductor and is measured in amps.

FUSE A safety device found in older homes that protects circuits from overloading. When a circuit overloads, a metal wire or strip inside the fuse melts or "blows," cutting off power to the circuit.

GROUND Any conducting body, such as a small metal rod driven into the earth, that gives electrical current a path to the ground.

GFCI Stands for ground-fault circuit interrupter. A GFCI receptacle protects against electric shock, and is required in areas that could be wet, such as bathrooms and kitchens. A GFCI breaker is installed in the main service panel and monitors the amount of current going to and from a circuit.

GFCI

GROUNDING WIRE Conductor that grounds a metal component but does not carry current during normal operation. Grounding wires are usually bare copper or green wires.

HOT WIRE Anyone who has had too much coffee. Heh-heh. But really, a hot wire is the star player in carrying electrical current from its source to a receptacle, switch, or whatever. Hot wires are usually identified by black or red insulation, but may be any color other than white, gray, or green.

HOUSING BOX Connection points for joining wires or mounting receptacles, fixtures, and switches. Boxes can be metal or plastic. The box sits just inside the wall and houses the connections so you can have access to them when you need to. Depending on its intended usage, a housing box is also referred to as receptacle box, junction box, cut-in box, or pancake box.

INSULATION The thermoplastic material that covers bare wires.

KILOWATT-HOUR (KWH) Unit used for metering and selling electricity. One kilowatt-hour equals 1,000 watts used for one hour.

NEUTRAL WIRE Grounded conductor that completes a circuit by providing a return path to the source. Neutral wires are usually identified by white or gray insulation.

PIGTAIL SPLICE A connection of three or more electrical wires.

RECEPTACLE Fancy name for what you plug stuff into. The terms "receptacle" and "outlet" can be used interchangeably.

TERMINALS Screws on the side of a switch or receptacle that you wrap wires around to transfer electrical power to that switch or receptacle.

VOLT (OR VOLTAGE) The force causing electrical current to flow is measured by the utility company in volts.

WATT Unit of measurement for electrical power. The energy per second consumed by a lightbulb or appliance is expressed in watts.

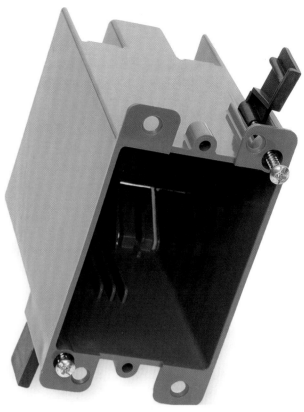

PLASTIC HOUSING BOX

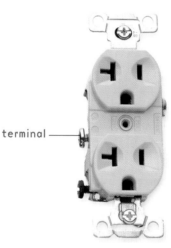

terminal

METAL HOUSING BOX

PERMITS

You don't need a permit for any of the projects in this chapter, but if you plan to do other work, check with your local building department to see if a permit is necessary. Please don't avoid the permit process out of fear. The inspectors are there to help make sure work is carried out properly and safely; they're making sure your house won't burn to the ground. So pay the fee (which is often nominal), get your work inspected, and sleep well at night.

CREATING A CIRCUIT MAP

The next time you host a brunch, I have the perfect party game for you: creating a circuit map that shows which lights, appliances, and receptacles are controlled by which circuit or fuse in your main service panel. Put one person in each room of the house, hand them a walkie-talkie and a circuit tester, and then go to the main service panel and start flipping circuits or removing fuses. Hilarity ensues!

No? All right, but this chore is much easier if you have one or more helpers. Creating a circuit map is important because you will occasionally need to shut off power to a certain light fixture or receptacle to repair or upgrade it, and if you don't know which circuit or fuse controls that fixture, it will take you a lot of time to figure it out. Check your main service panel to see if a previous homeowner has already taken care of this task for you. Look for numbers next to each circuit or fuse and a list that correlates each number to a room or area it controls. If you don't see a list like this, then you'll have to make one yourself.

Before you start, turn off anything that could be damaged from having the power turn on and off, like computers and televisions. Then turn on every light and ceiling fixture in the house. A pair of walkie-talkies will make this job a lot easier. With them, you can stand at the main service panel and your helper can walk around the house and let you know what's going on. Otherwise, you'll have to yell back and forth or run to each room to see what happened.

Go to the main service panel and make sure the ground is completely dry. Open the panel with one hand while keeping your other hand at your side. Make a list of how many circuits or fuses there are from left to right or top to bottom, and number them on a pad of paper. Then turn off the first circuit breaker or fuse (see page 175). See what turned off inside the house and make a note of it next to the number you assigned to that circuit or fuse. Remember to check receptacles too. Have your helper try each one in the room by plugging in a radio or clock. It sounds like overkill, but some wiring gets downright goofy. Sometimes the receptacles in a room will be on one circuit while the ceiling fixtures are on another. Remember to check major appliances like ovens and dryers too, as they have circuits of their own (called dedicated circuits).

Once you've gone through the entire house, you'll have a list of what each circuit or fuse controls. Some main service panels have a grid on the inside of the door where you can create your map. If not, write the numbers you've assigned on pieces of masking tape and stick them on the flat metal area next to the appropriate breaker or fuse. Then keep the notes about which number controls what near the panel or in a file.

AND ANOTHER THING ...
If you can't recruit a helper for this project, plug in a radio that you can hear at the service panel. You'll know you've turned off the power when you can't hear the music anymore.

REPLACING A LIGHT SWITCH

Replacing a light switch is a straightforward job; you just have to make sure the replacement switch is the same type you had before. People replace light switches because they're old and grimy, don't flip easily, aren't working at all, or because they want to change the color of the switch. If you want to install a dimmer switch, see page 181.

The most common types of switches are single pole and three way. A single-pole switch turns one or more lights on and off from one location. A three-way switch allows you to turn lights off and on from two locations. If a room has two access points and you can turn the lights on as you enter and off at the other side when you exit (and vice versa), then those are three-way switches.

There is another way to tell whether a switch is single pole or a three way. Once you've pulled the wires out of the housing box (safely, of course!), you'll see brass screws (called terminals) and one green grounding screw on the sides of the switch. If the total count of terminals is three, it's a single-pole. If there's a total of four terminals, you have a three way. You also need to get a replacement switch that is rated for the same voltage and amperage as the old one. The ratings will be written on the back of the old switch.

TIME & TALENT

No heavy lifting required! You can get this completed in 15 minutes, plus a trip to the store for the new switch.

**HOW TO REPLACE
A LIGHT SWITCH**

1. Turn off the power to the circuit that powers this switch (see page 175). Then unscrew the switch plate and store it and the screws in the plastic bag if you plan to reuse them.

2. Use the voltage tester to verify that the power is off before going any further (see page 174).

3. Once you're absolutely, positively, most assuredly sure the power is off, unscrew the switch from the housing box. You can now pull the switch toward you so you can reach the wires more easily.

4. For three-way switches, it's important that you connect the wires in exactly the same way they were before. Mark which wire is going to which side of the switch by writing "left" and "right" on pieces of masking tape and wrapping the tape around the proper wire. Don't skip this step. For single-pole switches, both wires are hot, and it doesn't matter which is on the left or right.

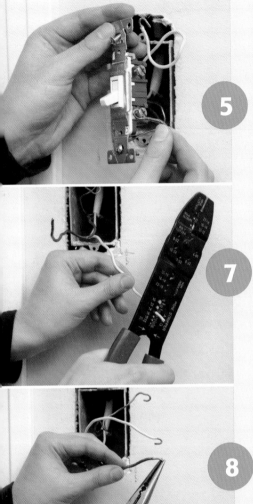

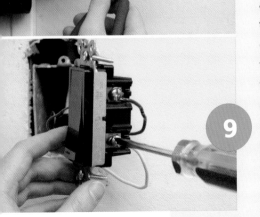

5. Loosen the terminals on the sides of the old switch and then detach the wires with your fingers (as shown). If your switch doesn't have wires attached to terminals on the side, then the connections were made using a push-in terminal at the back of the switch. In this case, use the screwdriver to open up the slots next to each hole. That will release the wires (or you may have to use wire cutters to cut them loose).

6. Now that the old switch is out, check the back for the voltage and amperage ratings, and buy a replacement switch with those same numbers.

7. If you cut the wires to remove them from the old switch, you may need to use the wire stripper to trim back the insulation. You want about ½ inch of bare wire exposed or your connections will fail. A wire stripper has holes for different-sized wires. Slip the wire into the hole that fits around it. Hold the wire firmly with one hand and press the handles of the stripper together with the other hand to penetrate the insulation. Then pull the stripper away from the wire to remove the insulation. It makes quick work of this task.

8. Use needle-nose pliers to bend each wire into a J-shaped half loop that will hook around the terminals. Connect the grounding wire (if there is one—it will be either bare or have green insulation) by hooking it around the green grounding terminal on the switch. This may take a few tries, as the wire is less malleable than you'd think. Once you've got it in place, use the screwdriver to tighten the terminal down, squeezing the wire between the screw head and the switch.

9. If you're wiring a single-pole switch, hook the remaining two wires around the two terminals in any order (top or bottom doesn't matter). If you're wiring a three way, hook the wires around the terminals according to your masking-tape notes. Tighten all connections with the screwdriver.

10. Now that all the wires are connected, push the switch into place. The wires are a little stiff and ornery, so it helps to curve them back into the box. Align the switch vertically, making sure "on" is at the top, and tighten the screws that hold the switch to the box.

11. Turn on the power at the main service panel. Then touch the terminals behind the light switch with the voltage tester. If they aren't receiving power, turn the main breaker off again and retrace your steps. If you can't figure out the problem, leave the power off and call an electrician. Otherwise, put the switch plate on and you're finished.

TECHNIQUE
If you're having trouble stuffing all the wires back into the housing box, use the butt end of the screwdriver to push them in.

installing a dimmer switch

Looking for a little mood lighting? Who isn't? I don't know about you, but in dim light I look as if I'm in my 30s again. You can replace a single-pole light switch with a dimmer switch very easily. And you may want to before that next romantic dinner you host. Not all light fixtures can be controlled by a standard dimmer switch, however. Fluorescent lights need special dimmers, as do ceiling fans, so be sure to read the packaging before you buy.

Dimmer switches come in different styles. Some look like regular light switches with a small dimming control next to the switch. Or they can have a round knob, or a wide, flat knob that moves up and down. Read the instructions carefully. They're all a bit different, so if any part of these instructions doesn't make sense, refer to those that came with the dimmer.

JUST SO YOU KNOW ...

If you get a dimmer switch with a small control on the right, you should be able to use your old switch plate. If not, you'll have to buy a new one.

STUFF YOU'LL NEED
- Screwdriver
- Ziplock plastic bag (if necessary)
- Voltage tester
- Wire cutters (if necessary)
- Wire stripper
- Wire nut
- Dimmer switch
- New switch plate (if necessary)

TIME & TALENT

Really not much harder than installing a regular light switch. Be sure to read the directions that came with the dimmer you purchased.

HOW TO INSTALL A DIMMER SWITCH

1. Turn off the power to the circuit that powers this switch (see page 175). Unscrew the switch plate and put the cover and screws in the plastic bag if you plan to reuse them.

2. Use the voltage tester to verify that the power is off before going any further. If the indicator lights up or beeps continuously when you touch the terminals and wires, then the power is still on and you have to turn it off before moving on.

3. Once you're sure the power is off, unscrew the switch from the electrical box. Pull the switch toward you so you can reach the wires more easily.

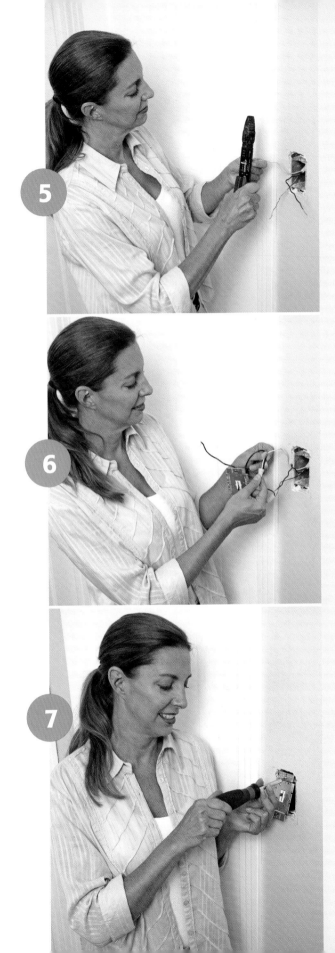

4. Loosen the terminals on the sides of the old switch and detach the wires with your fingers. If your switch doesn't have wires attached to terminals on the side, then the connections were made using a push-in terminal at the back of the switch. In this case, use the screwdriver to open up the slots next to each hole and that will release the wires (or you may have to use wire cutters to cut them loose).

5. If you need to, use the wire stripper to remove about ½ inch of insulation from the wires coming out of the electrical box (see step 7, page 180). Some dimmer switches have you stick a straight wire into the back of the switch, while others have you wrap a curved wire around a terminal. Refer to the instructions that came with your switch.

6. Connect the grounding wire (or wires) first, either by hooking the grounding wire (which will be bare copper wire or have green insulation) around the green terminal or using a wire nut to join the grounding wire in the box with the grounding wire from the dimmer. To connect them with a wire nut, twist the two bare wires together, put the wire nut over the twisted wires, and turn the nut clockwise until it's tight and no bare wire is exposed. Tug on the wires to see if they come loose. If they do, you'll need to start again. Then connect the two black wires and the two white wires. Again, refer to your specific directions.

7. Once all the wires from the dimmer switch are connected to their partner wires in the electrical box, you can push the wires back into the box and screw the switch in place. Make sure you've got it right side up!

8. Restore the power and see if the dimmer switch is working. If it isn't, shut off the power again and retrace your steps. If you can't figure out the problem, leave the power off and call an electrician. Otherwise, put on a switch plate and voilà, you've got mood lighting.

INSTALLING A GFCI RECEPTACLE

Ground-fault circuit interrupter (or GFCI)—the name is enough to make your eyes glaze over. But once you understand its important safety features, a GFCI assumes more interest. In new construction, GFCIs are required in kitchens, bathrooms, garages, and any place that may have wet or damp conditions. If you live in an older home, it's possible that there are no GFCI receptacles in these areas, and even more likely that you have ungrounded receptacles throughout the house (which will always have two prongs instead of three—and no, just changing them to three-pronged receptacles doesn't make them grounded).

"Ground fault" is when electricity leaks from a circuit and looks for the quickest path to the ground. If you're using that circuit at the time, *you* may become the conduit between the receptacle and the ground, which could result in a bad shock or even electrocution. GFCIs are like hyperalert electrical cops. They monitor any imbalance between the hot and neutral wires running through your home. If a GFCI detects abnormal behavior (like leaking electricity), it "trips," or shuts down. GFCIs, in effect, take the "zap" for you.

For your safety, you should replace ungrounded receptacles and those in potentially wet areas with GFCIs. It's almost as easy as replacing a light switch.

You won't discover this until you turn off the power and remove the old receptacle, but if you have a metal housing box that's only 2 inches deep, it's not big enough for a GFCI receptacle, so don't even attempt it. Call an electrician instead.

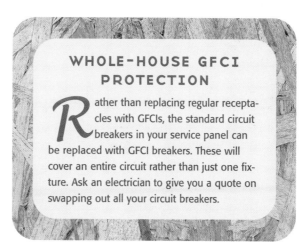

WHOLE-HOUSE GFCI PROTECTION

Rather than replacing regular receptacles with GFCIs, the standard circuit breakers in your service panel can be replaced with GFCI breakers. These will cover an entire circuit rather than just one fixture. Ask an electrician to give you a quote on swapping out all your circuit breakers.

TIME & TALENT

This project has a couple more steps than replacing a switch, but it's not any more complicated. You should be able to accomplish this for the first time in about 45 minutes, and it will get much faster after that.

HOW TO INSTALL A GFCI RECEPTACLE

1. Turn off the power to the circuit for the receptacle you're replacing (see page 175). Make sure it's really off by plugging the circuit tester into the receptacle. If the light doesn't come on, then the power is off.

2. Use the screwdriver to remove the cover plate and the screws holding the old receptacle to the housing box. Then pull the receptacle out of the wall and see how many wires are connected to it. There could be as few as two or as many as six, depending on whether the current receptacle is grounded and whether it's in the middle of a circuit or at the end of a circuit. You don't really have to understand the ins and outs of this—the important thing is to note how the wires are hooked up to the old receptacle before you take them off. Make a rough sketch of it, and then use the screwdriver to disconnect the wires from the terminals.

3. If you only have two wires (a hot and a neutral) or three wires (a hot, a neutral, and a bare copper grounding wire) coming out of the box, then you can jump to step 4. If you have two or three wires coming into the box and another two or three going out (as shown), then you need to test the wires to figure out which ones are coming from the main service panel, and which connect this receptacle to others in the same circuit. Spread out the wires and make sure they aren't touching each other or anything else. Then go back to the main service panel and turn that circuit back on. Back at the housing box, touch each wire with a voltage tester to determine which is hot. Most often, hot wires are black or red and neutral wires are white, but they could be other colors so check all of them. You should only find one hot wire. Once you know which it is, flip the circuit back off and then mark the wire with masking tape.

4. On the back of the GFCI receptacle, you'll see markings next to the terminals that say "Line" and "Load." If you only have two wires, hook the hot wire around the brass terminal that's on one side of the word "Line," and the neutral wire around the silver terminal that's on the other side of the word "Line." If you also have a grounding wire, hook it around the green terminal on the GFCI.

5. If you only had two or three wires, jump to step 6. If you have two groups of wires in the box and you tested them as described in step 3, wrap the wire you determined was hot around the brass terminal next to the word "Line" and the other wire in that same sheathing around the silver terminal on the other side of the word "Line." Hook the wires that both tested neutral in step 4 around the terminals next to the word "Load." The black wire again connects to the brass terminal and the white wire connects to the silver terminal. In this case, you probably have two grounding wires coming out of the box, and you'll need to attach them to each other (which may already be done for you) and to the GFCI. Do this with a grounding jumper, which is a short grounding wire you can buy at the hardware store (see illustration at right). Wrap one end of the grounding jumper around the GFCI's grounding terminal, and then use a wire nut to connect the other end of the grounding jumper with the two grounding wires coming out of the box.

6. Once everything is connected, push all the wires back into the housing box and screw it into place. Restore the power to this circuit and test with a circuit tester. If everything is fine, put the cover plate back on. To test the GFCI, plug in an electrical device, turn it on, and press the "test" button. This should turn the appliance off. When you press the "reset" button, it should turn the appliance back on.

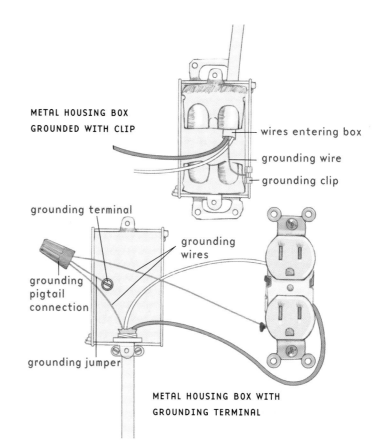

METAL HOUSING BOX GROUNDED WITH CLIP

wires entering box

grounding wire

grounding clip

grounding terminal

grounding wires

grounding pigtail connection

grounding jumper

METAL HOUSING BOX WITH GROUNDING TERMINAL

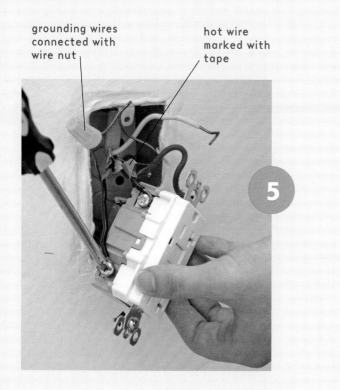

grounding wires connected with wire nut

hot wire marked with tape

5

GROUNDING A METAL BOX If you're installing the GFCI in a metal box, as we are in these photos, you'll need to ground the box itself in addition to the GFCI. With any luck, that part has already been done for you by the person who installed the original receptacle, but if not, you'll need to take care of it now. If one cable enters the box, attach a short grounding wire from the GFCI to the grounding terminal in the back of the box. If the box has no grounding terminal, use a grounding clip made for this purpose (as shown in the top illustration above). If more than one cable enters the box and it has a grounding terminal, use a grounding jumper (a short grounding wire) to connect the grounding wires together with a wire nut (as shown in the bottom illustration above). This connection is called a grounding pigtail.

REPLACING A CEILING FIXTURE

When it comes to ceiling fixtures, some people are real cheapskates. They'll buy an unimaginative frosted globe for $3.99 and call it a day. I say, "Fight back against lazy design!" You can doll up a hallway or bedroom pretty easily with a new ceiling fixture. Just pick one you like and get out your screwdriver.

The new fixture will come with installation instructions, so take the time to read them and understand which part is which as you take everything out of the box. Then follow these general instructions.

STUFF YOU'LL NEED
- Ladder
- Screwdriver
- Wire cutters
- Wire stripper
- New fixture
- Wire nuts

JUST SO YOU KNOW ...

If your current fixture touches the ceiling, someone may have painted up to but not under it. Therefore, if the new fixture hangs just below the ceiling, you might have some touch-up painting to do.

TIME & TALENT

You may need a helper on a second ladder if the new or old fixture is terribly heavy; otherwise, it can be tough to simultaneously loosen the screws and hold the fixture so it doesn't crash to the floor. This project should take less than an hour.

HOW TO REPLACE A CEILING FIXTURE

1. Shut off the power to the circuit that controls this fixture (see page 175). Then try the light switch to make sure the power is off.

2. Remove the old globe from the ceiling fixture. Some have decorative knobs at the base that unscrew. Others have screws on the sides. Hold the globe up with one hand as you unscrew it with the other (use a helper if you can't support the weight of it with one hand).

3. Once the old globe is off, remove the lightbulbs and unscrew the mounting bracket that's attached to the housing box. Find the wire groupings connected with wire nuts in the housing box. You can unscrew the wire nuts and untangle the wires, or use the wire cutters to cut them. But only cut the wires if it looks as if you've got plenty of wire slack for the new fixture. Sometimes there's barely enough wire to make the connections.

4. Refer to the instructions that came with the new fixture to install it. The one we're installing has a grounding plate that's first attached to the housing box with mounting bolts.

5. The grounding plate has a green grounding terminal (or screw) on it. Wrap the grounding wire (it will be bare copper or green) coming out of the housing box around the terminal and tighten with a screwdriver.

6. Connect the black wire from the fixture to the black wire in the housing box by twisting the ends of the two wires together. (If you don't have enough exposed wire, strip the ends as described in step 7 on page 180.) Then snip about ½ inch of the wires off so the tips are even.

7. Place a wire nut over the wires and twist clockwise until it's tight and no bare wire is exposed. Tug on the wires to see if they come loose. If they do, you'll need to start again. Connect the white wires in the same way.

8. Carefully fold all the connected wires into the housing box and secure the canopy (the base of the fixture) to the housing box. Assemble the fixture according to the instructions that came with it. Put in new lightbulbs that are no brighter than the wattage indicated on the fixture.

9. Attach the globe or bowl to the canopy, which is usually done by tightening a decorative screw at its base. Restore the power to the circuit and turn on the light. If it doesn't come on, and you're sure the lightbulbs are good, say, "uh-oh," and call an electrician to troubleshoot it for you.

INSTALLING A CEILING FAN

Ceiling fans are great when you want to reduce your dependence on air-conditioning or simply circulate air throughout the house. On warm nights, it's nice to turn the ceiling fan on low instead of having ice-cold air blowing on you. And because most models include lights, you don't have to give up a light source. You're getting a two-fer—breezy air and illumination. Ceiling fans come in a variety of styles and finishes, so shop around to find one that works with the décor in the room. More expensive models will run quieter and last longer.

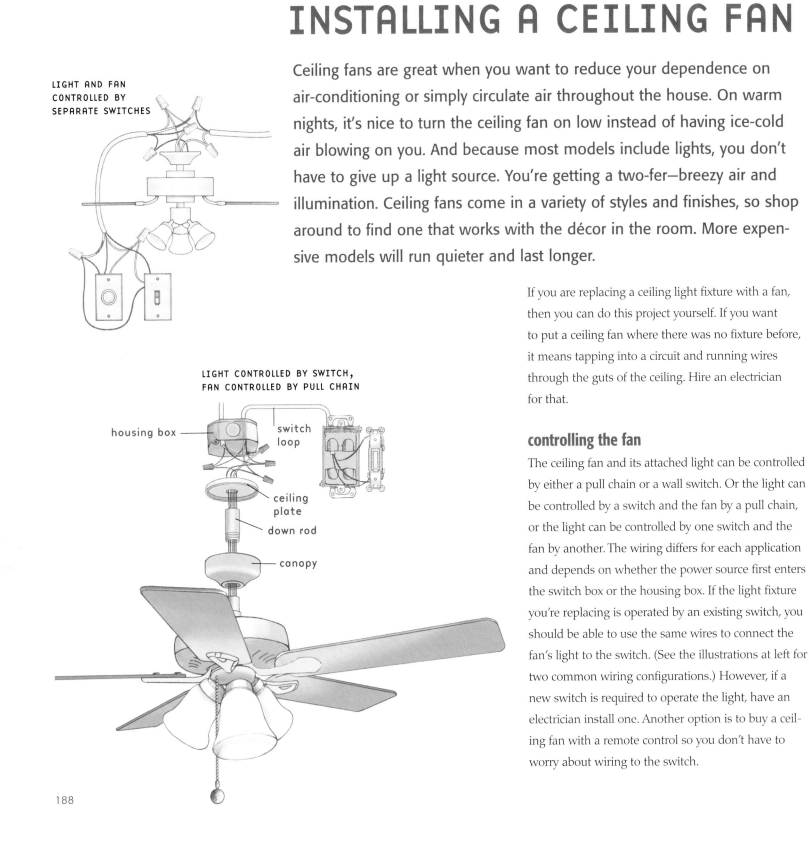

LIGHT AND FAN CONTROLLED BY SEPARATE SWITCHES

LIGHT CONTROLLED BY SWITCH, FAN CONTROLLED BY PULL CHAIN

housing box

switch loop

ceiling plate

down rod

canopy

If you are replacing a ceiling light fixture with a fan, then you can do this project yourself. If you want to put a ceiling fan where there was no fixture before, it means tapping into a circuit and running wires through the guts of the ceiling. Hire an electrician for that.

controlling the fan

The ceiling fan and its attached light can be controlled by either a pull chain or a wall switch. Or the light can be controlled by a switch and the fan by a pull chain, or the light can be controlled by one switch and the fan by another. The wiring differs for each application and depends on whether the power source first enters the switch box or the housing box. If the light fixture you're replacing is operated by an existing switch, you should be able to use the same wires to connect the fan's light to the switch. (See the illustrations at left for two common wiring configurations.) However, if a new switch is required to operate the light, have an electrician install one. Another option is to buy a ceiling fan with a remote control so you don't have to worry about wiring to the switch.

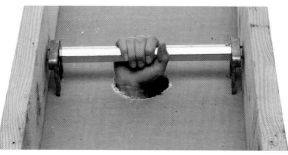

EXPANDABLE FAN BRACE

supporting the weight

Ceiling fans are heavy and need more support than light fixtures. If you know that your housing box is metal and firmly attached to the ceiling joists on either side, then you'll be fine. If not, remove the existing housing box and buy an expandable fan brace (sometimes called a hanger bar) that you can insert into the ceiling opening and align between two joists (as shown above). As you rotate the center of the brace, it lengthens and drives the barbed end brackets into the wood. Get a matching housing box with a mounting strap you can tighten from inside the box.

STUFF YOU'LL NEED
- Ladder
- Screwdriver or drill
- Expandable fan brace and housing box (if necessary)
- Ceiling fan
- Wire coat hanger (if necessary)
- Wire stripper
- Wire cutters
- Wire nuts

TIME & TALENT

This project is only slightly more complicated than installing a ceiling fixture. You should be finished in an hour or so.

HOW TO INSTALL A CEILING FAN

1. Turn off the circuit that powers the light fixture you're replacing (see page 175). Flip the switch that controls that fixture a few times to be sure the power is off.

2. Remove the old fixture by following steps 2 and 3 on page 186. Carefully read the instructions that come with the ceiling fan to figure out what parts you have and how they fit together. (If you need to install an expandable fan brace and new housing box, as described at left, now is the time.)

3. Before you climb back up the ladder, insert the down rod of the fan, if your model has one, into the canopy (see bottom illustration, page 188). Feed the wires from the motor through the down rod and/or canopy. Tighten the screws that secure the fan to the down rod.

4. Standing on the ladder, feed the wires from the housing box through the ceiling plate, which holds the weight of the fan against the housing box. Use the screwdriver or drill to attach the plate to the box. (Most ceiling plates have a hook for holding up the fan during installation so you don't have to hold it. If yours doesn't, you can concoct something from a wire coat hanger.)

ceiling plate

4

5. Ceiling fans with attached lights can have a number of different-colored wires in them. Refer to the manufacturer's instructions to figure out which is which. You'll need to connect each wire to its mate in the housing box. Use the wire stripper (see step 7, page 180) to remove enough of each wire's insulation to connect them together. Start by connecting the black wire from the fixture to the black wire in the housing box by twisting the ends of the two wires together. Then snip about ½ inch of the wires off so the ends are even.

6. Place a wire nut over the wires and twist clockwise until it's tight and no bare wire is exposed. Tug on the wires to see if they come loose. If they do, you'll need to start again.

7. Connect the white wires, the grounding wires, and any other matching wires (refer to the instructions for your fixture) in the same way.

8. Attach the canopy to the ceiling plate and tighten the screws.

9. If your fan has a light fixture, connect the socket to the bottom of the switch housing, following the manufacturer's instructions.

10. At this point, it's a good idea to restore power to the circuit and test to make sure the fan motor will turn on. Otherwise, you'll have to dismantle more parts to troubleshoot it. If all is well, attach the fan blades and lightbulbs. If not, refer back to the instructions to see if you can figure out what's wrong, and if you can't, call an electrician.

REWIRING A LAMP

A cool table lamp can cost a small fortune, but if you like to shop, you can find beautiful lamps at flea markets, estate sales, and even garage sales for a fraction of the price. The only downside? They often don't work. But that's a fixable problem, and a nice project for a rainy afternoon.

Even if your lamp does work, you should replace the cord if it looks frayed or damaged, and the plug if it's cracked or loose. Otherwise, you could get a shock when you use it, or it could even start a fire. Cut off a portion of the old cord and take it to the store to find a replacement that's the same size and has the same type of insulation. If you plan to replace the plug too, see if you can find a new cord with a plug already attached. Otherwise you can buy a separate plug that will clip onto the new cord.

SHORTCUT
If your lamp needs a total overhaul, look for wiring kits that give you everything you need in one package, plus detailed instructions on how to do it.

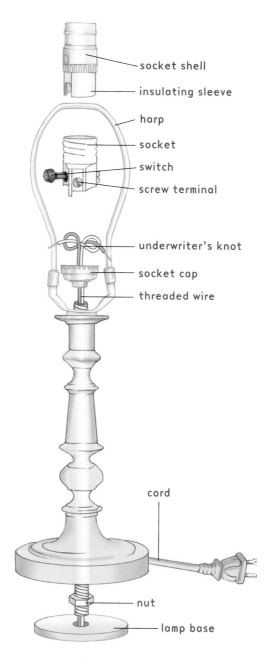

socket shell
insulating sleeve
harp
socket
switch
screw terminal
underwriter's knot
socket cap
threaded wire
cord
nut
lamp base

STUFF YOU'LL NEED
- Wire cutters
- New lamp cord and plug
- Scrap wood
- Utility knife
- Wire stripper
- Needle-nose pliers (optional)
- Screwdriver

TIME & TALENT

Give yourself a couple of hours to figure this out. The great thing about this project is that there are no time constraints on getting it completed. The lamp will sit quietly waiting for you to fix it without interrupting the household.

HOW TO REWIRE A LAMP

1. Most lamp cords have two strands of wire that are each covered with insulation. In order to strip the wire, you first need to separate the two strands. Use wire cutters to cut the new cord to length, with a little slack. Place one side on a piece of scrap wood. Use a utility knife to slice the center groove until the blade digs into the wood, and then split the cord a few inches. Repeat this process on the other end of the cord, unless the plug is already attached.

2. Remove about $\frac{1}{2}$ inch of insulation from both ends of each wire with the wire stripper. Note: If you're using a clip-on switch, you don't need to strip the wires on that end.

3. Lamp cord wires are fairly malleable, so you can either use your fingers or needle-nose pliers to shape both ends of each wire into the shape of a hook.

4. With the new replacement cord ready to go, remove the old one. This means you'll have to loosen—and maybe completely disassemble—the lamp's components. There may be a fabric (often felt) covering under the lamp. You'll need to remove this. It's likely that a nut holds the lamp's components together near the base. Loosen the nut. At this point, all the lamp's components will become jiggly and loose, so if it's glass, be careful!

5. Rewiring a lamp is like restringing a bead necklace; everything goes back on in the same order it came off. So, if you have to completely disassemble the lamp, place all the new parts in the same order. Detach the old wires on the socket, then attach the new ones by tightening the terminals onto each wire with the screwdriver.

6. Next, remove the old cord by tugging at it from the base. Throw it away. Feed the new cord that's already attached to the socket through the lamp's center. If you pull it taut once it's all the way through, you can replace the socket shell and tighten the nut (and any other connections) at the base of the lamp. If there's a switch, reinstall that.

7. The final step is to connect the plug (if there isn't one already attached to your replacement cord). There are some really easy ones that merely snap onto the lamp cord. Buy one of these and you've got new life for a vintage lamp.

TECHNIQUE

If the lamp still won't work, unplug it and use the screwdriver to slightly lift up the tab in the lightbulb socket, which can flatten and impede the connection to the bulb.

INSTALLING A PROGRAMMABLE THERMOSTAT

Conserving energy is more important than ever. So if you're limping along with an old thermostat that's heating and cooling your house when you aren't even home, then shame on you! Replacing it with a programmable thermostat is easy to do, will save you money on your utility bill, and is quite simply your responsibility as a conscientious citizen of the planet. Have I made you feel guilty enough yet? Then let's get to work!

JUST SO YOU KNOW ...

Programmable thermostats will work with most heating and air-conditioning systems, but they don't work for electric baseboard heaters.

STUFF YOU'LL NEED

- Voltage tester
- Screwdriver
- Masking tape
- Pencil
- Nonexpanding insulating foam
- Programmable thermostat
- Torpedo level
- Drill and drill bits
- Plastic screw anchors (if necessary)
- Batteries

FUN FEATURES

Programmable thermostats allow you to set different temperatures for weekdays and weekends. Normally there are four cycles per day for which you can set times and temperatures: when you first wake up; when you leave the house; when you come home; and when you go to sleep. Look for a model that offers manual override and hold-temperature features so you can easily turn off the system when you'll be away for a few days.

TIME & TALENT

You'll be finished and saving money on your energy bill within 30 minutes.

HOW TO INSTALL A PROGRAMMABLE THERMOSTAT

1. Turn off the power to the circuit for the furnace and air conditioner. Then remove the cover of the old thermostat. Touch the wires with a voltage tester to make sure the power is off.

2. You'll see up to five wires coming out of the wall that are connected to the old thermostat. Use masking tape to label each one with the letter next to its terminal, and then disconnect them one at a time. Keep the wires from touching each other as you work, and bend each wire so it doesn't fall back into the hole. Then unscrew the old thermostat base from the wall. (Warning: Some old thermostats have glass tubes that contain mercury. Ask your local waste disposal facility how you can dispose of it, as you can't just throw it in the trash.)

3. Wrap the wires around a pencil so they won't slip away. Spray nonexpanding insulating foam in the hole surrounding the wires to protect the thermostat from drafts, which may cause it to misread the room's temperature.

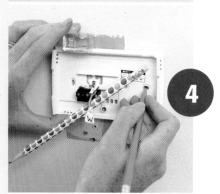

4. Read the installation instructions that came with your programmable thermostat (seriously). Take the base of the thermostat and slide the pencil and wires through the opening so it can sit flush against the wall. Put a torpedo level over the base, check that it's level, and mark the wall for mounting holes. Then remove the base.

5. Drill pilot holes for plastic screw anchors (which probably came with your thermostat) and insert the anchors in the wall. Then put the base back on the wall, check again for level, and screw the base to the wall.

6. The instructions for your thermostat will tell you which wire connects to which terminal. Generally speaking, you'll need to connect each wire to a specific terminal and use a screwdriver to tighten the terminal.

7. Once you're finished, put in backup batteries so that in case of a power outage, you won't lose the information you programmed. Attach the cover, and restore power to the heating and cooling system. If the thermostat won't turn on, call an electrician to troubleshoot it.

chapter 8

EXTERIOR MAINTENANCE

....

IT'S EASY TO PROCRASTINATE on minor home repairs. If it's not something that interferes with the operation of the house—like a clogged bathtub—you tend to ignore it.

Growing up, we had a storm door like that. It had a pane of lightweight glass in the bottom and a screen on top. The problem with that door was that it never caught the latch and completely closed. We kids learned to simply push it open as we tore out to the backyard to play.

One day, our paperboy, Chuckie Peterson, stopped by the house. I liked Chuckie. Along with Mr. Green Jeans from *Captain Kangaroo,* he was my first crush. When I heard he was there, I went tearing through the screen door to see him. Unfortunately, it was the only time the door had actually latched and closed. Fueled by puppy love, I pushed the door, expecting it to swing open. I plunged through the glass pane instead. Kinda gives new meaning to those song lyrics, "love hurts."

Now I know that a simple adjustment on the hinge would've fixed that door. Read on as we tackle that and other home-exterior issues, such as windows and doors, gutters and grading, siding fixes, and painting.

197

WINDOWS

I'm pretty sure I would've been a lousy pioneer—especially if I had to live in a sod house. Those houses didn't have bupkus for windows and doors. Imagine being cooped up in all that dank, dirty darkness all winter. It's no wonder some of those prairie people went a little cuckoo.

You only have to put yourself in the shoes of an American pioneer to begin to appreciate the comforts of modern homes. Windows that provide a clear view of the great outdoors—while keeping the weather out—are one of those comforts.

Windows are the gateway for natural light and views. They provide architectural and design interest and breathe ventilation into the house. And they are stalwart protectors, doing their best to keep out rain, snow, and ice. But because they are pelted incessantly with changes in heat, humidity, and so on, they do wear out. Before we get into whether or not you have any windows that need to be replaced, let's go over a few basics.

window construction

A window is one or more panes of glass (also called a light) surrounded by a support frame (the sash). This sash is affixed to a larger frame that fits inside an opening in the house. The vertical sides of the frame are called jambs, the top horizontal piece is the header, and the bottom is a sill. (See the illustration on page 204.)

Windows can be constructed of wood, vinyl, metal, or composite materials. Newer wooden windows often come with a weather-resistant exterior "jacket" wrapped around the wood framing that's called cladding. Wooden windows don't conduct as much cold or have as much condensation as other materials, so they're a good choice for northern climates and for older homes if you're trying to preserve the architectural character.

Metal windows, such as aluminum, are thinner, lighter, and easier to handle. They're not prone to the expansion and contraction that wooden windows are; however, the material can fall victim to corrosion in extremely moist and salty air. Vinyl windows are also lightweight and are built to resist heat loss and condensation.

Glazing is another word for the glass in a window, as well as for the act of putting glass in a sash. If you live in a severe climate, you should double or even triple your glazing. In other words, you'll want windows with two or three panes of glass. Dual- or triple-paned windows also increase energy efficiency and reduce noise. The air pocket between the panes of glass has insulating value.

Window professionals will sling around jargon like a short-order cook with hash. They might say, "Oh yeah, that's a low-e two with argon." Huh? The translation is that the window has argon gas sandwiched between two panes of glass, and a low-emissivity (or low-e for short) coating has been applied to the glass to prevent certain solar rays from penetrating the home. If you're going to buy a new window, don't be afraid to ask for constant translations.

window styles

Window technology continues to advance. Whether it's increasing the energy efficiency or creating imaginative new designs, window manufacturers are all highly competitive with each other in devising innovations. This is a good thing for consumers. Almost every new window you get now is going to be better than it was 10 years ago. Windows 10 years from now will have features today's windows don't. Pretty soon windows might even be able to pop themselves out of their frames and do the grocery shopping and laundry while we're at work. Cool! Give that window a raise.

Here's a breakdown of some of the most common window types:

DOUBLE-HUNG WINDOWS Many older homes have double-hung wooden windows. Two sashes stack on top of each other to create a single window unit. Each sash can slide up or down to let in air. Windows with only one operating sash are called single-hung windows.

Aging double-hung wooden windows can be ornery in their operation. They swell and get bloated with changes in humidity and refuse to budge. When they dry out again and shrink, they can refuse to stay open, plus they'll leak air. New double-hung windows don't have these problems.

CASEMENT WINDOWS These windows open from the side—like a book—with a crank or push bar. Casement windows come in a couple of varieties. Awning and hopper windows function almost like the little vent windows in older cars. Awning windows are hinged at the top and open up at the bottom; hopper windows are hinged at the bottom and open at the top.

DOUBLE-HUNG WINDOWS

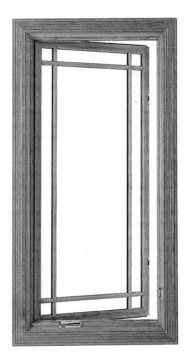

CASEMENT WINDOW

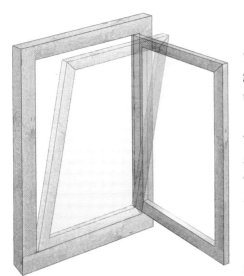

TILT-TURN WINDOW

LOUVERED WINDOW

GLIDERS OR SLIDING WINDOWS Like sliding glass doors in miniature, one window slides over the other on a metal, wood, or vinyl track.

TILT-TURN WINDOWS These windows are like acrobats with their dual-functioning capabilities. They can tip open (like an awning) to provide ventilation, but can also be opened from the side.

BAY AND BOW WINDOWS These are the showgirls of the window world—glamorous and dramatic. A bay window consists of three windows joined together: a nonoperational window in the center flanked by two side windows. Bow windows have several windows joined together to form a gentle, arcing curve.

LOUVERED OR JALOUSIE WINDOWS As kids, we called these "Florida windows" because we thought that was the only place they existed. Small, horizontal glass slats sit in metal frames that are stacked vertically to form a window unit. Louvered windows are great for ventilation, but as my friend Pam will attest, "they're a drag to clean." She would know—she has a three-season porch with 195 individual panes in her jalousie windows.

DECORATIVE FIXED WINDOWS These windows are typically used as design accents and come in shapes like half-moons, trapezoids, triangles, or octagons.

you just might need a new window

Jeff Foxworthy is a talented comedian from the South. Part of his routine involves a humorous checklist of how to determine when or if "you just might be a redneck." So in respectful homage to Foxworthy's routine, a variation on his theme:

If the frame around your wood window is so soft and rotted that even the carpenter ants don't bother to eat there, you just might need a new window. If the window sashes chronically stick, busting off your $50 acrylic nail fill every time you open one, you just might need a new window. If the condensation on the glass is like a frosty mug of Bud, you just might need a new window. If your metal window has more rust than an abandoned steel mill, you just might need a new window. If you can gauge the outdoor temperature and humidity by passing your hand over the glass, you just might need a new window. If your glass builds up enough ice for a margarita, you just might need a new window. If the design of your window has less style than your granny's seersucker housecoat, you just might need a new window.

Seriously, windows can't last forever. Mother Nature and even the fluctuations of your indoor air quality take their toll. Luckily, window manufacturers have devised all kinds of systems to easily replace poor-quality or rotted windows. Check

FREEING CASEMENT WINDOWS

Casement windows open and close with a crank or push bar. Grime and dirt can build up on that hardware and make these windows tough to open. By applying a lightweight oil or silicone spray on the moving parts, you can often free up operation.

window manufacturers' websites and you'll find more information to help you determine if "you just might need a new window."

freeing a stuck sash

A sash that won't budge is a common and persistent malady for double- and single-hung windows, especially those made of wood. The sashes operate by traveling up and down on tracks. When there are changes in temperature and humidity, the sashes get PMS. They become ornery, crabby, and bloated.

STUFF YOU'LL NEED
- Utility knife
- Putty knife
- Hammer
- Pry bar
- Scrap block of wood
- 180-grit sandpaper
- Paraffin or beeswax

TIME & TALENT

If the window is merely painted shut, or just experiencing too much humidity, this fix should only take a few minutes. If the frame and sashes are warped and out of square because the house has settled, well... you just might need a new window.

HOW TO OPEN A STUCK SASH

1. The sash may be sticking because it is painted shut, either from the inside or the outside. Take a utility knife with a new, sharp blade and carefully score the seam between the sash and frame. If the sash still won't operate, go on to step 2.

2. From the inside of the house, wedge the flexible blade of the putty knife between the sash and the frame. Use the hammer to lightly tap the knife blade around the entire perimeter of the frame and sash.

3. If this still doesn't free the sash, you may have to attack the problem from the window's exterior. Assuming the window is accessible and not four stories up, gently wedge a pry bar under the sill along the corner of the window. You may need to tap it with the hammer to get it in place. Stick the block of wood under the pry bar so you don't mar the sill. Using the leverage of the pry bar, try lifting the sash—working it evenly from one corner to the other to prevent damaging the window.

4. With luck, the window is now open and you can examine the tracks. There may be paint buildup or burrs (rough areas on the metal). If that's the case, lightly sand the area and apply paraffin or beeswax to keep things moving smoothly.

repairing window screens

This is a satisfying slam dunk of a job. There are a number of reasons why a screen might tear (like, uh, somebody walked through a screen door they didn't see at a nighttime party). The fix depends on the size of the tear or hole.

Window screening is made out of fiberglass or metal. If your tear is large enough to merit a patch, look for matching material at the hardware store.

SMALL TEARS For small tears in metal screens, use tweezers to twist the strands into shape (as shown below) and then seal them with a dab of superglue. With a fiberglass screen, use the needle and fishing line to stitch the tear, then seal it with superglue. Don't pull too hard, or the screen will buckle and you'll create an uneven pattern.

STUFF YOU'LL NEED

For small repairs :
- Tweezers
- Superglue
- Large sewing needle
- Clear fishing line

For medium to large repairs :
- Utility knife
- Replacement screen material
- Adhesive rated for use with your screen material
- Flat-head screwdriver
- Screen spline roller or putty knife
- Screen spline (if necessary)

TIME & TALENT

If you're a crafty gal, you will feel right at home. The fix should be completed in less than an hour. If you don't know how to use a needle and thread, and glue leaves you all sticky, it will take much longer.

HOW TO FIX MEDIUM-SIZE HOLES AND TEARS

1. If the damage is more than an inch on a metal screen, you'll want to make a patch. Remove the screen from the window and place it on a flat surface. Use a sharp utility knife to cut out a clean square where the damage is.

2. From the replacement screening, cut a patch that's slightly larger than the damaged portion. Unravel the edges and bend the strands through the existing screen until they're interwoven. Glue the border with the adhesive.

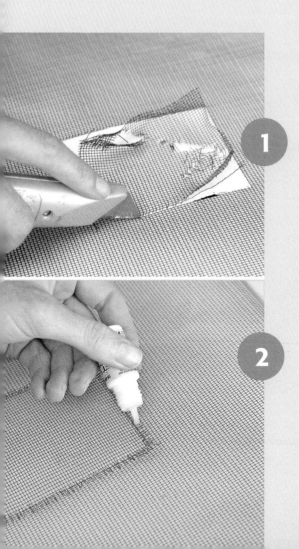

HOW TO FIX LARGE HOLES OR TEARS

1. For large holes or tears that are longer than a few inches in fiberglass mesh-type screening, you'll want to replace the whole piece of screen fabric. Lay the screen on a flat work surface. Use the flat-head screwdriver to pry up the spline that runs around the perimeter of the frame, holding the fabric in place. Remove the old spline and the screen fabric.

2. You'll need a piece of screen that's larger than the size of the frame, because the excess is trimmed to fit. While you're at the store, also buy a spline roller and new spline material that will fit the groove of your screen (you can use the old spline if it's not damaged). You could also use a putty knife instead of a spline roller so you don't need to buy a new tool. Lay the new screen over the frame, making sure you have a couple inches of overlap on all four sides. Starting on the top edge, place the spline into the groove and press it in place with the spline roller or putty knife, letting the excess hang over. Check to make sure the screen material is not crooked.

3. Once the top is secure, stretch the screen fabric taut and secure it along the bottom. Then secure each side. Trim off the excess material with the utility knife.

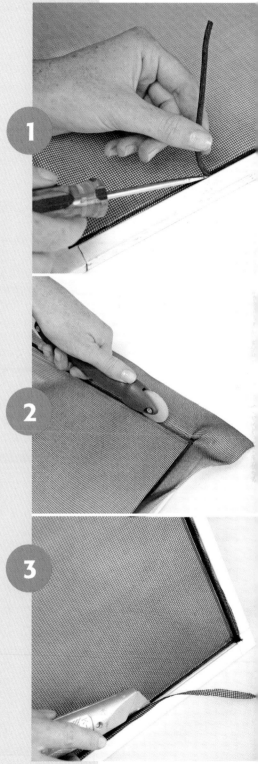

header

bottom
edge of
sash

jamb   sill   top edge of sash

jambs   sill

weather-stripping windows

Weather stripping is the placement of sealing materials around windows and doors to keep out rain, snow, or cold air. You'll find weather-stripping materials in the form of self-stick tapes and nail-on strips. The self-stick versions come in rubber, foam, or vinyl. For metal and vinyl windows that can't be nailed into, self-stick weather stripping is the only choice. Look for EPDM rubber weather stripping (EPDM is a kind of synthetic rubber), as it lasts the longest. High-density foam tape is also a good choice, but open-cell foam tape won't stand up to the elements for long. Vinyl V-strips also wear out quickly.

For wooden windows, nail-on strips are best. Use spring bronze weather strips that are nailed in place and spring open to close air gaps.

APPLYING SELF-STICK WEATHER STRIPPING For double-hung windows, start by cleaning the jambs, the bottom edge of the sash (where it meets the sill), and the back of the bottom sash with a solution of mild dish detergent and water. Rinse and let it dry. The adhesive material won't stick to a gritty or dirty surface.

Starting with the sash bottom, cut the self-stick weather stripping of your choice to length and peel back the adhesive tape. Keep a straight line in affixing the weather stripping to the bottom edge. Next, you'll do the sides, or jambs. With the bottom

sash raised all the way up, cut two lengths of weather stripping and work it between the sash and the jamb. Finally, cut some weather stripping for the top edge of the sash. Raise the sash up 3 to 4 inches and press the strip firmly onto the back of the sash so that it's even with the top edge (as shown in the top left inset illustration).

For casement windows, open the window and clean the edges with a solution of mild dish detergent and water. Once all the surfaces are dry, cut the self-stick weather stripping to length, peel back the tape, and press it onto the jambs and sill where the window makes contact (see bottom illustration at left).

APPLYING NAIL-ON WEATHER STRIPPING
If you have wood windows, and want to weather-strip with a material that's long-lasting and has some architectural character to boot, spend the extra dough for spring bronze weather stripping. The spring in these bronze strips compresses so that when the window closes, a weathertight seal is created. This type of weather stripping lasts longer than foam types, but the installation is a little more laborious.

Spring bronze strips come in different widths, so make sure you measure your sashes and jambs

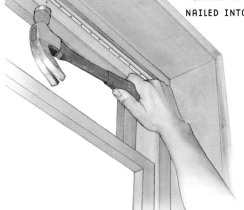

before purchasing. Use tin snips to cut the strips to length. You'll secure them to all the moving or operational parts of the window. (If it's a double-hung window, you'll attach it around all four sides, and the top rail of the bottom sash.) Ideally the strips have small holes you'll nail into. If not, sinking the tiny heads on the tiny nails, or brads, is persnickety and time-consuming.

sealing windows with plastic

If buying new windows isn't in the financial cards, you can at least seal leaky windows temporarily with clear, heat-shrink plastic film. It's advisable to use this application on the window's interior. Doing it on the exterior could trap moisture and compromise the sill.

There are kits you can buy for under $10 that have just about everything you need. Follow the kit instructions, but in general, this is the routine. Clean the trim around your window with a solution of mild dish detergent and water to remove dirt and grease. If the trim is just a little dusty, try electrostatic cleaning cloths; oil-based cleaners

won't let the adhesive stick. Apply the double-stick tape around the outside edge of the window trim (not the face of the trim). Cut your plastic covering so that it's 2 inches bigger than the window on all four sides. Remove the protective backing on the double-stick tape on the top edge and affix the film to it. Stretch the film as you go so it's taut. Secure the film along the sides and bottom. Then use a hair dryer to shrink the film. The heat should take out any wrinkles or creases, giving you a clear, transparent result.

STORM WINDOWS

*D*ecades ago, installing storm windows was a fall rite of passage. The good fathers of America would take a Saturday afternoon to put down their pipes and *Popular Science* magazines, and put up their storm windows.

The principle of storm windows is a sound one: when you overlay windows with an extra pane of glass, old man winter has a harder time penetrating your home. But that extra pane is a pain. Old storm windows are heavy and cumbersome. Hoisting them up to second-floor windows is tricky at best, dangerous at worst. Storing storm windows during spring and summer is also problematic.

Fortunately, there's a new generation of storm windows available at home centers and hardware stores. They're lighter weight and have built-in screens. These storm windows are available in standard sizes, but most homeowners will need to custom-order to fit their windows. You can measure your window openings to get an idea of what it would cost to put storms on all of your windows. But the final measuring and installing is better left to a professional, especially if you're working with a brick, stucco, or masonry exterior.

DOORS

You should adore your front door. It welcomes in loved ones and keeps out intruders, pests, and lousy weather. Your front door makes an architectural statement about your house, so it behooves you to keep it well maintained and nice-looking.

Exterior doors are often larger and made of more heavy-duty materials than interior doors. Steel doors are the least expensive option. Some have a finish that mimics wood, but the door can dent and the sun can make it hot to the touch. Vinyl and fiberglass doors are the next tier up in price. Both require less maintenance than wood doors. Some versions never need to be painted, and others have a wood-grain finish that can be stained. Hardwood doors are beautiful, but they need to be sealed regularly with marine-grade varnish. More expensive wood doors have mortise-and-tenon joints, which will hold up much longer than doors whose parts are merely glued together.

If you're in the market for a new door, ask local millwork shops for recommendations on door installers. Contractors should visit your home before quoting a price in order to check out your door frame and let you know whether you can buy just a new door, or if you need to buy a prehung door with a new frame. If your current frame shows no signs of rot, it should be fine. Keep in mind that when you replace the entire door frame, you may need to patch some scars on your exterior siding that will occur during installation.

Unattractive front doors can be given an inexpensive face-lift with paint or stain. Also consider adding or changing the trim around the door.

Glass fabricators can change out the windows in your door if you don't like the color or style, or add windows to your current door.

out, damn squeak!

Doors that announce each visitor with a high-pitched squeak can quickly get on your nerves. There are many products on the market that claim to solve this problem, and you don't even have to remove your door from the hinges to do it.

Before tackling this fix, cover the surrounding floors with a tarp or plastic just in case you spill.

STUFF YOU'LL NEED
- Tarp or plastic
- Flat-head screwdriver
- Hammer
- Disposable plastic gloves
- Steel wool
- Graphite powder, lubricating spray, or ball-bearing grease

TIME & TALENT

No helper is required because the door stays on at least one hinge at all times. In about 15 minutes, you should have a squeak-free door.

HOW TO FIX A SQUEAKY DOOR

1. If you listen closely, you might be able to tell which hinge is squeaking. To remove the hinge, place the tip of the flat-head screwdriver under the hinge pin. Lightly tap the base of the screwdriver with the hammer until the pin comes all the way out.

2. Put on the gloves and clean the hinge with the steel wool.

3. Silence the squeak with the product of your choice. Pour graphite powder into the hinge (as shown here), coat the hinge and pin with lubricating spray, or rub ball-bearing grease on the pin and hinge joints.

4. Reinstall the hinge pin by tapping it into place with the hammer. Then follow the same steps for the other hinges if need be.

fixing a loose or binding door

Front doors should open and close with ease. If your door won't latch shut, or is hard to open, you'll need to investigate the problem in order to find the right solution. Most often, it means the door is slightly out of square because a hinge has pulled loose. Try tightening the screws on the hinge plates with a screwdriver. If that doesn't work, the screws might be stripped (meaning you can no longer get your screwdriver to fit in the recessed part of the screw head because the face of the screw head has been scratched or damaged). If the old screws are stripped, you need to buy new ones in a finish that matches your hinge. Buy screws that are 3 inches long as they guard better against forced entry.

Another cause could be that the wood around one or more of the screws has worn away so much, they don't have anything solid to grab onto. To fix that problem, you'll need to remove the door from its frame.

HOW TO STRENGTHEN A LOOSE HINGE

1. Have a helper hold the door steady while you do this job, or shove towels underneath the door and be ready to grab it once you remove the last hinge pin. Remove the hinge pins as described in step 1 on page 207. Lift the door off the hinges and set it aside.

2. Unscrew the hinge plate from the doorjamb. Dip the ends of the matchsticks or the golf tees in carpenter's glue and press them into the screw holes. Wipe off excess glue with a wet rag. Once the glue dries, use the utility knife to trim the pieces flush with the jamb.

3. Hold the hinge plate in place with one hand while you use a pencil to mark the screw holes with the other hand. Then put the hinge plate down and drill pilot holes over the pencil marks, using a bit that's slightly smaller than your screws.

4. Put the hinge plate back up and drive in the new screws. The screws should "bite" into the patched wood and feel strong.

5. To get the door back on, have your helper lift the door up and align it with the hinge plate. The two sides of the hinge plates will interlock so you can rest the weight of the door on them. Once the hinge plates are lined up, drop the hinge pins partway into place. Then tap them with a hammer until they're all the way into each hinge.

TIME & TALENT

Get someone to hold the door while you remove it from its hinges. The fix doesn't take much time, but you'll have to wait for the glue to dry before putting the door back on. Start in the morning so you can have the door back in place by the end of the day.

MOVING THE STRIKE PLATE If your hinges don't appear to be loose, or if fixing the loose hinge hasn't solved your problem, you might need to adjust the strike plate. Close the door and watch the latch try to catch the strike plate. See if it's hitting too high or too low. Try to measure the difference and then measure up or down on the door frame and make a mark where the edge of the strike plate needs to be. Unscrew the strike plate and fill in the old screw holes as described in step 2 on page 208. Use a chisel to enlarge the mortise in the direction you want to move the strike plate. Take the sharp blade of the chisel directly perpendicular to the door edge and score a line either up or down for the strike plate's new position. Only chisel to the existing depth. Hold the blade at a 45-degree angle to chisel away the wood. Reposition and reinstall the strike plate. You may need to patch part of the old mortise with wood putty if the strike plate moved significantly.

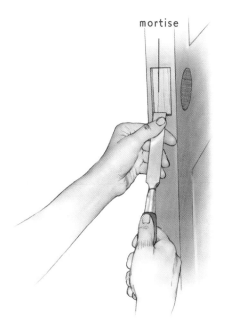

mortise

Dead bolts can be purchased on their own or in a set with matching handle. Look for a designer series to find a finish that matches the metal used elsewhere in the house.

dead bolts

The best way to keep intruders from breaking in through your front door is with a solid dead bolt. Don't have one at all? You should run out and get one, but don't pinch pennies. Buy a dead bolt with at least a grade 2 rating. Grade 1 is a commercial rating and usually more than you'll need. Just make sure the one you buy has a six-pin keying system, a heavy-gauge steel or brass strike plate, 3-inch-long screws, a bolt that extends 1 inch into the jamb, and a housing that goes into the door face rather than being attached flush to the door.

You can get all the security features you need with a stand-alone lock set that costs under $30. Or you might pay over $100 for one with a pretty finish and better style. If you want to replace your doorknob as well, look for a keyed-entry lock set. This has a knob or thumb latch (see below) and a keyed lock on the outside. On the inside you could either turn a latch to unlock the dead bolt, or you could buy a model where the hand lever unlocks the dead bolt for you. Although they seem safest, avoid dead bolts that require a key even to leave the house. In an emergency, you want to be able to get out quickly without fumbling for a key.

Replacing an existing dead bolt with one that's the exact same size is pretty straightforward. You'd only do this if you don't like the look or finish of your current one. If you just want to change the lock, a locksmith can re-key it for about $85. If your current dead bolt doesn't have the safety features described at left, consider replacing it. But if its dimensions are different than your existing dead bolt, the job should be done by a professional.

Sure, you could install it yourself, but I'm guessing you don't currently own a router, a hole saw, or a spade bit. A router is the cleanest way to install the strike plate. You could do it with a chisel, but one mistake and you've gouged your door frame. Patching it won't look so hot. For $75 to $150, a professional locksmith will come to your home and install the new lock in a fraction of the time it would take you to do it, and the results will most likely be cleaner. This is a security feature and you want it done right. Your job is to find the best-quality dead bolt. Hire out the rest.

weather-stripping doors

Put your hand right next to the small gap between your front door and the surrounding doorjamb. Feel a breeze? If so, your doors are releasing heated and cooled air, and letting in outside air as well. That naughty door! A well-sealed home has lower energy bills, so it pays to fix the problem.

This lock set features an easy-to-use thumb latch and hand lever combination. A key is needed only to enter; the dead bolt unlocks by turning a latch from the inside.

Newer doors often have built-in weather stripping in the form of thick rubber gaskets. Older doors might not have any at all, or might have brittle or painted-over strips that aren't doing any good. You'll have to remove old weather stripping before installing new material.

Go to your local hardware store or home improvement center and you'll be amazed at how many products are on the market to weather-strip doors and windows. Most of them will work just fine, though solutions like foam tape may only last one season. They're all easy to install, including vinyl V-seal weather strips, and vinyl or felt weather strips that are nailed into place. Each option comes with installation instructions.

If your door frame doesn't already have spring bronze weather stripping (see page 204), it's worth installing it. Cut the strip to size and nail it in place with brads (very small nails) along the hinge side, latch side, and top of the door. Around the latch, apply the bronze weather stripping to the side that the door closes into. Bronze weather stripping should do the trick because the spring compresses to make an airtight seal.

If you have a gap underneath your door, install a door sweep to keep air and bugs out. Leave the door on its hinges. Buy a door sweep and cut it to size. Use a drill to screw the door sweep to the base of the door. Position it so it brushes across the threshold but still allows the door to move freely.

WEATHER STRIPPING AROUND A DOOR

spring bronze weather stripping

door sweep

ROOFING

You probably don't spend much time pondering your roof. A functioning roof is generally outta sight, outta mind. But it pays to look up every once in a while. You might catch a problem in its infancy, rather than waking up one night with water dripping on your head.

Roofs are generally constructed of plywood sheathing that's attached to your home's rafters. Over the sheathing is a layer of roofing felt, which protects the plywood and acts as a water barrier. Over the felt is the roofing itself. Roofing materials include asphalt shingles, wood shakes, clay tiles, metal, or composite materials. Asphalt shingles are the most common; they're affordable and come in a variety of colors and shapes.

Around roof protrusions such as vent stacks, skylights, and chimneys, metal flashing is required to shed water so it doesn't sneak under the roofing material. You'll also see flashing in areas where one roof line meets another. With any luck, your roofer wasn't a lazy flasher. This is one occasion where you *want* to be flashed! Flashing that hasn't been installed or maintained properly is a common culprit for leaks.

preventing problems

There are a few things you can do to prevent roofing failure. Keep large trees pruned back so your roof gets enough sunlight—this prevents moss and mold from growing on the shingles. It also cuts down on leaves and debris in your gutters. If your roofing material is wood, hire a roofing company to apply a wood preservative once a year to prevent the wood from drying and cracking.

inspect from below

Climbing up on the roof to inspect or repair it is inherently dangerous. If you have access to your attic, a better idea is to examine the roof's underbelly. With flashlight in hand, look for any dark spots or areas that look wet. Poke those areas with a flat-head screwdriver. If the screwdriver easily penetrates the wood, it may be rotted. If the wood is

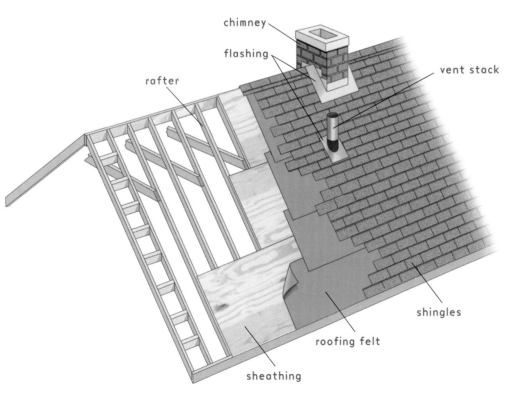

chimney

flashing

rafter

vent stack

shingles

roofing felt

sheathing

obviously wet, call in a professional right away. Another way to find problems is to turn off all the lights and see if you can find any beams of sunlight peeking though.

need a new roof?

If shingles are missing or curled, or if you have asphalt shingles and they've lost their granular coating, you may need to replace your roof. Obviously if you have repeated leaks from mysterious sources, your roof may need to be replaced. And remember, roofs age quickly. Like professional gymnasts, when a roof gets to be about 20 years old it may no longer be able to compete.

When it comes time to replace your roof, it's wise to call four or five contractors to bid on the job. But if it's winter and you've got a leak, you might not have time to go through that process. In an emergency, it's any port in a storm. This is another reason to stay on top of the state of your roof—if you're not in a hurry, you can take the time to interview several candidates.

If you have asphalt shingles, your roofer might offer to add another layer of shingles rather than remove the old roof first. This costs less and can generally be done unless you already have three or more layers of shingles. Some experts, however, do not recommend adding another layer. If your roof is leaking, it might be a problem with the sheathing or the roofing felt, and new shingles won't solve the problem. Ask the roofing contractors for their thoughts on this matter when you're getting estimates, and then make an educated decision that factors in your particular situation and budget.

ice dams

Those of you who live where it never snows can have a little laugh and skip this part. The rest of you may be all too familiar with ice dams, which is what happens when ice forms along the roof edge and blocks melting snow from running off. The melting water can't drip to the ground, so it creeps backwards up your roof, sneaking under shingles that are meant to shed water. Roofs with damaged flashing or other points of entry might leak from this backed-up water and penetrate attic walls and insulation.

There's a low-tech way to deal with ice dams: rake your roof to clear the snow a few feet back from the eaves. Most snow rakes are about 15 to 17 feet long and can be purchased with extensions.

There are also more sophisticated products on the market like electric heating cables and mats. These are installed at the base of your roof, underneath the shingles, to keep water from penetrating the roof's sheathing. It's a job best left to a roofer or general contractor. They may suggest installation only in problem areas (which can be done as a retrofit). But if your roof has a low slope or gets a lot of sun, they might recommend covering the whole surface when you reroof.

Ice dams are created by a complex recipe of heat loss from the house, snow cover, and the outdoor temperature. You can help prevent ice dams by making sure there isn't a lot of heat loss from your attic or upper rooms. Too much warm air can cause snow to melt even if there is no sunlight on it. Make sure your attic has adequate insulation, and stop the flow of warm air around vent pipes and other fixtures in the roof with caulk or insulating foam.

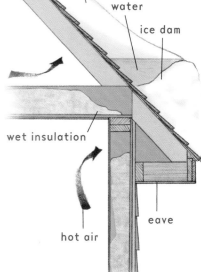

snow

water

ice dam

wet insulation

hot air

eave

GUTTERS

Gutter contractors in Phoenix must feel as lonely as the Maytag repairman. After all, if you live in a city that gets less than 9 inches of precipitation a year, you probably don't need gutters and downspouts. Of course, who knows what global warming will do to arid climates? For all we know, Phoenix could end up wetter than Seattle someday.

Gutters and downspouts are invaluable for catching and funneling water away from one of your home's largest surface areas—the roof. Why is this important? Because water that drips unabated all over your windows, doors, siding, and foundation will cause damage over the long run. Water is the reigning (or raining?) champion of the Erosion Play-Offs. So you want to do everything you can to keep it contained and directed away from your house.

Some homes don't need gutters. If your home is constructed with big, broad overhangs, water probably falls far enough away from your foundation. But anyone who lives in a climate with regular amounts of snow and rain should have gutters. It's simple preventive maintenance.

materials

Gutters can be constructed of steel, vinyl, aluminum, copper, and even wood. Steel gutters are durable, but can rust over time. Vinyl or plastic gutters are a favorite for do-it-yourselfers because they're lightweight. But longtime exposure to wind, sun, and rain can cause them to fade and degrade. Aluminum gutters are probably the most

popular these days because they can be fabricated on-site and without seams. Seamless gutters are preferable to ones where sections must be joined together because there's less chance of leaking. Copper gutters are beautiful and long-lasting, but they cost a lot more than just copper pennies. Wood gutters are practically obsolete, but you can still find them on historic homes.

regular inspection

It's a good idea to inspect gutters a couple times a year to make sure they're operating efficiently. Gutters are typically secured to something called a fascia board. This board hangs just under the

A downspout extender leads water away from your foundation.

Diagram labels:
- spike-and-ferrule hanger
- fascia bracket
- strap hanger
- gutter
- end cap
- fascia board
- downspout

214

roofline and is typically made of wood. Make sure the fascia isn't deteriorating or rotting when you're on a ladder checking the gutters. Here are a few other things to keep in mind:

• Check the straps or hangers that secure the gutters to the fascia; these should be sturdy and not pulling away.

• Examine seams for rust or signs of leaking.

• Check to see if there's a slight downward pitch to the gutters. Gutters should slope slightly toward the downspouts.

• Make sure the downspouts direct water at least 4 feet away from your foundation. Many downspouts have an extra "tailpiece" called an extender that helps to do this. Extenders should rest on splash blocks that are slightly sloped.

maintenance and repairs

If your gutters are full of rust and show signs of deterioration and leaking, they should be replaced. But if there are just a few bad spots here and there, you can make repairs and squeeze another few years out of them.

Gutters can develop leaky seams or holes along the trough's bottom. Patches and fixes will hold things at bay for a while. But if you're mending gutters every year, you might want to start budgeting for a full replacement.

You should only consider maintaining your own gutters if you live in a one-story home. Climbing up to reach gutters on a second or third story is extremely dangerous and should only be done by professionals.

TIME & TALENT

Patching holes doesn't take much skill or expertise, but you do need to be comfortable working from a ladder. Again, if your gutters are more than one story up, hire someone else to do this.

HOW TO REPAIR DAMAGED GUTTERS

1. Anchor your ladder securely and climb up to the gutter. Clear away any debris from the leaking area. There can be exposed screws and jagged metal parts in gutters, so be sure to wear the heavy-duty work gloves.

2. If the hole is small, a smattering of roofing cement ought to do the trick. If there's rust, sand the area, wipe away the particles with a rag, and use a putty knife to apply the cement. (Only use cement when it's warm enough outside for it to be malleable.)

3. Holes larger than an inch but narrower than the width of the gutter trough can be patched with a small piece of sheet metal. If you're lucky, you have a piece of sheet metal lying around! If not, you may have to buy a large piece from a home center and then cut it to size with tin snips. Spread the roofing cement around the hole and embed the patch over it. Slather more roofing cement over the seams of the patch, so it will be watertight.

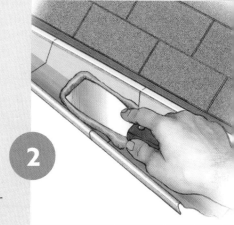

CLEANING GUTTERS Gutters should be cleaned at least twice a year. If your home is on a heavily wooded lot, you'll need to do it more often. The idea here is to keep gutter channels free of debris so water can be free-flowing.

TIME & TALENT

Some people are afraid of heights, even just 8 feet up. If you fall into this category, consider hiring a professional. Otherwise, cleaning the gutters of a single-story home will take a few hours.

STUFF YOU'LL NEED
- 8- to 12-foot stepladder
- Heavy-duty work gloves
- Garden trowel (optional)
- Garden hose with high-pressure nozzle attachment
- Safety glasses
- Scrub brush (if necessary)

HOW TO CLEAN GUTTERS

1. Start at the drain or downspout area and anchor your ladder securely. With the heavy-duty gloves on, scoop out the loose debris with your hands or a garden trowel.

2. Once you've removed all the debris you can, take the hose to the middle of a gutter run. Wearing the safety glasses, turn the nozzle on "jet" and flush the trough with water. Direct the stream toward the downspouts.

3. If there are large chunks of debris that won't dislodge, loosen them with the scrub brush.

4. Finally, go to each downspout and spray water down into it to clear any built-up mud or debris.

SHORTCUT

If you clean gutters a day o[r] two after it rains, the mois[t] muck is easier to scoop up. If the muck dries out and adheres to the gutter, it's more time-consuming.

GRADING

Once, during a particularly bad rainstorm, the basement flooded in a home I was renting. Water accumulating around the home's foundation suddenly began weeping from the basement's concrete block walls. It was like a scene from *Fantasia* without the benefit of a cartoon mouse to make it cute. As I scooped up bucket after bucket full of water, I thanked my lucky stars I didn't own that home.

That house had a problem with its grading. In fact, its grading deserved a D+. Grading refers to the gentle slope of the ground away from a home's foundation. The general rule is that the ground should slope down between 6 to 10 inches the first 10 feet it travels from the foundation walls. This allows water to flow merrily away from your home instead of getting sucked down to the foundation.

It might be very obvious to your eye if the ground surrounding your home pitches slightly downward. But if you can't tell, use this method. Find an unobstructed area next to your foundation. You'll have to find a space where a 10-foot-long 2 by 4 can stretch out from the foundation into the yard without hitting anything. Put a level on top of the 2 by 4. Now lift up the 2 by 4 until it hits its level point, and have a helper measure from the end of the 2 by 4 to the ground. If the tape measure reads 6 inches or more, you're OK.

Check the grading on all sides of your home, including the corners. Just because you've got A+ grading on one side doesn't mean you've got it all the way around.

If your home doesn't have the proper grade, or any grade at all, it's possible to build it up with topsoil. Stone mulch will not build up your grade. You need to remove any existing mulch,

build up the grade with soil, and replace the mulch. Make sure the new mulch won't hold water like bark will (gravel or pebbles are best).

You should also buy a soil-testing kit to see if your soil type retains too much water. Soil with a balanced recipe of sand, silt, and clay is best. If there's too much clay, water tends to pool and drain poorly. Amend your soil if you have to.

Finally, be sure not to cover any portion of your siding if you have to build up the grade. Soil should be 4 to 6 inches below the siding's bottom edge. If you can't keep that distance and still fix the grade, then the perimeter of the house needs to be excavated, which is a job for a professional.

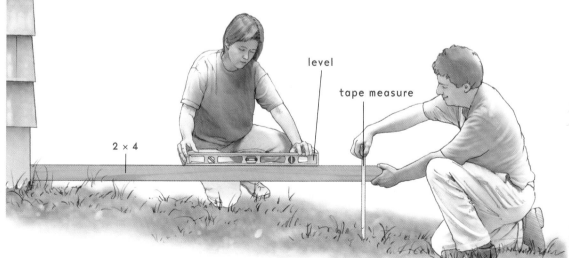

level

tape measure

2 × 4

EXTERIOR CAULKING

Water doesn't exactly enter your house with a Snidely Whiplash moustache and an evil laugh. But it could. It is one of your home's worst enemies. So it's up to you to be Dudley Do-Right and keep water from imperiling your home.

Each spring and fall, make sure you walk around the house and look for cracks and holes where water could penetrate the siding. Check areas where two surfaces meet, such as two pieces of trim around a window or where a deck meets up with the house. Make sure there's a solid bead of caulk connecting them. If the caulk is loose or missing, you'll need to dig out the old stuff and reapply.

When you go shopping for caulk, look for latex-silicone or acrylic-silicone types rated for outdoor use. Silicone has more flexibility and will last over the long haul. Latex-only caulk has a tendency to shrink and become brittle over time, so spend the extra dollar or two on quality caulk. Buy one that says "paintable" if you plan to paint over it, or find one that comes in a color that blends with the surrounding surfaces.

applying caulk

Before applying new caulk, you need to remove the old stuff. It's tempting to skip this step, but the new caulk will perform worse than Enron stock if you put it on top of already-failed caulk. You can pretty much use any thin tool to dig out the old caulk, such as a putty knife or flat-head screwdriver. Once

the majority of it is out, use a wire brush to scrape off any remnants. Then clean the area with a wet towel. Be sure it's warm enough outside (but not too warm) to get this job completed. It needs to be between 50 and 80 degrees for the caulk to set properly.

Creating a smooth and even caulk line takes some practice. Caulk comes out of the tube in a thick bead, so the idea is to get that bead where you want it, and then wipe it with a wet rag or your finger to smooth it out. Caulk is sticky, so it's good to wear skintight rubber gloves for this task. If you use paper towels or rags, have plenty of extras.

Caulk tubes look as if they'd be squeezable, but most aren't. (You can buy small squeezable tubes for some uses, so if you have just a few areas to caulk you might look into those.) For nonsqueez-able caulk tubes, you also need a caulk gun.

FOAM IT UP

Once a crack is larger than ⅜ inch, caulk won't work. To seal holes where pipes or wires are coming through the siding, spray some aerosol foam into the crack. Using this stuff is addictive—you'll be spraying foam into everything. Once it dries, you can scrape off the excess, and you can even paint over it. But be ready to fill all the holes you have in one session, because once you leave the can unused for a couple of hours, the material hardens and you can't spray any more. Read the can to find out which surfaces the foam won't adhere to.

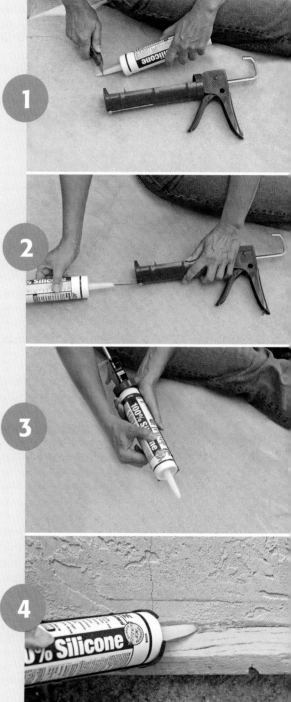

TIME & TALENT

If you're a perfectionist, you'll love this job. If not, trying to get that caulk line smooth and even might drive you nuts. It will take more time than you'd think to remove the old stuff and apply the new—how long depends on how much you're caulking.

HOW TO LOAD A CAULK GUN AND APPLY CAULK

1. Lay the nozzle of the tube on a flat surface that you can cut into, and use a utility knife to cut off the tip. The closer you cut to the tip, the narrower the caulk bead will be. Cut close to the tip to begin with, and if it's too hard to get the caulk out or the line is too thin for what you're caulking, you can always cut more off later.

2. Most caulk guns are equipped with a piercing tool that swings out from either the bottom or side of the gun. Use it to poke through the tip and pierce the caulk tube.

3. Pull the plunger at the back of the caulk gun all the way out so you can fit the caulk tube into the center, with the nozzle facing away from the plunger. Then squeeze the trigger a few times until the flat plate rests against the back of the caulk tube.

4. Put on the rubber gloves. If you're right-handed, hold the trigger of the caulk gun with your right hand and guide the end with your left (reverse this if you're a southpaw). Place the tip of the caulk tube against the opening, squeeze the trigger slowly until you see caulk coming out, and, if you're filling a crack or seam, start to move backward (or down) with the caulk gun so you can see the bead coming out. If you squeeze the trigger too hard, you'll get more caulk that you need and it's sloppy-gloppy going to get the excess off.

5. After a foot or so, put the gun down and run a wet rag, paper towel, or gloved finger across the bead of caulk to smoosh it down so it adheres to the surface on both sides. (Some guns have a release at the gun's back end that you need to press to keep the caulk from flowing.)

CLEANING SIDING

Over the years, dirt and grime can accumulate on your house and make it look shabby. Luckily, it's fairly straightforward to clean most types of siding. The only concern is that you'll be spraying water onto your entire house, including parts that your eaves usually keep dry when it rains. So before you douse the house, make sure that all the cracks and holes are sealed and caulked (see pages 218–219). You don't want water to penetrate your siding and cause damage.

Buy or rent either a power sprayer attachment for your garden hose or a pressure washer with an integrated soap dispenser. If you go with the pressure washer, be sure to keep it turned down to 400 psi (pounds per square inch). Set it any higher than that, and the pressure washer could damage your paint and siding. If you're using a power sprayer attachment on your garden hose, keep the water flowing in multiple jet lines, rather than setting it up to spray one hard jet of water.

Although there are chemical cleaners you can use for this, it's safest to use water and liquid dish detergent. This soap shouldn't harm the plants around the perimeter of the house.

Put on rubber gloves and eye protection. If you're using a pressure washer, squirt some liquid dish detergent into the soap dispenser. If you're using a sprayer attachment without a dispenser, you will have to combine water and detergent in a bucket and sponge it on the walls, which is certainly more labor intensive. Start spraying from the bottom of the house up. The soapy water will drip down. Use a bristle brush to get any areas the spray doesn't seem to dislodge.

Once you finish soaping, go back and rinse each side of the house before moving on to the next so the soapy, dirty water doesn't dry in place. Spray clean water from the top down.

When you're finished, go inside and make sure there aren't any puddles around doors and windows. If there are, that's an "uh-oh" and you'll need to fix that problem.

JUST DUST IT

If your house is just a little dusty, it may be enough to sweep the siding and windows and underneath the eaves instead of power washing. Dust every couple of months and you might be able to avoid major cleaning altogether. A large, soft-bristled brush on a long handle is all you need.

REPAIRING SIDING

While you can repair damaged areas of siding yourself, think about whether the time it will take is worth it. Not that the repairs themselves are hard, but finding individual pieces of siding that match what you currently have might be. Perhaps you won't be able to buy just one piece, whereas a siding contractor would. You may decide you'd rather hire this out.

repairing wood siding

Before replacing a damaged section of wood siding, determine what's at the root of the problem. If it's water-related, that needs to be fixed first. Call a professional if you can't figure out where the leak is coming from. Beyond wood rot, other likely damage includes holes and cracks. Small areas can be filled with exterior spackling compound or wood filler. Easy! Larger damaged areas need to be cut out and replaced. Less easy.

TIME & TALENT

Cutting into your house is stressful, but not hard. If you see any water damage on the building paper underneath the damaged siding, call a professional for help.

STUFF YOU'LL NEED
- Level
- Pencil
- Wood shims
- Keyhole saw
- Miniature hacksaw or small pry bar
- Roofing cement (if necessary)
- Tape measure
- Circular saw or other power saw
- Replacement piece of siding
- Piece of scrap wood
- Hammer
- 3" nails
- Nail set
- Putty knife
- Wood filler
- Medium-grit sandpaper
- Painting or staining supplies

HOW TO REPAIR WOOD SIDING

1. Determine how wide a section you want to remove, and draw straight lines on either side of it. Push the wood shims into the piece of siding directly above the lines you drew to lift it off the part you need to cut. Then use the keyhole saw to cut out the damaged piece.

2. If there are nails holding the damaged piece in place, use a miniature hacksaw to cut them off, or use a small pry bar to remove the piece.

3. Once the old piece is off, you'll see building paper underneath. If the paper is torn, repair with roofing cement.

4. Measure the area, then use a circular saw or other power saw to cut your replacement piece to fit. Position it on the lines you drew, hold the scrap piece of wood underneath it, and hit the scrap piece with a hammer to drive the replacement piece into place. Drive two nails on top and two on the bottom of the replacement piece. Countersink the nails with the nail set.

5. Use a putty knife to fill the cracks with wood filler. Once dry, sand smooth, prime, and paint (or stain).

repairing vinyl siding

Vinyl siding comes in interlocking panels: the top is nailed to the plywood sheathing and the bottom connects to the panel below. You'll need to remove the top portion of your replacement piece to make it blend in.

STUFF YOU'LL NEED
- Ladder (if necessary)
- Utility knife
- Polyurethane caulk (or siding sealant)
- Caulk gun
- Replacement piece of vinyl siding
- Tin snips
- Tape measure

TIME & TALENT

As with other siding repairs, the hard part will be finding a matching piece of siding. The repair itself is straightforward and shouldn't take more than an hour.

HOW TO REPAIR VINYL SIDING

1. Using the utility knife, make cuts to the left and right of the damage, and remove the damaged piece. Remember the bottom edge is latched onto a lip beneath it. You may have to tug down to free the piece.

2. Apply polyurethane caulk to the top of the damaged panel. To load and use the caulk gun, see page 219.

3. The replacement piece will have a nailing strip at the top. Trim that off with the utility knife or tin snips. Then cut the new piece about 6 inches longer than the opening so it overlaps it by 3 inches on either side.

4. Lock the flange on the bottom into the piece underneath it. Then press the new piece in place, making sure it overlaps the existing siding by 3 inches on each side. Use a ladder or whatever's handy to hold the piece in place until it's dry.

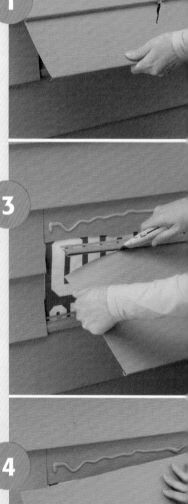

repairing stucco siding

Cracks and holes in stucco siding should be repaired right away. If not, moisture weasels its way through to your home's structure and will cause damage. The fixes are pretty easy, and the materials are readily available and inexpensive. The only trick is matching the finish to the surrounding area. You may need to practice on a piece of plywood to get the right look, as stucco finishes can vary from spattered (often achieved by flicking the stucco mix onto the wall with a broom) to swirled (a whisk broom is used to swirl a circular pattern over the wet stucco) to knock down (spattered with the broom, then the surface is lightly smoothed with a trowel). If, even after practice, you can't release your inner artist and match the existing texture, call a professional.

Once the area is fixed, the stucco must cure before you paint it. Small holes and cracks only need about 4 days, but large areas could take a month before they're fully cured.

FILLING NARROW CRACKS Fill narrow cracks with stucco caulk. First clean the area with a wire brush and clear any debris. Then load the tube of caulk into a caulk gun (see page 219), and fill the crack as shown below left. Read the label for drying and finishing information.

FILLING LARGE CRACKS The stucco patching compound will stay in the crack better if you first enlarge the crack a bit (counterintuitive, I know). Use a cold chisel and hammer to open up the crack, and brush away the loose material with a wire brush. Then use a foam brush to apply a liquid concrete bonding agent. As the name implies, this helps the stucco patch to adhere. Mix up a small batch of stucco patching compound according to the directions on the bag, and use a small putty knife or trowel to spread some over the crack. Then try to match the surrounding finish as best you can.

PATCHING SMALL TO MEDIUM-SIZE HOLES Holes up to 6 inches wide can be filled with stucco patching compound as well. Larger holes are best filled by a professional, who will apply three coats of regular stucco mix and probably blend the patched area with the old surface much better than a first-timer would be able to do. But for a hole 6 inches or less in an inconspicuous place, try the steps on page 224.

STUFF YOU'LL NEED

- Cold chisel
- Hammer
- Wire brush
- Foam brush
- Liquid concrete bonding agent
- Stucco patching compound
- Plastic bucket
- Putty knife or trowel
- Whisk broom
- Scrap plywood
- Garden hose
- Piece of plastic
- Painter's tape
- Priming and painting supplies

TIME & TALENT

The trick is getting the finish right. Practice, practice! The fix itself can be done in no time, but remember it will need about 4 days to cure before you can prime and paint.

HOW TO REPAIR A HOLE IN STUCCO

1. Use a cold chisel and hammer to remove old stucco from the damaged area. Clean the area with a wire brush, then use the foam brush to apply the bonding agent.

2. Mix up a small batch of stucco patching compound according to the directions on the bag. Apply a thin layer with a trowel or putty knife, pressing down as you go and feathering the edges.

3. While the stucco patch is still wet, try to match the finish that's on the surrounding wall with a whisk broom or other tool (practice first on a piece of plywood to get the right texture).

4. Keep the area damp for about 4 days to let the stucco cure before priming and painting. Do this by misting the area with water and taping a piece of plastic over it with painter's tape. Check on it each day to see if another spray is needed.

EXTERIOR PAINTING

Painting the exterior of your home is a big job. You can't simply slap new paint on exterior siding and expect good results. Just like painting indoors, you have to prepare—a process that often takes more time than the actual painting does. To achieve a good finish, your siding may need to be sanded, scraped, patched, and primed. Two-story houses will require working on a ladder, which can be difficult and dangerous. Feeling discouraged yet?

There are some situations where you should just throw in the brush and get a professional to do the work. For homes that have significant paint problems (such as wrinkling or blistering), or are two or more stories high, or have oodles of ornate trimwork, you really should call in the pros—they can do it faster and better than you can. One-story homes with siding that's in pretty good shape, however, can be tackled by an ambitious homeowner.

preparing to paint

You'll first need to wash your existing siding, scrape or sand away any loose paint, and fill holes and dents. Walk around the house and locate problem areas so you know in advance how much time you'll need to set aside for these preparations.

STUFF YOU'LL NEED
- *Rubber gloves*
- *Safety glasses*
- *Garden hose*
- *Stiff-bristle brush and extension pole*
- *Bucket*
- *Mild dishwashing detergent*
- *Power sander with medium-grit and fine-grit sandpaper (if necessary)*
- *Exterior spackling compound*
- *Putty knife*
- *Soft-bristle brush*
- *Painter's tape*
- *Drop cloths or plastic*
- *Pruning shears, rope, and fine netting (if necessary)*
- *Primer*
- *Wide paintbrush*
- *Paint*
- *Paint roller and tray (if necessary)*
- *Patience!*

TIME & TALENT

You need at least a day to prepare a small, one-story house—more if there's significant patching and scraping to do. Then it may take several weekends to prime and paint the house. The only special talents required are patience and persistence.

HOW TO PREP A HOUSE FOR PAINT

1. Wearing the rubber gloves and eye protection, hose down one side of the house with a light spray of water. Using the stiff-bristle brush mounted on an extension pole, wash the siding with a solution of water and mild dish detergent. Just dip the brush into the solution and scrub away. When you're finished, rinse from the top down with fresh water, and move on to the next side.

225

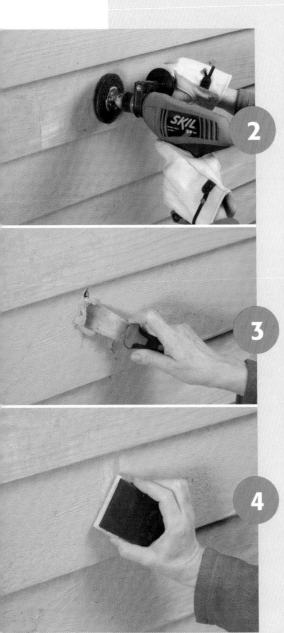

2. If you have wood siding, check for areas with loose or peeling paint. If you just paint over them, the new paint will soon suffer the same result. So you need to sand down to bare wood with a power sander equipped with medium-grit sandpaper. Move the sander horizontally over the top portion of the board, then up and down across the middle of the board. Finish with a few passes of fine-grit sandpaper.

3. Fill any holes or dents with exterior spackling compound. Scoop some of the compound out and spread it into the hole with a small putty knife.

4. Once the spackling compound has dried, use fine-grit sandpaper to smooth it out flush with the surrounding surface. Wipe away any dust with a soft-bristle brush.

painting

Once everything is cleaned and prepared, you're ready to paint…almost. Use painter's tape to cover any surfaces you aren't painting, and put drop cloths or plastic around the perimeter of the house. You may need to prune or tie back some plants that are in the way. For unwieldy shrubs, buy some fine netting to drape over them.

Exterior painting must be done in fair, dry weather (at least 50 degrees), and you should make sure to finish 2 hours before nightfall, when some moisture may be in the air. You don't want to paint in direct sun, or where the sun will heat the surface right after you paint. For best results, paint an area right after the sun has left it.

To paint stucco siding, use a brush to cut in on the top, bottom, and sides, and then fill in the middle with a roller. Paint lap siding with a brush.

HOW TO PAINT A HOUSE

1. It's best to start with a coat of primer. You have to prime any spots of bare wood and newly spackled areas. Even if you don't have bare wood, you'll get better results this way. Ask your paint store to tint the primer a color close to your final color so there's more of a chance you'll only have to do one final coat of paint. Apply the primer with the wide brush.

2. Once the primer is dry, start by painting the edges of the horizontal boards with the wide brush. Dip the brush 1 inch into the paint, tap it against the side of the can (don't wipe it), tuck the bristles under the edge of a board as shown here, and then brush across the board horizontally.

3. Reload the brush, this time dipping about 2 inches down, and again tap the brush on the side of the can. Brush the paint over the boards you "cut in" in step 2. Keep going, and going, and going, and going, and going until you've completed one side of the house. Exterior painting takes time. You'll get frustrated if you think you can get it all done in a day or two, although using a roller on other types of siding will certainly make the process faster.

4. Days or weeks or even next Labor Day, when you've finally painted all the siding, you'll be ready to tackle the trim. Protect your newly painted siding with painter's tape and use a brush to paint the trim, going with the grain of the wood.

chapter 9

PESTS, CRITTERS, AND NUISANCES

SUSAN WAS IN A DEEP, sweet summer sleep when she was startled awake by a banging noise. *Ku-thwump, ku-thwump!* She quickly went into protective Doberman mode, attuning her ears to the noise. She determined it wasn't a human intruder— no one is that ridiculously noisy. She padded down to the kitchen in her slippers to investigate and turned on the light. Perched on the kitchen sink, a full loaf of French bread in its mouth, was a raccoon. It was trying to exit the torn screen the same way it had come in—only the bread was too wide and wouldn't fit through the opening. Raccoon and Susan briefly stared each other down before the intruder hissed, dropped the bread, and escaped. Susan repaired the screen the next day.

You know, it's nice to appreciate Mother Nature and all her critters, but not in the house. Read on to learn how to combat creepy-crawlies and furry fiends that do damage to our yards and sometimes dare to find their way into our homes.

chapter contents

PREVENTING PEST INFESTATION

I live adjacent to a wetlands area. I've seen foxes, coyotes, wild turkeys, and deer from my back door. So I figured my house was a good candidate for a pest professional's assessment. My local Humane Society (a good resource, by the way) recommended someone they called "a walking encyclopedia" and "a compassionate animal-control guy." They were right.

Sean Francis of Falls Creek Animal Control spent hours showing me a home's potential pest access points. There are a lot more of them than you may think. It doesn't take much of an opening for pests to get into your home. Mice can compress their lithe little skeletons into a ¼-inch opening. Bats can squeeze through an area the size of a dime. Red squirrels—nattering, nasty, and destructive—can get through a 1¾-inch-diameter hole.

The best offense for pest infiltration is a good defense. Keep these general tips in mind to help pest-proof your home:

• Trim all tree branches and limbs so they're at least 8 feet away from your roof. When cold weather hits, squirrels will leap onto roofs and look for openings under loose shingles and flashing.

• All openings and vents on the roof—like chimneys—should be capped with ¼-inch rigid mesh screening.

• The area where the chimney meets the siding is a common entry point for insects. Make sure this area is sealed with a high-grade silicone caulk.

• Attic vents should have screening that is free of dust and debris (to maximize ventilation) and no holes. Any holes, tears, or openings in these screens should be patched or replaced (see pages 202–203).

• Vines and ivy look beautiful as they creep up the sides of your home. But they attract insects (and can damage siding). They're also vertical runways for certain kinds of rodents. Keep this quaint feature to a minimum, and away from your eaves.

• Lumber piles attract boring insects (that's "boring" the verb, not the adjective). They also make great hideouts for groundhogs, chipmunks, and other critters. Keep lumber and firewood piles far away from the house, and if you have a woodstove, don't stack firewood in the basement.

• Check all your service entry points—the places where the cable TV, gas, phone, and water lines enter the house. Even the teensiest opening should be sealed with high-grade silicone caulk (see pages 218–219).

• Dryer vents, which exhaust warm air, are particularly attractive to animals looking for shelter from cold air. Make sure your vent is wrapped in rigid mesh screening or replace it with a special type of vent cap that closes when it's not in use.

• Examine the areas where your exterior doors meet the threshold. If you can see light coming through, seal the gap by installing a door sweep (see page 211). Also check the areas around the door framing. All cracks, gaps, and openings should be stuffed with steel wool (mice and rats won't chew through it) and then caulked. The same goes for windows.

- Garage doors should have rubber bottom seals.
- Keep your garage door shut. It's warmer in a garage than it is outside, so critters will wander in looking for shelter.
- The spaces behind shutters and exterior light fixtures are nice, dark harbors for bats and spiders. If the shutters are nonoperational, caulk the gap around them. Seal the area where a light fixture meets the siding.
- Bird feeders provide as much entertainment as a PBS nature special. But they should be located a good distance away from the house because rodents are attracted to the birdseed.
- Don't leave ripe fruit or vegetables from your garden to rot naturally on the ground. Rodents are attracted to it. Use it or lose it.
- It's a gross job because it means crawling under a house, but homes with crawl spaces should be thoroughly examined and all openings sealed. A friend of mine had an opossum sneak through the crawl-space skirting. It died and made a rotten stink for weeks.
- Examine the perimeter of your home for signs of tunneling or holes. If you see them, chances are that rodents are nearby.

This is Sean Francis, showing me what to look for outside my house.

GETTING RID OF CREEPY-CRAWLIES

Mice, rats, spiders, termites, ants, and roaches are everywhere. They skulk, slither, scuttle, scamper, creep, crawl, and fly. With verbs like that, these are things you don't want in your house, so you want to do everything you can to keep these creatures where they belong—outside.

mice and rats

Consider the following mouse trivia: the common house mouse should wear diapers because it deposits microdroplets of urine constantly. Plus, it leaves its little trademark calling cards of solid waste wherever it goes. Rabbits look celibate compared with mice—the female mouse can produce 6 to 10 litters a year, with approximately 6 mice born in each litter. The house mouse is found in all 50 states and is most active between October and February when it seeks warmth and shelter. Oh, and they don't just scamper; mice are adept at climbing, jumping, swimming, and gnawing. Yuck!

Now, on to our next star rodent…the rat. The two most common rats are the roof rat and Norway rat. As the name implies, roof rats go high, rooting around in attics and on rooftops. Closer to the ground, Norway rats (also called the brown rat, sewer rat, or barn rat) can burrow 3 feet straight into the earth and are able to chew through building materials like glass, cinder block, wires, and aluminum. Double yuck.

The best way to handle mice and rats is to make sure they don't gain access in the first place. How do you know if there's a mouse in the house? Here's a list.

- Rodents are most active at dawn and dusk. Do you hear any scampering activity in your walls or ceilings?
- Burrows and runways are typically located around concrete slabs or foundations, or even along fence lines. Mouse burrows are small; rat burrows will have an irregular rounded opening that's at least 2 inches in diameter.
- Urine stains or odor can be an indication of rodent infestation.
- Gnaw marks or chewed materials mean something's been doing some illicit snacking.
- Droppings mean that rodents have been present. Gross.
- Mice and rats travel along baseboards and walls; look for oily rubbings from their fur.

All I can say is, "Super platinum yuck to the third power."

If you think you've got a big problem with mice or rats, get a professional exterminator. Otherwise, set traps and kill them yourself. Obviously, if you have pets or children, you need to exercise extreme care in dealing with traps and poisons. Find a way to secure the area so curious kiddies and kitties don't come across them.

Trapping mice is gross. And it's even kind of sad because when you look closely at a little mouse face, it's kind of cute. Heck, Disney made gazillions exploiting a cute mouse image. But in reality, mice are dirty and smelly, so shove your Mickey sentiment aside and get busy.

SNAP TRAPS These traps are cheap and effective. Those with the larger paddle-type bait bar are supposedly more effective. If you're setting one of these in an area where a pet might come in contact with it, place a shoe box over it and cut out openings on the back side so the mouse can gain access, but the pet can't.

STUFF YOU'LL NEED
- *Snap trap*
- *Bait of your choice*
- *Knife*

TIME & TALENT

Setting a snap trap does require some hand strength and dexterity. And of course you need to be very careful not to pinch your fingers. Takes a minute.

JUST SO YOU KNOW ...
A clever mouse may lick off peanut butter bait without snapping the trap. Try gluing a chunk of apple or a gumdrop down so it can't get lunch without getting busted.

HOW TO SET A MOUSETRAP

1. Take the trap and bait to the area where you want to set it. Load the bait on the bait bar. Peanut butter, apples, bacon, cheese, and chewy candy (like gumdrops) all work.

2. If you're right-handed, hold the trap in your left hand (reverse this if you're a southpaw). Hold the trap like a guitar—with the thumb along the left edge, and all four fingers on the other edge. Pull back the spring-loaded bar to the opposite end of the trap and hold it down with your thumb and fingers.

3. Angle the brace against the catch in the bait bar until it's hooked.

4. Slowly release the bar you were holding down. The trap should now be set. Place it at a perpendicular angle to the wall base. Be very careful in setting the trap down. The slightest movement can snap it.

OTHER "SNAPPY" OPTIONS There are other snap traps that are quick and easy to set and pose no risk to your fingers. These traps encase the mouse in a plastic housing so you don't need to handle the dead mouse to dispose of it. They cost about twice as much as the other snap traps, but they are reusable.

Catch-and-release traps won't hurt the mouse at all. Once you've got the little fella, you can always drive out into the woods and release him. Then there's no blood on your hands!

If you suspect rats, you'll need to buy the much larger rat trap. Rats are supposedly more suspicious than mice when it comes to investigating bait, but the snap traps work. My friend Blanche bagged five rats in her attic using snap traps and beef jerky. Disposing of a dead rat is disgusting, but she's a Nebraska farm girl and just copped a can-do attitude. You need it with this stuff. That and a good pair of gloves.

BAIT STATIONS The principle behind baiting is that by ingesting the pellets, the mouse is eventually poisoned and dies. This might be fine for pests in your garage, but it's icky to think there's a poisoned mouse carcass somewhere in your house. If you use bait stations (shown below), place them

every 8 feet or so and use them in an area where you're fairly sure you'll be able to locate the carcasses and dispose of them. Otherwise, you'll have a couple of months worth of stink on your hands.

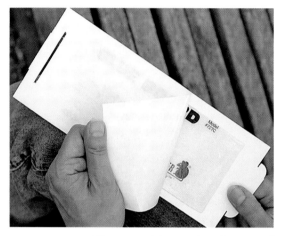

GLUE TRAPS Glue traps (shown above) are used not only for mice, but for insects and spiders too. They're typically scented (I got a whiff of one that smelled like popcorn), which is what attracts the rodent or insect to the trap. These are probably the most user-friendly traps because they don't involve poison. However, it can be a torturous death because the mouse will struggle to free itself. If you catch one on a glue trap, place it in a plastic bag, seal it, and dispose of it. It's pretty Cruella DeVille–like, but if you've declared war on mice, you might not have a problem with the glue traps.

Glue traps don't work very well in wet or dusty areas because these conditions compromise the quality of the adhesive. They also don't work well in attics with blown-in insulation because there are so many free-floating fibers present.

termites and carpenter ants

Suppose you're relaxing on the couch with a good sci-fi novel one spring afternoon and all of a sudden, a swarm of flying insects appears out of nowhere. Guess what? That ain't science fiction; you've got real-life trouble. A swarm of winged insects inside your home probably means you've got termites.

Contrary to popular belief, termites don't live in the wood of your house, they work there. They live in a nest where a king and queen hold reign and worry about reproducing. Meanwhile, the worker termites march through protective mud tunnels to their wood-munching jobs. At the end of their shift, they come back to the nest, and excrete the food they ate. This is dinner for the other termites. Termiticides (termite poisons) interrupt this digestive process. The worker termites ingest poison, and excrete it to their buddies, who eat it and die.

A termite is the most destructive wood-destroying insect there is, and dealing with an infestation is best left to a professional. But you can try to detect for yourself whether or not your house has a termite problem. Start your inspection down low; termites are typically found in basements and crawl spaces. Here's what to look for:

- The presence of mudlike "patches" on exposed wood framing.
- Pencil-thin mudlike tunnels on basement walls, wood posts, or trim boards. These tunnels are the termite's "hallways."
- Buckling paint or tiny holes on exposed wood.

- Crumbling or soft wood (which could also be due to moisture). Pick at the soft wood with a screwdriver. If you see tunnels running parallel with the grain, that's an indication of termites.

The swarming (I wasn't kidding earlier) is another indication. Winged ants and termites look an awful lot alike, but ants have a narrow, wasp-like waist and their wings are about the same length as their bodies. Termite wings are twice as long as these insects' thick-waisted bodies. Guess it's spandex for those curvy ants and an empire waist for those shapeless termites.

Termites eat wood; carpenter ants set up house-keeping in it. They establish nests in either rotting or structurally sound wood. The problem is, once they've settled into their "house," the wood member can lose its structural integrity.

Carpenter ants aren't as sneaky as termites in that they're often visible. They're big ants that are either black or red. But just because you see one or two of them in the house doesn't necessarily mean they've established condos in your framing. Here are indications that carpenter ants are nesting in your home:

- Fibrous, sawdust-like deposits at the base of wood members. Carpenter ants like moisture, so common nesting sites are porch posts and damp basements.
- Signs of tunneling. Carpenter ant wood tunnels are clean and smooth—almost as if they were whittled and sanded down.

Finding and getting rid of the nest is best left to a professional, but there are certainly measures you can take to prevent carpenter ants from getting into the house. Eliminate all woodpiles next to your house, seal up all cracks and gaps along the foundation with caulk, and make sure there's adequate ventilation in moist areas.

roaches

I once moved into an apartment that turned out to be infested with roaches. The landlord sprayed some noxious chemicals and then never bothered to clean up the scores of dead roach bodies. Welcome to Los Angeles!

Countertops that are never fully wiped down and spilled beverages that are never quite wiped up are prime feeding grounds for roaches. They also like fermented foods (i.e., garbage).

And they are attracted to moisture, which is why they're such a problem in kitchens.

There are many varieties of roaches, but the most common are the German cockroach and the flying palmetto bug. They are primarily nocturnal and will emerge when the house is dark to forage for food and water.

Roaches typically live in cracks and crevices, but they might also take up residence under the sink, underneath countertops, in cabinets, and even in the motor compartments of refrigerators. Although totally eliminating roaches will take

patience and persistence, start with some immediate measures:

- Pare down the roaches' food supply. Buy trash cans with tight-fitting lids, make sure dishes are thoroughly washed with no residual grease, wipe up spills immediately, and sweep or vacuum the floor after meal preparation and eating.

- Roaches will go for Fido or Fluffy's food, so once pets have eaten, pick up their dishes and wash them.

- Roaches like water, so it's a good idea to keep drains plugged at night, and to fix dripping faucets.

- Use boric acid or a roach killer of your choice along the baseboards, in cabinets, behind appliances, under sinks, and anyplace else you've noted activity. But don't put any poison where you keep food, obviously.

- Seal up cracks and crevices using a combination of steel wool (if the opening is big enough) and silicone caulk or nonexpanding foam spray.

- Glue traps are a good bellwether of how you're doing in your war against roaches. Set them against baseboards and monitor the activity. Ideally, a couple of weeks after your all-out assault, you should be finding nothing but vacancies in your roach hotels.

spiders

I used to have night terrors about daddy longlegs when I was a kid. Now I realize that most spiders are beneficial and help balance nature by feeding on insects. But they still give me the creeps.

All spiders have venom, but only two types have the fangs and venom to do serious damage to humans—the brown recluse and the black widow.

I've known a couple of people who have been bitten by recluse spiders. It's serious stuff. The lesion often becomes necrotic, meaning your living tissue keeps dying.

Spiders like quiet, dark, damp, dusty places. That's why they're found in attics, basements, utility rooms, closets, sheds, woodpiles, and under roof eaves. Of course there are sprays that will kill spiders, but if you can handle it, you can avoid using poisons by just catching them and releasing them outside. Glue traps and sticky boards are effective at catching insects and spiders; you can give those a try. Or better yet, make sure they don't find a way inside your home.

PREVENTING SPIDER INFILTRATION Most spiders prefer to live outside. Use these methods to keep them there:

- Use tight-fitting window and door screens.
- Install door sweeps and seal any openings along the doors, windows, and foundation walls.

- Destroy webs by vacuuming, or knock them down with a broom. Eliminate outdoor webs by spraying them with a high-pressure garden hose.
- Keep the foundation of your home free of debris (especially those lumber piles!).
- Eliminate clutter in closets, basements, and attics. Store items off the floor.

And finally, a word about cardboard. Apparently spiders like cardboard. If you're short on storage space and keep items in cardboard boxes under your bed, switch to plastic containers, or seal the cardboard edges with tape. Nothing worse than opening a memory box and finding a spider that's bigger than your head staring back at you!

yellow jackets

Yellow jackets are a type of wasp; they are not bees. While bees sting you once and then die, a yellow jacket or wasp can sting repeatedly. Not only that, they'll attack you if angered and will call all their friends to attack you as well. Not cool.

Their favorite foods are sweet liquids like plant nectar or fruit, and meat. This is why they're particularly interested in your picnic and will attack your food so fiercely. In fact, there is a type of yellow jacket called a scavenger that isn't interested in plant food or insects at all—it only wants to eat *your* food.

You'll often find yellow jacket nests under roof eaves, hanging from a tree branch, or in the ground. But they have also been known to nest in the attic, crawl space, and walls of a home. There have even been cases where yellow jackets looking

for food actually chewed through the walls to get into a house. Yikes! They can also get in through small holes or gaps around windows and doors, or where plumbing or wiring enters the house, which is why it's so important to keep the house well sealed (see pages 218–219).

When the weather is warm, yellow jackets are far more likely to search for food outside. But as it gets cooler, they can be drawn to the warm house and sweet smells of your food. Luckily, the ones that make it into your house probably haven't eaten for a while and will therefore be pretty slow and sluggish. But they can still sting, so exercise extreme caution around them.

DEALING WITH YELLOW JACKETS OUTSIDE The best way to ensure that yellow jackets never make their way into your house is to keep them from nesting outside your house. They are drawn to sweet food, so pick up any fallen fruit instead of leaving it to rot. If you eat outdoors, clean up any spilled food right away.

You can buy hanging traps that lure them in with a sweet scent and then don't let them back out. Be sure to hang these traps away from where people usually gather—you don't want the feeding frenzy happening right outside your front door.

If you see a nest, buy a wasp spray (look for the nonpoisonous variety that's safe for use around children and pets) to kill the entire colony. Never spray a nest in the middle of the day. There aren't going to be as many yellow jackets inside, and the ones that are hanging around could attack you. The best time to spray is at dawn or dusk. Stand a safe distance from the nest with your back to the wind, and saturate the nest with spray. Wait a couple of days before removing the nest with a stick. For multiple or large nests, it's much safer to hire a professional exterminator.

DEALING WITH YELLOW JACKETS INSIDE
Nests are only used once, so if one has formed inside your wall or attic, it will only be a hassle this year. In areas with freezing winters, the cold will kill any remaining yellow jackets if they haven't already died of starvation. The few that get into the house, though, will need to be dealt with.

• Though tempting, it's not a good idea to spray a yellow jacket inside. Instead, wait for it to land and then hit it with a magazine or flyswatter. It should be lethargic from being inside.

• If you saw one but can't find it again, coax it into plain sight by leaving a piece of meat or fish on a plate. Let the food reach room temperature, and your visitor will smell it and show up for supper.

• No food in the house? Turn off all the lights except for one room. The yellow jacket will be drawn to the light.

• Not the killing type? Wait for it to land low on a wall, put a glass over it, slide a piece of cardboard underneath the opening, walk outside, and let it go (you're too kind).

• Scared to death? Put the long hose attachment on your vacuum cleaner and suck up the wasp from a safe distance. Work up your nerve first with a primal yell. Once the wasp is inside, tape up the hose opening and wait a few days for the insect to die.

ENCOURAGING CRITTERS TO LEAVE

Wildlife is beautiful, at least on *National Geographic*. But when it encroaches on our living space, it can be unnerving at the least and physically dangerous at worst. Trapping and removing animals from your yard generally doesn't do the trick, as new ones will soon take their place. The only things you can do are seal any openings to your house so wild animals can't come inside, and make your yard less desirable to them.

Skunks, squirrels, opossums, and raccoons might have found a friend in *The Beverly Hillbillies'* Elly May, but they can wreak havoc in your yard. They can also camp out in your attic, crawl space, or chimney if those areas aren't sealed off (see the bulleted list on pages 230–231).

raccoons

Raccoons will go where they can find food. If they can't find any in your yard, they'll remember and won't come back. Raccoons come out a couple of hours after the sun goes down, and generally are not afraid of people. You can temporarily scare them away with motion-sensor lights, but to discourage them from visiting in the future, try one of these techniques:

- Place bowls of water and ammonia around the yard where raccoons visit. They don't like the smell. Keep them off the grass though—ammonia will damage it.
- Secure the lids to your trash cans with rubber straps, or get locking lids.
- If raccoons are digging up your sod looking for worms, sprinkle a generous amount of cayenne pepper on the lawn.
- If a raccoon has taken up residence under your house, put a loud radio—with an annoying station of your choice—near the nest and keep it there all day. Sprinkle some flour around the entrance to the crawl space and wait until you see footprints leading away from the door. Then block off the opening. (Do this only if you suspect one adult raccoon; see the note about babies below.)
- Chimneys and attics are favorite places for raccoons to give birth. Wait a few weeks until the babies are mobile and then blast a radio to get them out. A mother with babies may take several days to evacuate, so don't block her entry until you know she's got everyone moved.

skunks

The advice above also applies to skunks. But while skunks will go after your garbage, they are mostly interested in rodents and insects. Again, keep the openings to your crawl space sealed, even small holes. Skunks will follow rodents in there.

- Skunks don't like water, so motion-sensor sprinklers often shoo them away.
- Unlike raccoons, skunks don't climb. So you can fence off a problematic area and bury chicken wire underneath the fence to prevent them from digging under it.
- Keep your pets inside at night to avoid having them getting into a scuffle with a skunk and coming home stinky.

opossums

These cat-size creatures with a long tail come out at night and can wreak havoc just like raccoons and skunks. They like fruit trees and vegetable gardens, but will eat your garbage as well. Luckily, opossums are wanderers, and generally don't revisit the same place. Use the same tricks recommended for skunks to deter them.

squirrels

Don't be fooled by those cute fuzzy tails! Squirrels are rodents, and rodents are born to chew. When squirrels get in your house, they can go nuts chewing on electrical wires, wood, or anything else they find.

A common problem is for a squirrel to get stuck in your chimney. First, shame on you for not having a chimney cap! That said, you can try hanging a rope that's secured to something on the roof down the chimney. Squirrels only go out during the day, so after a few daylight hours the squirrel will hopefully climb up the rope and leave. Then quickly get that chimney cap installed.

Don't try to smoke the squirrel out, as the mother and babies may die and then you will have another problem on your hands. If the squirrel won't leave, close all the interior doors in the room and open a nearby exterior door or window. Then open the damper and the fireplace doors and the squirrel should instinctively head for the outdoors.

Squirrels that get into attics can cause real damage. Red squirrels especially are gangsta-tough and are difficult to deal with. If you hire a professional exterminator, make sure he or she has experience with squirrels.

deer

My sister declared war on the deer that ate her hostas every summer. As she later ruminated, "Hostas for deer?! It's the same as a chocolate smorgasbord for a woman with PMS."

She tried stinky-smelling mulch, but still the deer ate the hostas. She heard hair sweepings from a barber shop would deter them and spread those around. But still the deer ate the hostas. She sprayed the leaves with a commercial deer repellent. But still the deer ate the hostas.

Finally she found a product called Milorganite (a fertilizer). Although the manufacturer doesn't claim Milorganite is a deer deterrent, it worked. The deer left her hostas alone. The only other way to keep deer out of your yard is to erect tall fences.

BIRDS AND BATS

Ah, the twitter of sweet sparrows, the distinctive call of a cardinal. For the most part, having birds in your yard is a pleasant experience. But if too many birds are congregating and leaving piles of poo as their calling cards, it's time to take action. And unless you're Elvira, the Mistress of the Dark, I doubt you want bats roosting under your eaves. Here are a few ways to outsmart our flying friends.

birds

If birds are taking over a spot in the yard that you'd rather they didn't, try placing bird-repellent spikes or a small statue of an owl or other large bird there. Also look for products called "scare-eye balloons" that look like Halloween decorations. Birds apparently don't like them.

A BIRD IN THE HOUSE When a wild bird gets into your house, it's easy for both of you to get your feathers ruffled. The bird will be scared and if there are mirrors or reflective surfaces, the animal can get disoriented and start bashing into walls and windows.

First, close all the interior doors in the room and open the windows and exterior doors. If the bird isn't going in the right direction, sprinkle cracker crumbs near the doors or windows to lure it out. Birds that are up high or trying to get out through a skylight can be hard to redirect. Waiting them out is one option. Another is to use a fishing net to grab them and then release outdoors.

If the bird is injured, gently pick it up in a towel, place it in a box with some air holes, and bring it to your local SPCA or wildlife-rehabilitation facility. Try not to touch the bird or do any damage to its wings. Be particularly gentle with small and delicate birds.

WOODPECKERS DAMAGING SIDING If you have aged or damaged cedar or redwood siding, you can practically hear the mocking laugh of Woody Woodpecker as he drills away on your house. Woodpeckers love this stuff and go at it with zeal and fury. If there are many holes larger than $\frac{1}{2}$ inch in diameter, you'll need to eventually replace that section of siding. But to mitigate damage in the meantime, try the following:

• Patch holes with wood putty and caulk, and then prime and paint. With really large holes, you might want to consider sheet-metal patches. It won't look good, but as a temporary measure, it might suffice.

• Woodpeckers supposedly can't get their beaks through $\frac{3}{4}$-inch netting. Try securing that over damaged areas until the birds are discouraged.

• Mylar or fabric streamers, balloons, and wind chimes might scare the birds away.

• You can find products that emit high-pitched sounds that scare woodpeckers away. Either that, or play a continuous loop of Eric Carmen's "All by Myself." That'll spook 'em!

getting bats to move out

The most common bats are also the variety that like to nest within structures rather than outdoors. That's right, nest! Bats living in your walls, attic, or crawl space can present serious health hazards and are downright creepy, too. When bats live near humans, the possibility of being bitten increases, and bats are common carriers of rabies. Also, where bats live you will find their droppings, which are full of bacteria and viruses that can become hazardous as airborne dust.

If you have bats in or around your home, the only thing you can do is wait for them to leave and then block the opening they're using so they can't get back in. Yeah, you'll feel a little like Bill Murray tracking down gophers in *Caddyshack,* but bats are lousy houseguests.

First, you'll need to wait until dusk, then sit outside and watch for the bats to escape. They usually enter a structure high up, so look around the roof and eaves. A small bat can squeeze through an opening as small as a dime, so this is another reminder that you need to examine the entire house and fill every crack and hole with caulk or nonexpanding foam (see the bulleted list on pages 230–231). Bats can't chew through walls like rodents, so they need to find an existing opening.

Don't close up the hole once you've determined the main pathway for the bats—at least not yet. If you close the hole immediately, especially during spring and early summer, it's possible that you'll be trapping baby bats inside. When they die, you'll have a horrible smell and fly problem on your hands. So the thing to do is create a door where bats can fly out, but not back in. Use a flap of any stiff material that only swings one way. Once you're sure all the bats are out, even the babies (which may take a week or two), you can close the hole permanently.

If the bats have lived there for a while, they'll be desperate to get back in, so be particularly vigilant during the next month or so. Once all the holes are permanently closed, you'll need to clean up the droppings left behind, if they're accessible. Make sure you wear full protective gear and a respirator so none of the dust gets into your system. Don't vacuum this type of thing up. The germ-laden dust will be spit out of your vacuum cleaner and inhaled. Wet everything down before you begin so that the least amount of dust is kicked up. But really, if you have a significant area to clean, it's better to call in a professional.

PET DOORS

How many times a day do you get up to let your pet in or out of the house? When you're preoccupied with tasks or business at home, it's a hassle to drop everything for an insistent pet's demands. You might've considered a pet door, but what about safety and giving other animals access to your home? Well, today's high-tech pet doors are more than just a flap of plastic blowin' in the wind. They're made to keep out the weather, and also come with special lock features so they won't let in other animals or intruders. In fact, a well-made pet door might be more energy efficient and safer than opening the entire door to let Fido in (and out…and in…).

Installing a pet door is an easy do-it-yourself project. It comes with a template and detailed instructions that walk you through the installation. Beware of the cheap models, though, as they won't have the features described below. Expect to pay between $100 and $200 for a well-made model, depending on the size you need.

where can I put it?

The most common place to install a pet door is in an exterior door made of wood. Before you decide on doing this, however, be aware that you'll be cutting a hole in the door, which can't be undone. Some manufacturers make pet doors that can be installed in sliding glass doors. These come with a panel above the pet door that reaches the full height of the glass door opening. The sliding door will be open to the width of the panel, but it can still be locked with the pet door in place. Plus, the panel will make the door weathertight. Glass-paneled doors can accept a pet door, but the installation can be tricky. It's best to hire a professional if this is your only option.

You can also install pet doors in an exterior wall. Patching the hole from inside is easy (see pages 62–63). Patching a hole in an exterior wall is more complicated. Stucco, brick, and stone exteriors are more difficult than wood to cut through and patch (see pages 221–224). If you choose to install your pet door through a wall rather than a door, be sure to buy a wall-mount unit that comes with a frame. Otherwise, you'll have to frame out the opening yourself to keep moisture, air, and critters out.

safety and privacy

Look for a pet door that gives you several locking options. Some can be locked manually, while others have automatic locks that can be set up for incoming and/or outgoing traffic. You can also find models that will only let pets out but not back in. You won't have to worry about intruders or other animals getting in, but you'll still have to get up to let your pet back inside.

The most advanced versions use programmable infrared technology, the same kind used for magnetic key systems, to allow only your pet access to the door. (I think this is what Astro from *The Jetsons* must've had cuz' it's pretty high tech.) The door comes with a key that your pet wears around its collar. As the pet approaches, the door unlocks. Any other pet or critter trying to gain access will be shut out.

There are also remote-control pet doors that use the same technology. You can set them to "in only," "out only," "open," or "locked." If you want to keep your pet from using the door at certain times of day, this might be the best option.

Generally, wild animals don't seem to use pet doors. It's not their instinct to look for them. If raccoons and possums regularly traipse through your yard, though, install one of the high-tech doors described above so these wild animals won't be able to get into the house. This solution would also work if you're concerned about neighborhood cats and dogs.

Worried about intruders of the nonanimal variety? One idea is to put the pet door in an exterior wall and then place a doghouse up against the wall, covering the pet door. A passerby wouldn't be able to see that there is a pet door inside the doghouse.

installing a pet door

Before you buy a pet door, measure your animal to determine the size you need. For the width, use the widest point of your animal and then add a few inches. For the height, measure from the bottom of its rib cage to the top of the shoulders, and add a few inches to that number as well. You don't need a door that reaches from your pet's feet to its head; animals will crouch and lift their feet to get through the door.

Double-check your measurements by holding an exterior door open at the right width and blocking off the entry at the height you've determined. Coax your pet through the opening. If your pet won't fit through or has to squeeze through, increase the dimensions of the opening.

Pet doors are usually sold by the animal's weight and shoulder height. If your pet hasn't reached full size, you'll need to guesstimate and use those measurements rather than the ones you've taken now. Otherwise, the pet door may be too small next year.

Most animals only need a couple of days at most to learn how to use a pet door. Teach your pet how it works by standing on the other side and offering a treat. Do this a few times and he or she should get the picture and a belly full of yum-yums.

The following instructions will give you a general idea of the installation process, but each pet door is a little different, so be sure to carefully read the instructions that came with the model you bought.

TIME & TALENT

This is a simple in-and-out procedure (sorry). The jigsaw is easy to use, and the whole job can be finished in an hour, as long as your pet isn't vying for attention while you're trying to work.

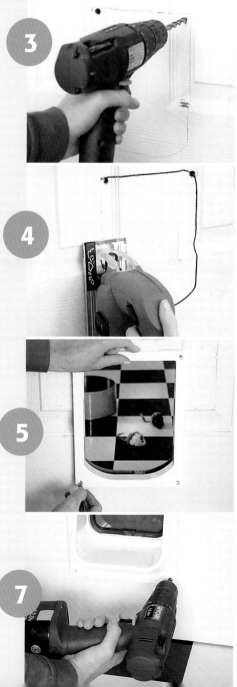

HOW TO INSTALL A PET DOOR

1. Measure from the floor to the bottom of your pet's abdomen. Then transfer that measurement to the door and mark it with a pencil. That's where the bottom of the pet door will go. Use the level to draw a straight and level line across the door at that point.

2. Tape the template that came with the pet door to your door so that the bottom touches the level line you drew. Trace around the template, which will later guide your cut.

3. Using a ½-inch drill bit, drill a hole all the way through the door in the top two corners of your trace marks.

4. Insert the blade of the jigsaw into one of the holes and cut from that hole to the next, and then around the rest of the marked area.

5. Put the interior frame into the opening and make sure it's not binding. Mark the four screw locations with a pencil.

6. Remove the interior frame and drill pilot holes over your pencil marks.

7. Place the interior frame on the inside of the door and the exterior frame on the outside of the door. Working from the inside, screw the two pieces together through the door, using the screws that came with the pet door.

TECHNIQUE
If you have a paneled door, you may have to build up the recessed area with shims so the pet door sits flush against the exterior door from top to bottom.

SEASONAL MAINTENANCE

Keeping up on seasonal maintenance chores will often prevent small problems from becoming big ones. The chart below lists common procedures that you can use as a starting point, but every house has its own issues. Just don't turn a blind eye when something starts to show warning signs, and you should be fine. Consult the user's manual for how to clean and repair your appliances.

WATCH OUT!
Before doing any electrical work, be sure to shut off the power (see pages 174–175). Some plumbing repairs also require that you shut off the water (see pages 12–13).

WHEN	WHERE TO CHECK	WHAT TO DO
Every month	Fire extinguisher	Check that it's fully charged; recharge or replace if needed.
	Sink and tub stoppers and drain holes	Clean out debris.
	Garbage disposal	Flush with hot water and baking soda.
	Water softener	Check water softener salt drum and replenish salt if necessary.
	Forced-air heating system	Change filters once a month if user's manual recommends fiberglass filters.
Every 2 months	Wall furnace	Clean grills.
	Range hood	Clean grease filter.
Every 3 months	Faucet	Clean aerator.
	Tub drain assembly	Clean out debris; inspect rubber seal and replace if needed.
	Floor and outdoor drain grates	Clean out debris.
Every 6 months	Smoke detector	Test batteries and replace if needed.
	Toilet	Check for leaks and water run-on.
	Interior caulking	Inspect caulking around tubs, showers, and sinks; replace any if it is deteriorating.
	Forced-air heating system	Change semiannually if user's manual recommends high-efficiency pleated or HEPA-style filters.
	Garbage disposal	Tighten drain connections and fasteners.
	Clothes washer	Clean water inlet filters; check hoses and replace them if they are leaking.
	Clothes dryer	Vacuum lint from ducts and surrounding areas.

WHEN	WHERE TO CHECK	WHAT TO DO
	Wiring	Check for frayed cords and wires; repair or replace them as needed.
	Range hood	Wash fan blades and housing.
Every spring	Roof	Inspect roof surface, flashing, eaves, and soffits; repair if needed.
	Gutters and downspouts	Clean them out or install no-clean version. Inspect and repair weak areas; check for proper drainage and make repairs if needed.
	Siding	Inspect and clean siding and repair if needed.
	Exterior caulking	Inspect caulking and replace any that is deteriorating.
	Windowsills, doorsills, thresholds	Fill cracks, caulk edges, repaint; replace if needed.
	Window and door screens	Clean screening and repair or replace if needed; tighten or repair any loose or damaged frames and repaint if needed; replace broken, worn, or missing hardware; tighten and lubricate door hinges and closers.
Every fall	Roof	Inspect roof surface, flashing, eaves, and soffits; repair if needed.
	Gutters and downspouts	Clean out. Inspect and repair weak points; check for proper slope.
	Chimney or stovepipe	Clean flue (more frequently if needed); repair any cracks in flue or any loose or crumbling mortar.
	Siding	Inspect and clean siding and repair if needed.
	Exterior caulking	Inspect caulking and replace any that is deteriorating.
	Storm windows and doors	Replace any cracked or broken glass; tighten or repair any loose or damaged frames and repaint if needed. Replace damaged hardware; tighten and lubricate door hinges and closers.
	Window and door weather stripping	Inspect and repair or replace if it is deteriorating or if it does not seal.
	Thermostat	Clean heat sensor, contact points, and contacts; check accuracy and replace the thermostat if it is not functioning properly.
	Outdoor faucets	If you live in an area with freezing winters, shut off valves to outdoor faucets. Open spigots and drain, store hoses.
Annually	Septic tank	Have a professional check the tank (watch for backup throughout the year). In many areas, it is recommended that the tank be pumped every year.
	Main cleanout drain	Have a "rooter" professional clean out the main line, particularly if there are mature trees in your yard whose roots could have cracked the pipe in their search for moisture.
	Water heater	Drain water until it is clear of sediment; test temperature pressure relief valve; clean burner and ports (gas heater).
	HVAC system	Have a professional tune up your heat/air-conditioning system.

RESOURCE GUIDE

Angie's List
(find and rate contractors nationwide)
www.angieslist.com

Aprilaire
(indoor air quality products)
www.aprilaire.com
(800) 334-6011

Baldwin
(door and window hardware)
www.baldwinhardware.com
(800) 566-1986

Barbara K
(tools for women)
www.barbarak.com
(800) 803-5657

Black and Decker
(power tools)
www.blackanddecker.com

Brookstone
(tools, detectors, and gadgets)
www.brookstone.com
(800) 846-3000

Bruce
(hardwood and laminate flooring)
www.bruce.com
(800) 233-3823

DIF Gel Wallpaper Stripper by Zinsser
www.zinsser.com

The Humane Society
(information on dealing with pests and critters)
www.hsus.org

Manda Mudd
www.mandamudd.com
(877) 626-3268

Mr. Rooter
(full-service national plumbing chain)
www.mrrooter.com
(877) 766-8305

Pella
(windows and doors)
www.pella.com
(800) 374-4758

Pergo
(laminate flooring)
www.pergo.com
(888) 393-5667

Tomboy Tools
(tools for women)
www.tomboytools.com
(866) 260-1893

CREDITS

photography

Unless otherwise credited, all photographs are by **Michele Lee Willson** with styling by **Laura del Fava**.

Courtesy of **Belwith**: 27 all; **Courtesy of Bruce Hardwood**: 132 bottom; **Wayne Cable**: 45 bottom, 51 middle left, 52 middle left, 52 bottom left, 53 left, 53 top middle, 53 top right, 53 bottom right, 79–81; **Jayson Carpenter**: 89; **Stephen Carver for David Schiff**: 50 bottom right, 51 bottom; **Courtesy of Certainteed**: 11 right; **Steve Cory**: 25 bottom; **Cheryl Fenton**: 87; **Scott Fitzgerrell**: 46 top right; **Courtesy of Forbo Linoleum**: 132 left; **Jamie Hadley**: 28; **Margot Hartford**: 123 bottom, 132 right; **Alex Hayden**: 30, 31; **Tom Haynes**: 118 left, 133 bottom, 134 left, 122 left, 124 top left, 124 middle left, 124 bottom left; **Scott Hirko**: 49 top left, 49 top middle, 49 top right, 49 middle right, 49 bottom right, 49 bottom left, 51 top right, 90 top, 90 bottom; **HomeTips, Inc.**: 54 bottom left; **Rob Karosis**: 64 left; **Muffy Kibbey**: 135 bottom; **David Duncan Livingston**: 96; **Courtesy of Manda Mudd**: 64 right; **Sandy May**: 216 all, 219 all, 230, 231, 233 all, 234 all; **E. Andrew McKinney**: 83–85 all; **Stephen O'Hara**: 43 bottom right, 48 top left, 50 bottom left, 51 top left; **Sharon Risedorph**: 134 right; **Eric Roth**: 15 top; **Mark Rutherford**: 3 bottom, 4 top left, 43 top right, 44 middle left, 54 top right, 54 bottom right, 55 top right, 55 middle right, 55 bottom right, 55 bottom middle, 55 top middle, 55 left; **Mark Samu**: 124 right; **Michael Skott**: 130; **Dan Stultz**: 42 left, 47 bottom, 51 middle right, 44 top left, 49 bottom middle, 50 top left, 50 bottom middle, 52 top left, 54 top left; **Dan Stultz for Dave Toht**: 4 bottom left; **Michel Thibaut**: 103–106; **Dave Toht**: 13 bottom, 16 top, 16 bottom, 24; **Courtesy of U.S. Fish and Wildlife**: 239, 240; **Don Vandervort**: 48 bottom left; **Christopher Vendetta**: 111; **Jessie Walker**: 123 top; **Courtesy of Werner Ladder Co.**: 48 bottom right; **Ron West**: 237; **Courtesy of Wicanders Cork Flooring**: 133 top; **Karen Witynski**: 88; **Courtesy of Zinsser**: 69

design

Design by **Jane Antonacci/ Jane Antonacci and Associates**: 28; Interior design by **Debi Cekosh, Cekosh Design Studio**: 130; **Annie Cronin, Verde Design and Janet Costa, A Work of Art**: 87; **David S. Gast & Associates**: 132 right; **Reynolds Gualco Architecture-Interior Design, www.rgaid.com**: 123 bottom; **Courtesy of Hearst Publications**: 124 right; **Steve Knutson of Knutson Designs**: 123 top; **Louie Leu Architect, Inc., www.louieleuarch.com**: 134 right; Interior design by **Patricia McDonald and Marcia Moore**: 135 bottom; **Anne Olson, architect**: 64 left

merci, danke schoen, gracias —a world of thanks

Thanks to every single one of you who just bought this book. Let's go out and have nachos sometime! Thanks to Ben for opening the publishing door, Bridget and Bob for holding my hand and letting my voice riff and roil, and to all the women who contributed their talents to this book. This book is 100% Chick-Produced!

Thanks to dozens of contractors whose knowledge, intelligence, and humor have been imparted to me over the years, and shared in this book—Doug Dormanen, Doug Anderson, Sean Francis, Dave Frederixon, Dean, Dan and the Hometime gang, Mikkael, and Brian Essig. A humble thanks to the healers, helpers, family, and friends who are always there for me, with a special shout out to the greatest Builder/Designer of all. I'm grateful You always have a master plan.

INDEX